Time to Journey

Religion for Senior Cycle Students

Claire Breen & Fiona Hedderman

GILL EDUCATION

Gill Education
Hume Avenue
Park West
Dublin 12
www.gilleducation.ie

Gill Education is an imprint of M.H. Gill & Co.

978 07171 5605 4

Design and print origination in Ireland by Design Image

For permission to reproduce photographs, the authors and publisher gratefully acknowledge the following:

© Alamy: 6, 9TL, 9TCL, 9TCR, 9TR, 22, 28, 33T, 33C, 33B, 49, 52, 58T, 58B, 58R, 59TL, 67, 77B, 89T, 94, 96BR, 97C, 97BR, 98TL, 98TR, 98BR, 110, 122, 125, 127, 134TL, 134TR, 135, 135, 140T, 140B, 143T, 143R, 153C, 164TC, 164TR, 165TR, 165BC, 167T, 167B, 170, 171L, 171T, 172BR, 175, 177, 185, 193B, 195; © The Bridgeman Art Library / Moment I, 1999 (oil on board), Macneill, Jane (b.1971) / Private Collection / Photo © Peter Nahum at The Leicester Galleries, London: 205TL; © The Bridgeman Art Library / God the Father loves us as His children with a tender and unfailing love, 2000 (oil on panel), Wang, Elizabeth (Contemporary Artist) / Private Collection / © Radiant Light: 205TR; © The Bridgeman Art Library / St. Jerome Checking the Stigmata on the Body of St. Francis, 1296-97 (fresco), Giotto di Bondone (c.1266-1337) / San Francesco, Upper Church, Assisi, Italy / Giraudon: 205B; © Collins Agency: 103B, 107; © Corbis: 59TR; © Getty Images: 153R, 208, 210; © Lalage Snow – photos of Second Lieutenant Adam Petzsch, Private Dylan Hughes and Corporal Steven Gibson from the series We Are The Not Dead: 128; © Photocall Ireland: 14, 113, 148; © Shutterstock: 9BL, 9BCL, 9BC, 9BCR, 9BR, 11R, 11BL, 27, 48, 77T, 77T, 81, 82, 83, 90, 88, 89B, 92, 96TL, 96TR, 96BL, 97T, 97BL, 98BL, 126, 142, 143B, 153TL, 153BL, 164TL, 164B, 165BR, 165BL, 169, 172TR, 172TL, 172BL, 173L, 173R, 178, 179, 193T, 1993R; © Shutterstock/kunanon: 183; © Shutterstock/Paul Prescott: 165TL; © Shutterstock/Prometheus72: 11T; © Shutterstock/Spirit of America: 59B.

The authors and publisher have made every effort to trace all copyright holders, but if any has been inadvertently overlooked we would be pleased to make the necessary arrangement at the first opportunity.

Contents

Foreword

Time to Journey has been designed for Senior Cycle non-exam Religion. The book has been divided into 6 sections taken from the NCCA guidelines. In each section, the objective is to engage the students with the material. The aim for each section is to allow teachers to set their own pace on the length of time they want to spend on each one. The activities and resources in each section will give the students a great opportunity to engage with each topic in depth. The end of section activities will also enable teachers to cover the topic in as much detail as they want to fulfil the needs of their class group. This book, along with the extra resources and topics online covers a two year senior cycle. We hope you and your students enjoy your *Time to Journey* through Senior Cycle Religion.

How to Use this Book

Questions

These questions can be answered individually (I), in pairs (P) or in groups (G), depending on what the teacher deems appropriate.

Long Questions

This activity allows for more in-depth questioning for students. Questions should be answered in detail using references from the relevant section.

Debates

Debates allow the students to express their opinions on the material in the section. Debates can be written individually by students, they can also be argued aloud in class or they can be answered using a walking debate.

Research

This activity allows for further research by the students either in school, in the library or at home.

Projects

Larger research projects for students to complete.

Journal

This activity allows the students to record their personal responses to certain aspects of each section. Journals can be kept by the student/teacher and used for all sections. This ensures each student will have a completed journal for all sections at the end of the book.

Interview

This activity encourages students to reach out into the wider community to explore the topic in more detail. This enables students to explore a range of different opinions.

Extra Resources

A list of recommended films, books and websites to expand on your understanding once you have completed a section.

Section 1

The Search *for* Meaning

Context

The search for meaning involves human beings looking for answers. In this section, we will explore the search for meaning in our lives and we will examine contemporary searches for meaning. Through this chapter we hope students will become more aware of the importance of the search for meaning in their lives.

Searching

Each of us will, at some point, wonder what the meaning of life really is. We may question why we are here or what our role in life might be. This is perfectly normal: as humans, we have the ability to ask questions about the meaning of life. As we get older and we experience new things, the questions we ask might become more difficult to answer. However, this is all part of human nature and we must realise that we have the ability to ask and to answer these questions.

THE SEARCH FOR MEANING

Consider the following questions.

- Why are we here?
- What is the purpose of life?
- What gives meaning to our lives?
- What is most important in life?
- What happens when we die?
- Who helps you in times of need?

1 What is your personal response to these questions? Write two paragraphs based on your answers to these questions and your own search for meaning in life.

2 Share your answer to Question 1 with your classmates and compile the thoughts of the group.

Read the following quotes and research what other people have said about their search for meaning in life.

'Love one person, take care of them until you die. You know, raise kids. Have a good life. Be a good friend. And try to be completely who you are. And figure out what you personally love. And go after it with everything you've got no matter how much it takes.'

Angelina Jolie

'Till I loved I never lived—Enough.'

Emily Dickinson

'Breathe. Let go. And remind yourself that this very moment is the only one you know you have for sure. I believe that one of life's greatest risks is never daring to risk. Doing the best at this moment puts you in the best place for the next moment.'

Oprah

'Sing the melody line you hear in your own head. Remember: you don't owe anybody any explanations, you don't owe your parents any explanations, you don't owe your professors any explanations. You know I used to think the future was solid or fixed, something you inherited like an old building that you move into when the previous generation moves out or gets chased out. But it's not. The future is not fixed, it's fluid. You can build your own building, or hut or condo, whatever.'

Bono

'Yes, I sometimes fail, but at least I'm willing to experiment.'

Bono

'Those who are not looking for happiness are the most likely to find it, because those who are searching forget that the surest way to be happy is to seek happiness for others.'

Martin Luther King, Jr.

'We can discover meaning in life in three different ways: (i) by creating a work or doing a deed, (ii) by experiencing something or encountering someone (iii) by the attitude we take toward unavoidable suffering.'

Viktor Frankl

1. Which quote can you relate to the most?
2. What do you think Emily Dickinson meant by her quote?
3. Based on her quote, what attitude do you think Oprah has towards life?
4. What do you think Bono is trying to say in his quote?
5. How can you seek happiness for others, as suggested by Martin Luther King, Jr?
6. Would you agree with Viktor Frankl?
7. Write your own quote in relation to the meaning of life.

Choose five well-known people and research their views on the meaning of life. Find at least one quote from each person.

The Search for Meaning

Linda Sapadin

The last time many people took the time to ponder philosophical questions, such as: 'What's the meaning of life?' 'What values do I cherish?' 'What shall I do with my life?', it's likely they were with their college buddies, high on pot, contemplating the meaning of life, love, sex, truth, peace and more.

What a luxury it now seems to have that leisure to sit around to contemplate the meaning of life. For once one becomes immersed in the business of life – earning a living, raising a family, maintaining a residence – it's easy to shy away from reflecting on your philosophy of life. The typical consequence: a feeling of emptiness, alienation, purposelessness – despite being constantly busy and rushing around doing things.

A philosophy of life provides a compass, a direction, a guide to help us make our way through life. Knowing what you believe in not only creates a sense of purpose but also is a guide to practical matters such as how to make a difficult decision, how to develop a sense of personal organisation, how to be resilient – even in the most straining times.

Traditionally people turned to religion or principles of morality to provide meaning to their lives. Some still do. But others, despite religion, morality, education and wealth, feel little spirituality in their lives. Their deepest questions about why they are here on earth remain unanswered, typically resulting in feelings of loneliness, depression and reduced interest in anything except the pleasure of the moment.

'You cannot get enough of what you don't really need,' declared philosopher Eric Hoffer. But if you don't really know what you need, you've got to make it up as you go along. And what most people do is to accentuate the amorphous concept of 'more'. More money, more sex, more work, more drugs, more food, more clothes, more tech gizmos, more travel, more parties, more friends, more activities. And yet, despite having more than you ever dreamed of, you may still find less meaning in life.

So what should you do if you're not finding much meaning in life? Keep busy, keep active, keep moving, we are told. At times, these suggestions are helpful. But more often, we are busy enough. What we need, we don't even deem worthwhile. Qualities like acceptance, simplicity, solitude, tranquillity, stillness. If you devalue these qualities, it's likely you'll create little or no time for them. Indeed, you may be critical of yourself for 'wasting time', instead of feeling pleased that you allowed yourself space for quiet and solitude.

Let's return full circle to our original questions: 'What's the meaning of life?' 'What values do I cherish?' 'What shall I do with my life?' With the wisdom of experience, it's a good chance you'll respond to these questions in a more enlightened way. I hope you give yourself the time to revisit these questions and reflect on your answers.

1 Write down five points this article makes about the search for meaning.
2 Consider your own search in relation to the questions pondered in the article.

Can One Escape the Search?

Some people choose not to engage with the search for meaning: they may live in the present and give little thought to what life is all about in the end. Other people may question the search for meaning at certain times in their lives: after the death of a loved one or when they find themselves at a crossroad with difficult decisions to be made. For others, the search for meaning can be a process that is pushed to the back of their minds. However, as humans, it is in our nature to question our own existence. While we might want to escape the search for meaning, it is inevitable that at some point in our lives we will have to face it.

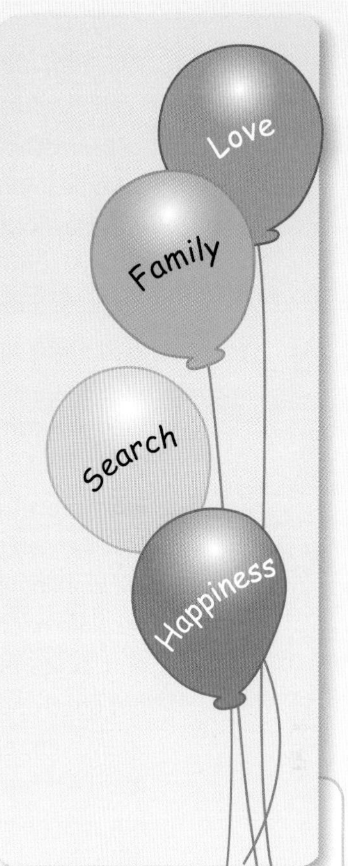

Contemporary Expressions: The Search for Meaning in Today's World

Below are two interviews from people who have found meaning in their lives through contemporary expressions: literature and film.

Ciaran Creagh

Director/Screenwriter

What role does film play in your life?

Film has a habit of sneaking up on you, infiltrating all aspects of your existence and before you realise it, taking over your life completely to a point to where everything you do or experience is related back in some way, shape or form to film. As a writer for the last decade, this has been the case for my writing but now since I have become more involved with film, all my experiences are now starting to relate more and more to film, i.e. pictures to go with the words. When you see something different or experience something new you assess that experience and catalogue it in your mind for use later in a film script.

Do you feel film brings meaning to your life?

As a writer or film maker you are in the position where you can select a topic which means something to you and then you can present this to the public. There is an onus on writers not to shy away from uncomfortable topics. The press are there to present the facts, the politicians are selling their dream but the writers and film makers are presenting ideas and images to get the public to think about their lives and experiences. I can't say it brings meaning to my life but it certainly gives me the opportunity to present my opinion on ideas which represent in some way my core values in life. The one thing I can say that does have meaning for me is that I will leave behind a body of work which will be accessible to the general public. I am not saying it is Shakespeare but it will exist forever.

Was film always important in your life?

I can't say that it was but I can imagine that it could have been for many people. Film was just something you went to on a very, very odd Saturday when I was young. It has only become important to me for the last number of years. All I did back when I was younger was play football on the road, all day – every day. The TV would have had more of an influence, especially those foreign channels of UTV and BBC! I can remember in 1978 sitting in a room full of Russian cyclists (who just won the Rás Tailtain) all glued to a TV with a very dodgy cable connection (homemade, of course) looking at the film *The Battle of Britain* with more fuzzy white lines than picture. Every one of those cyclists (born and bred in a communist restricted society) couldn't take their eyes from the screen.

How does film enhance your life on a daily basis?

Initially I can probably say that film does not enhance my life at all. I could sail through life working nine to five, a few pints at the weekend, a nice holiday in the summer and be quite happy with my lot. Instead you choose to be involved in film and all the stress and strains that this brings. Having people tell you to change this or change that; you're not good enough to make the grade; we won't fund you but will fund some 'artist' to spray themselves fifty different colours and hang backwards from some building (they call it art) – it is an extremely stressful, frustrating and thankless business to be involved with but strangely enough I love it.

One example of Ciaran Creagh's screenwriting work is the film Parked.

Watch *Parked* and journal your response to the message in the film. Comment on how the film made you feel.

Michael Preston

Poet/Writer

What role does literature/writing play in your life?

Writing is like my magic wand to express myself, or just simply to explain any event in one person's life. To write it down is a great gift for anybody to have and it is a natural gift.

Do you feel writing brings meaning to your life?

Yes, of course writing helps: it helps you to review your work, especially in poetry where you can reflect on what you have written. When you have completed a poem it is a great feeling and achievement and it is also good for the soul.

Was writing always important in your life?

Writing is very important to me. From a very young age I was writing about real people and real events. It is so fulfilling, it makes me feel I am worth something and always relaxes me and helps me through stressful times.

How does writing enhance your life on a daily basis?

Writing is like a release valve for me and it lets off steam and eases me when I am under pressure. Each day when we rise from our beds and set out on our journeys, we come across different people. I write about these everyday experiences and it is a very nice feeling. Putting reality into words and your thoughts from pen to paper is gift. That is a gift we all have and I thank God for that.

What else gives meaning to your life?

Staying positive and keeping on the move. Always set realistic goals and keep your journey simple. Don't get caught up in the madness of life. Stand up tall and be yourself, stay strong and be kind as well. I find that when you do good you feel good, when you do bad you feel bad. Sometimes life can be as simple as that. I have been writing poetry since the eighties and I have my own book published now.

One example of Michael Preston's work is his book of poetry 'Into the Light'.

Symbols

In our search for meaning, sometimes words fail us and we look to other things to help us to express ourselves. A lot of the time we use symbols or symbolic actions. Symbols have many meanings and they can affect each of us in different ways. Certain symbols take on extra significance for people because of their individual experiences.

There are personal symbols and group symbols. Personal symbols are unique to each person, e.g. their favourite song, book, poem, colour, place or photo. Group symbols are symbols that are of importance to more than one person because of a shared experience, e.g. supporting a football team, attending a certain school or following a specific band.

There are two aspects to every symbol:

★ The visible = what you can see
★ The hidden = what the symbol means for you.

Symbols can evoke different emotions in us and make us feel a certain way, e.g. listening to the national anthem at an important sporting event. Symbolic actions are mainly used when we cannot express ourselves, e.g. giving someone a hug when they have recently lost someone close to them. Symbols are of importance in both the religious and secular worlds.

1 What are symbols?
2 Can you list some of your personal symbols?
3 What is the difference between a personal and a group symbol?
4 Can you think of more examples of symbolic actions?
5 Do you think symbols are important?

1 Sketch or collect pictures of your personal symbols.
2 Gather all the symbols from the class and make a group collage.

			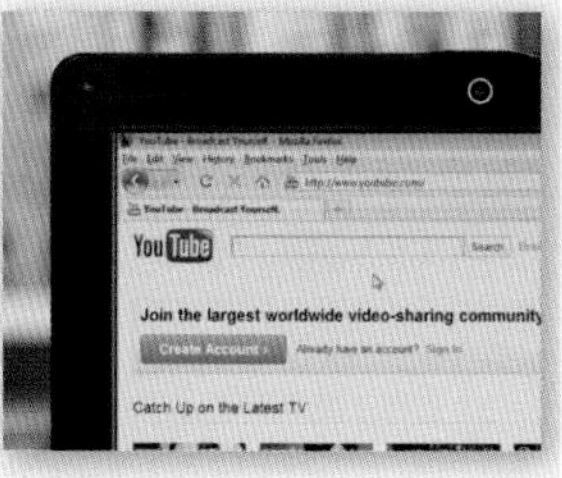
Facebook	Twitter	Coca-cola	YouTube

Modern symbols

Religious Symbols

Symbols are also of importance in the religious world. Certain phenomena occur in religions and these phenomena are often represented through symbols. These symbols then act as a permanent reminder of the event, e.g. when Christians see the crucifix, it signifies for them that Jesus died so that they would be saved.

Every faith has its own set of symbols for the purpose of representation. These symbols also allow for easy identification of a particular faith, e.g. during medieval times the colour green was used in Islam to identify fellow Muslims.

Symbols have always been important in teaching people about their faith, especially in times of illiteracy, e.g. Old Testament prophets used symbols to teach the Jewish people about the coming of the Messiah.

The five major world religions are easily identified by their symbols:

- ★ Christianity – crucifix
- ★ Judaism – menorah
- ★ Islam – star and crescent moon
- ★ Hinduism – aum
- ★ Buddhism – eight-spoke wheel.

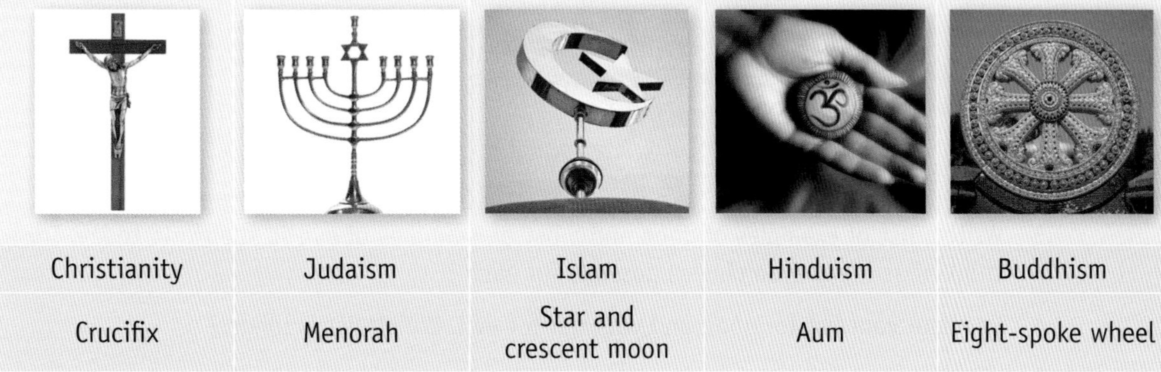

Christianity	Judaism	Islam	Hinduism	Buddhism
Crucifix	Menorah	Star and crescent moon	Aum	Eight-spoke wheel

Symbols from the five major world religions

1 Explain why world religions have symbols associated with them.
2 How many of the religious symbols are you familiar with?
3 Where might you see religious symbols?
4 How many of the modern symbols do you recognise?
5 Can you name any other modern symbols?
6 What does each symbol mean to you?

'Modern symbols have replaced religious symbols.'

Good and Evil

In our search for meaning, the concepts of good and evil emerge. We consider the meaning of good and evil in the world and the experience of suffering.

1 What is meant by good?
2 What is meant by evil?
3 Write a list of examples of good and a list of examples of evil in the world today. Try to think of as many examples as possible for each list.
4 Compare your list for good and your list for evil. Which list is longer?
5 Why do you think this is so?
6 Why, do you think, is there evil and suffering in the world?
7 Why do good people suffer?

All humans are created with free will and it is presumed that most people would use this free will for good. However, in our society today and in the past some people have abused this free will to act in a negative way towards others. The question of good and evil has been around since the beginning of time.

This poses a question: *Why is there evil in a world created by God?* This has always been a difficult question to answer because of its complexity.

Below are some theories that have been put forward to explain evil in the world.

- ★ God created the perfect world, which was spoiled by human disobedience and sin.
- ★ God has reasons for allowing evil to exist and these are reasons that we cannot understand.
- ★ God would not stop people from exercising their free will.
- ★ God allows evil to occur so that people can understand and acknowledge the difference between good and evil.

One theological dogma explaining how God can be just and righteous in the presence of pervasive sin in the world is Theodicy. It is a defence of God's goodness and presence in a world that contains evil.

An earthquake in Turkey

A volcanic eruption in Ecuador

The Great East Japan earthquake

Suffering

Unfortunately, suffering is a part of human life. Suffering affects everyone, even the most privileged of people. Our responses to suffering can be varied. Suffering can consume our lives but it can also be used as an experience from which we learn and move forward as a stronger person. This depends on the strength and circumstances of the individual. Each person will experience different suffering, e.g. the death of a loved one, an unforeseen tragedy or an unexplained illness. Each person will deal with suffering in their own way.

1 Categorise the following words into two lists:
- ★ Within human control
- ★ Outside of human control.

earthquake, terminal illness, tsunami, murder, hurricane, accident, flooding, holocaust, volcano, war

2 What is the difference between the two lists?

3 Why, do you think, do natural disasters happen?

4 Do you think natural disasters are outside of human control?

Religious Perspectives on Suffering

Each of the major world religions offers its own perspective on suffering. The following perspectives are offered by some people of the Hindu and Muslim faiths.

Hinduism

For most Hindus, suffering is viewed as a part of life and a consequence for previous negative actions. Hindus are accepting of their suffering: they do not question it. They know their suffering is not accidental and they believe that their individual suffering exists until they reach *Moksha* (freedom from the endless cycle of reincarnation). For many Hindus, suffering is viewed as a physical pain only: it does not affect one's soul. Consequently, there should be no concern over eternal suffering.

For Hindus, suffering is viewed as something that is not all bad. They know that everything comes from God, so their experience of suffering can be positive and can help them to progress spiritually. Hindus do not believe in becoming too attached to this world, since this can lead to suffering. They must remain detached in order to be brought towards their God.

Islam

It is noted that the Muslim view on suffering is similar to other monotheistic faiths such as Judaism and Christianity. For many Muslims, there are two perspectives on suffering: suffering that is a test of human character and suffering that comes as a result of sin.

The emphasis on suffering as a test of human character means that many Muslims believe that Allah tests their character through suffering. Allah sees it as a test of their faithfulness to him: throughout their struggles, their faith in Allah needs to remain strong. It is through suffering that Allah can see how people respond and he can examine the strength of their faith and character.

Within the Islamic faith, suffering also comes about as a result of sinful actions. These sinful actions are called *kufr*. A *kafir* is a person who has chosen to forget and turn away from Allah. This does not mean that the person is bad. Kufr comes about when people forget their faith and become consumed with money, power and other things that they think will bring them happiness. This can happen to anyone. Suffering occurs when the person realises their mistake. However, Allah will forgive the sinful actions when a kafir is truly remorseful and makes the necessary steps to make amends.

The Muslim faith acknowledges that people will struggle with sin and sinful actions. Muslims call this struggle *jihad*. Jihad is about trying to live a life of total submission to Allah and to act with the best intentions towards others. Muslims are accepting of their suffering because they truly believe that Allah would not allow them to suffer if they could not handle it adequately.

Life is sweet for Brian Keenan

Joanna Moorhead

As a hostage in Beirut, Brian Keenan knew that if he didn't survive, his biggest regret would be not having children. But twenty years on, the life he has with his wife and sons is the perfect antidote to the hell of four years in captivity.

It was as a hostage in Beirut, facing the possibility that he might be executed at any moment, that Brian Keenan realised how much being a father would mean to him. 'I remember thinking, if I'm going to die here, my biggest regret is that I haven't had any kids,' he says. 'The feeling quite overwhelmed me.'

Back then, as he and fellow hostage John McCarthy sat chained to a wall, half-starved, or were wrapped in sticky-tape and bundled into car boots, Keenan couldn't in his wildest dreams have foreseen how his life would pan out two decades on. Because today, with autumn starting to nip around Dublin Bay, Keenan is standing in his handsome, book-lined drawing room, stoking a roaring fire and doing a more than passable impression of a prosperous country gentleman. When the door opens and his wife, Audrey, 45, appears with coffee and perfect Irish scones, the idyll is almost complete. When it opens again and two good-looking sons – Jack, 11, and Cal, 9 – put their heads round to say hello politely, you realise he really did hit the jackpot.

Keenan admits that there are times when he looks at his picture-perfect family and can't believe life is this good. 'They'll be sitting there on the sofa opposite me, watching the television, and I see them and I think, how did I get all this?' During just over four years of captivity – from April 1986 to August 1990 – he wouldn't, couldn't, focus on what might happen if he ever got out. 'I remember thinking, this is where I am and I

Brian and his sisters upon his release

might be here for a long time – I might never get out. And thinking about the outside, about what might be going on and about a new life in the future, would have made it too difficult. Other hostages survived by thinking like that, by thinking outside their confinement, but I didn't.'

When he was finally released, Keenan famously told journalists that he intended to 'make love to every woman in the world', before realising that imprisonment had left him horribly vulnerable and that he should steer clear of a big love affair. Then, having decided after all not to leap into the arms of the first woman who crossed his newly liberated path, he ended up doing precisely that: Audrey Doyle, who became his wife in 1993, was the physiotherapist charged with helping to build up his muscles again.

'We were just friends for a long time, before it led to anything else,' says Audrey. 'All the same, some people thought I'd just emerged from nowhere and predicted it would never last.'

Sixteen years on, it's hard to believe anyone could have been pessimistic about their union: Audrey – warm-hearted, easygoing, open – is the perfect foil for the edgy, angst-ridden, complicated Keenan. Once, when she was still his physiotherapist and he her patient, she committed a faux pas by tying his leg to a gym bar, forgetting there would be connotations for a man who had been shackled so long. When she realised what she had done, she says, she 'went outside and laughed and laughed'. Today, as Keenan embarks on one of his serious, soul-searching stories, she interjects with perfectly pitched asides that manage to be both playful and respectful, and you sense that Keenan is immensely grateful for the sheer fun his wife has managed to inject into an existence that could easily have gone on being tortured long after his physical release. In fact, an ordinary life bringing up children is, Keenan admits, the perfect antidote to four years of hellish captivity in Beirut. 'Having kids is all about the here and now; there's no time to focus on the past.' He doesn't want, he says, to be defined by his hostage years. 'The years I was locked up were an incident in my personal history. They're not all of me.'

Yet for so many people those four years do define him, and will go on defining him. That is another reason family life is so precious. 'My children', he says, 'are among the few people in the world who don't think of me as an ex-hostage.' Jack and Cal don't know much about their dad's life before they came along but, from his point of view, becoming a father in his forties has obviously been fundamental to the new life Keenan, now 58, has forged for himself. After all those years spent living in his own head, forensically dissecting his own psychological makeup and then describing it, brilliantly and powerfully, in his bestselling book *An Evil Cradling*, he lives now in ordinary-dad mode, and is grateful that thoughts about paying the mortgage, helping his boys with their homework and what to make them for tea now take centrestage in his mind.

But when he allows his brain to wander, one of the things he is most struck by is the difference between the childhood his sons are having and his own. It was at least in part because he wanted to describe that difference for them that he decided to write about his own boyhood in Protestant east Belfast. Like *An Evil Cradling*, the new book is lyrical in parts, drawing on a depth of emotion that seems all the more raw and honest because it contrasts so radically with the picture he paints of his parents' unwillingness, or inability, to indulge in the self-reflection at which their son has become a master.

But it's the nuts and bolts of his early life, in a working-class neighbourhood in the 1950s, that strike you most forcefully. Keenan exquisitely describes the contrast between the exotic street names – his own was Evolina Street, next along was Syringa Street – and the ordinariness of life for its cash-strapped, often work-starved, inhabitants. His dad, who had been given up for dead after a plane crash in Africa while serving in the RAF during the war, later marrying his mother in a church in which his name had been carved prematurely on a war memorial, settled into life as a bus conductor and then a telephone engineer without complaint, never leaving the house without his cap and 'singing in the morning as he stood in his vest and trousers at the kitchen sink sloshing handfuls of soapy water into his face'.

Keenan remembers that his Sunday afternoon task was to cut up newspapers into six-inch squares as toilet paper for the outside loo. His mother, meanwhile, was at the heart of a street-centred community. In Evolina Street, no one locked the front door, even at night; other women came and went without knocking, simply blustering into one another's back rooms as if they were in their own homes. When Keenan was born, girls from the street were chosen to help Brenda, his older sister, take him for walks and look after him. 'Had I not had any sisters, the mothers of the street would have selected two of their own daughters for the job. In a very real sense the street was your family,' he writes.

That existence is light years from the spacious, comfortable, middle-class Dublin house in which Keenan is bringing up his own children (it even has electronic security gates) and one can only imagine the surprise with which it will eventually be read by Jack and Cal. All the same, though, their father's childhood isn't entirely another country: the values instilled in Evolina Street, says Keenan, are still the values he lives by and wants to pass on to his sons. 'My parents taught me to never just accept anything,' he says. 'To question everything, that was the spirit they instilled in me.' Audrey, beside him on the sofa, laughs happily. 'And oh, my God, did our kids inherit that!'

Keenan's parents are both dead – his father's death was pivotal in his decision to go to Beirut. It was as he carried his father's coffin that he made the decision to leave Belfast, and to seek a new life overseas as a teacher at the American University in Beirut. At the time of the kidnap he was wearing one of his father's shirts, and that connection was a crumb of comfort to him – in *An Evil Cradling*, he writes movingly about how his dad became 'not simply a memory but...a real presence...a presence I could feel more than see, a comforting reassurance that eased the hurt into a deeply filled sadness, yet that same sadness as it became reflective, lifted me'. His mother died in 2004 having survived his captivity – something she rarely spoke about, Keenan says. 'It was her way,' he explains. 'When I came home she didn't ask, and I didn't tell much at all. My sisters told me that when I was away she didn't speak much about what was happening. When there were rumours that I might be coming home, though, she knitted me a sweater.' She was always a great one for knitting, he says – in a way she both interpreted and dealt with the world through her clacking knitting needles.

In the new book, Keenan describes his mother's decline through Alzheimer's – and yet it wasn't entirely a decline, as he points out, because it seemed to take her back to a time and a place where she had been happiest: the world of her youth. It was a world her son had known nothing about – there was no memoir for him to read, as there will be for Jack and Cal – so he found, paradoxically, that what doctors might have labelled the confusion of his mother's old-age ramblings brought a clarity about his family's past that he had given up hope of ever hearing about. Against the odds, Alzheimer's seems to have strengthened Keenan's bond with his mother; even as she lay dying, having outstripped the doctors' expectations of how long she might survive, he felt she was asserting her independence of spirit one final time. It is clear that Keenan is as proud of his mother as she surely was, quietly, of him. 'She knitted me a sweater,' he says simply. 'I've written her a book.'

There were also his sisters: Brenda and Elaine – the former his elder by eight years, the latter his younger by ten – achieved global fame as they battled, through his captivity, to keep his plight in the public eye. Was he surprised by what they had done when he was released? 'I was amazed – I had no idea about the campaign,' he says. Then he says something in his lilting Belfast accent that is shot through with the sibling feeling none of us ever really manage to escape, however old or wise or clever we become. 'When they told me they'd been over to the US to talk to so-and-so and met Yasser Arafat and all that, I was a bit jealous, to be honest. I mean, there was me stuck in a prison the whole day long and my two sisters were on planes and living the high life.' He laughs at himself. 'We joke about it still.'

Today, Brenda and Elaine still live in Belfast, but the three siblings see one another regularly and he talks to them a lot on the phone. He keeps in close touch, too, with John McCarthy, the journalist who went to Beirut to cover Keenan's kidnapping, and instead became his cell-mate. He still considers McCarthy his closest friend and he and Audrey love seeing McCarthy, his wife, Anna, and their young daughter Lydia. 'We get together as families – the boys love Lydia,' he says. Both men have moved on, McCarthy like Keenan, helped significantly by having become a father. 'We never talk about the past any more. It's an irrelevant thing. We talk about kids or work – or our holidays.'

But inevitably there are reminders, some of them funny. 'We were in a taxi together in London, and the driver kept looking at us in his mirror,' says Keenan. 'And then he came through on his intercom and he said: "Sorry to interrupt you gentlemen, but I couldn't help asking...wouldn't you be more comfortable travelling in the boot?"'

He laughs for ages at the memory, then we go on to chat for a while about the family holiday two summers ago, when he and Audrey took the boys to Lebanon. It wasn't her first choice of destination, she's happy to admit, but she sent Brian along first to check out that it really was safe for the boys. 'We had a wonderful time,' she says, and Keenan nods his head. 'What we wanted was that they'd grow up with good memories of the place, that they'd find out that the people there are friendly and warm, before they found out the bad stuff,' he says. 'It all worked out really well in the end.' As indeed it all has for Keenan.

1. Comment on the suffering Brian experienced while he was held hostage.
2. What do you think brings meaning to Brian's life?
3. Comment on how Brian has remained so positive through all his suffering.
4. What do you think kept Brian going throughout his ordeal?

Another person who struggled with her search was Nuala O'Faolain. Research Nuala's radio interview with Marian Finucane and the RTÉ documentary about Nuala's life.
www.nualadocumentary.com

Spirituality

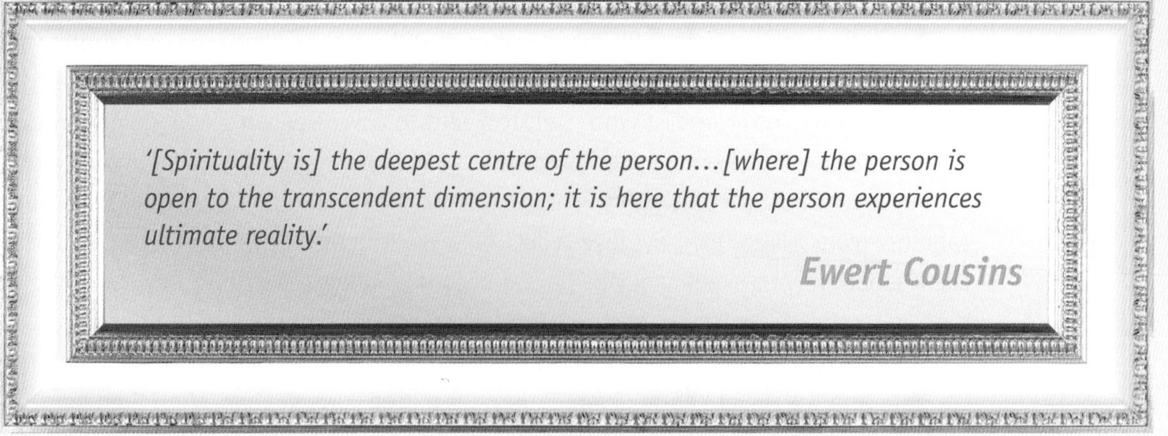

The quotation above touches on what is involved in spirituality; however, spirituality is not limited to any one definition. Spirituality can mean something to people of religion and people of no religion alike. For many people in previous generations in Ireland, spirituality was associated with the Roman Catholic Church. Nowadays it has become an important aspect of life on a broader scale: the twenty-first century has seen many people search for answers outside traditional religious structures.

Traditionally spirituality would have involved prayer, ritual and meditation (see Section 5). Today it is not limited to these three aspects alone. Spirituality involves a person being aware of the fact that there is more to life than what we can physically see and touch. Spirituality concerns the inner soul of a person and the connection that one may have to something beyond themselves.

It is worth questioning why spirituality exists today and why is it important. People choose spirituality so that they can:

- ★ Live their lives with a deeper meaning
- ★ Deal with everyday challenges
- ★ Feel supported during times of suffering and illness
- ★ Make a connection with something greater than themselves.

What Does it Mean to be a Spiritual Person?

Dr Margaret Paul

You go to church every Sunday and you say your prayers every day. Does this mean you are a spiritual person?
No.

You practise yoga and meditate every day. Does this mean you are a spiritual person?
No.

You belong to spiritual group and are devoted to following the teachings of the group. Does this mean you are a spiritual person?
No.

What, then, does it mean to be a spiritual person?

Being a spiritual person is synonymous with being a person whose highest priority is to be loving to oneself and others. A spiritual person cares about people, animals, and the planet. A spiritual person knows that we are all One, and consciously attempts to honour this Oneness. A spiritual person is a kind person.

So, you can go to church every Sunday and say your prayers every day, without caring about loving yourself, others and the planet. You can practise yoga and meditate every day without being conscious of what is loving and what is not loving in your thoughts and actions. You can belong to a spiritual group and devotedly follow the teachings, yet still be judgmental towards yourself and others in your daily life.

There are many people who do not practise a religion, who do not meditate, pray or belong to any group, who are very spiritual people. These people naturally do caring things for others. They think about how they can help. Their thoughts are kind rather than judgmental towards themselves and towards others. When you look at them, you see kindness in their eyes.

There are many religious people who are anything but kind. We all know of religious people who are extremely judgmental, righteous and outright mean. Can you be both religious and spiritual? Of course! But only when you are operating in your religion from your heart rather than from the learned dogma of your mind.

Years ago I very briefly attended a 'spiritual' group. People would meet in an auditorium to hear the leader of the group speak. The second time I attended I heard a number of parents yelling at their children and judging them to try to control them. These parents were being anything but kind with their children. That was the last time I attended the spiritual group. The focus of the group was surrender to God, but love was rarely in the picture! They obviously had a very different experience of God than I did.

My experience of God is that God is the energy of Love that created us and sustains us. In my experience, 'God is Spirit' (John 4:24) and 'God is love' (1 John 4:16). Anything that is not of love, peace, joy, truth and kindness is not of God. Praying to God does not mean that you are allowing the spirit that is God – the love, peace, joy, truth and kindness that is God – to guide your thoughts and actions. Practising yoga or meditating does not mean that you have invited the love that is God into your heart, or that you are turning to that ever-present love to learn about what is in your highest good, and the highest good of others and the planet.

If you want to be a spiritual person, then let kindness be your guiding light – kindness towards yourself, towards others, towards animals and towards this beautiful planet that is our home. Recognise that we all have the spark of love that is God within us, and learn to honour that love so that you can know and experience the Oneness of all that is.

1 According to this article, what does it mean to be a spiritual person?
2 Describe the author's experience of God.
3 What advice does the author give to people who want to be more spiritual?
4 What is your opinion of the views expressed in this article?

Comment on what you think it means to be a spiritual person.

God, Gold and Me

Katie Taylor

Inspired by faith and family, Katie Taylor blazed a trail for Irish sport and Irish women at the London Olympics.

Rituals Are Important

As far back as I can remember, I dreamed of becoming an Olympic champion and I imagined standing on the podium and having the gold medal placed around my neck. Most kids have big dreams like that, every child wants to be a professional footballer or a great champion or a movie star but for most people, life has a way of telling you that you're wasting your time with fanciful dreams. I guess I never got that memo! As I got older and became more involved with sport, my child-like dreams became my desires and my desires became my ambitions, until winning an Olympic gold medal became the most important personal goal of my life. I didn't even know what my sport would be at that time, I just knew there was an Olympic champion in my heart.

Mam was with me on the morning of the Olympic final against Sofya Ochigava. She had come over to my apartment in the athletes' village in Stratford in the east end of London to help me prepare for the bout. In a few hours' time I would fight against the Russian for the gold medal, and after that my Olympics would be over.

After nearly 150 fights and four World Championship gold medals, she doesn't need to ask me what I want her to do, our preparation is the same every time. She picked up my hairbrush, wet my hair as she always does, and began to put it into plaits.

I was standing with my back to her and, as she was doing my hair, she prayed out loud over me. I could sense the emotion in her voice but she had to hold it together for my sake, this is perhaps the most important part of my pre-fight ritual. Ma repeated some of Psalm 18 to me, which is one of my favourite pieces from the scriptures. This is a psalm that I regularly read when I am away in competition. It is a reminder that it is God that trains my mind for battle and He is my shield of victory. The focus of our prayers was to ask that I performed to the best of my ability and that I was able to express that ability when I stepped into the ring later. It was also about praying that God would help me deal with any negativity that might creep into my mind, or any comments from outside that might distract me. I tried to listen to what He was saying about me and not what other people were saying. It was important for me to be reminded that my Olympic dream began first in the heart of God before it ever began in me – this was my God-given destiny.

The night before, Mam had spent some time praying about what scripture she was going to read to me. It's never a random choice of words plucked from the pages of the Bible. She wants the meaning to be specific to the moment and to my needs, something that she could share with me that would give me assurance and confidence.

Mam is my spiritual rock and she is as much a part of my boxing team as anyone else, but she also has a great understanding of the sport. It may surprise you to learn that she was the first in our family to challenge the view that women and boxing don't mix, for in the late 1980s she became the first female judge to be appointed in Ireland. Needless to say, she faced a lot of opposition at that time from within the boxing community but now it is commonplace to see female judges and referees. I like to think that I have carried on her pioneering spirit.

Sofya Ochigava

For my final against Sofya Ochigava, Mam picked a scripture from the book of Isaiah that speaks about what God said about people with faith: 'That no weapon formed against you will prevail and that you will refute every tongue that accuses you and that this is the heritage of those that belong to the Lord.'

That might seem like a strange choice of scripture from all of the promises of the Bible, but it was exactly what I needed to hear, because my Russian opponent had been publicly saying some bad things about me in the days leading up to the final. I didn't know at the time exactly what she had said, but I knew she had been disrespectful.

These verses reminded me that Ochigava's critical words were just dirty tactics in an attempt to undermine my confidence in my Olympic dream. The words were a promise that God will shield me from any negativity and accusations that are thrown in my direction. If I had spent any energy before the fight dwelling on Ochigava's comments, then her tactics would have worked.

But the verses my mam gave me were telling me not to focus on who was standing opposite me in the ring, but to focus on the God who is always standing beside me, both in and out of the ring.

For those who think that I saw the fight as an opportunity to settle a score with Ochigava, I can honestly say that her words were not a motivating factor at all. Ochigava had said a lot of disrespectful things, but at the time I didn't fully realise the extent of what it was, as I had avoided the newspapers and was too focused on my own build-up to worry about anything else that might have been going on.

I had heard that negative words had been said only because a journalist came up to me after one of the earlier fights in the ExCeL Arena and mentioned it. Although it was in most of the newspapers and online, even now I don't fully know all the details. To be honest I was surprised with her, that sort of behaviour is usually more common in professional boxing than in the amateur code.

Over the last couple of years when we've boxed each other in big championships at European or world level, our rivalry has sharpened. Outside the ring, we say hello, we're not unfriendly, but that's about it. Years ago, when we were in different weight classes, we'd probably have gone out after the competition, sat around and had a coffee. We were friendly and I found her quite a funny person to be with. But now we are in the same weight division, that option has gone – it's difficult to be close to girls you are competing against on a regular basis. Regardless of what she said, I still think she's a nice girl and her comments were uncharacteristic. She is a very talented boxer who is great for the sport.

Under Pressure

All pressure is relative, but I'd be lying if I said I didn't feel it bearing down heavily on me. In every contest I've ever fought, there is some pressure to deal with. Often the greatest pressure is that which I put on myself. I knew the fans expected me to do well, and by now I was very aware of the massive support for me around London and back home in Ireland. So this time, I was feeling the pressure of other people's expectations creeping into my head in a way that I hadn't experienced to the same degree before. Normally, I'm strong at keeping out external things, but this Olympic final was something I had never faced before.

I wanted it to be over and done with, and that was a terrible way to think. On a couple of occasions in previous fights, when I haven't been able to enjoy the process of the build-up, I've fought and lost. I found it unnerving that on the most important day of my boxing life, and on the verge of fulfilling the dreams I've carried in my heart since I was a young girl, the nerves were knotting in my stomach and a part of me didn't want to face the battle.

Struggling to cope with finals is not what people expect of me. I think they believe that because I have won so many titles at European and world level, I'm mentally capable of coping with any boxing situation, and usually I am. It's one of the strongest facets of my game.

But, like anyone, I can have doubts, and it's at these times when it is so important to remind myself of the promises of God for my life. I remember speaking a verse from the book of Philippians to myself, it says: 'I can do all things through Christ who gives me strength.'

Family Support

In their support for me, my family members play different roles: Mam prays and Dad talks tactics. On the morning of the final, Dad came over to me in the Olympic Village. We wanted to make sure that Thursday 9 August 2012 was no different from over a dozen important finals I've been in, and we went for a walk as we always do. We walked for about 30 minutes, and it didn't matter where we went. We talked about the fight, how it was going to go, what might or might not happen, and how I was feeling – anything that we thought needed to be aired. This time was also about relaxing, getting prepared and being with someone I trusted, somewhere other than sat in my room.

Whatever city we are in, we have always found a route and we do the same walk over and over throughout the week. It's part of an unbreakable routine we have on competition day, and that day it began early at 8.00am when I had to get up for the weigh-in. After the scales, I went back to my room for breakfast instead of going to the main dining hall, because I wanted privacy and some space to do my own thing.

It was about 11 when Dad called so we could go for our walk, and we strolled out from the village up to Olympic Park and around by the athletics stadium, a vast, wide area where you can look across and see the velodrome, the aquatic centre and the basketball arena. When we came back, Mam arrived at about two o'clock to do my hair and pray.

It's the same ritual all the time and it has worked for me for years. It's a case of 'if it is not broke don't fix it'. We never change.

Throughout the day, I listen to the same worship songs on my iPod and I read the same Bible verses. When I'm boxing or preparing for a fight, it's when I feel closest to God.

This Olympic dream was too big for me to deal with on my own, so for the last 10 years, I have relied on God and I've put everything in His hands. It's hard to put everything you hold dear in the hands of someone else, because it's natural to want to be in control, but I've learned from experience that God will never let me down so I just try to trust Him.

The journey to the ExCeL centre from the village was about 30 minutes by bus. The team with me consisted of my dad, Irish head coach Billy Walsh and Zauri Antia, Ireland's technical coach. There were very few words spoken, except by Billy and Zauri, who were cracking a few jokes to try to lighten the mood.

Once inside the arena, I stuck to the same routine and did the same warm-up in the changing room as I'd done for my previous fights. I have quite a long warm-up session, which lasts maybe 45 or 50 minutes. I always wear the same warm-up tee-shirt, which says on the front 'It is God who arms me with strength' and on the back 'He trains my hands for battle'.

Before we left the tunnel for the final, my dad was constantly giving me instructions, reinforcing what he has been saying to me in the warm-up area.

He kept on repeating what he wanted me to do for the first 30 seconds of the first round, going over the tactics he had planned for the fight.

The warm-up

I used my long warm-up to focus on the fight and after that I practised some combinations and some shadow boxing specific to how I was going to try to fight against Ochigava. After the pads, I walked around stretching, trying to see things in my head. Dad was focused and so was I. Some people can joke and laugh minutes before a fight, but Dad and me are the opposite and are really intense people to be around during that time. He became so nervous I could see the colour of his face draining away.

It didn't help that from where we were in the locker room, we could hear everything that was going on outside in the boxing arena. The music was blaring and the crowd cheered and clapped every time they announced a celebrity in the arena. Before I went out for my final, I didn't know exactly who was in the crowd, but I was told afterwards that former heavyweight champion Evander Holyfield had attended, and so did the British prime minister David Cameron and Olympic silver medallist Amir Khan.

I could hear the interview former World Champion Barry McGuigan gave before my fight. Every introduction and announcement was audible, as the changing area was right beside the crowd. Ideally I like a quiet area to warm up in, but for an Olympic final you cannot expect to have such a luxury. Although I have no doubt it all added to the atmosphere, the last thing I wanted in my ear were the celebrity announcements coming in from the public address system; all I wanted to do was concentrate on the fight ahead. Much as I tried to shut myself off and detach myself, there was nothing I could do about it. In these situations when you can't control things, you just have to get on with it.

As I waited, I could sense the whole place was on edge; the atmosphere was so lively, more like a carnival or a concert than an amateur fight. I got my first direct taste of this when I walked out with Billy Walsh under the stands to have the bandages on my hands stamped by officials. The area where this was done was right out on the concourse of the arena, and when the crowd saw me at the official's table, everyone began screaming my name: 'Katie! Katie! Katie!' I realised then how many of the fans were Irish. It was crazy and on a completely different scale to anything I'd experienced at European or World Championship finals. When Billy Walsh came back into the warm-up area with me, he commented to my dad that the hairs on the back of his neck were standing up as the atmosphere was electric.

Into the ring

I had my mouthguard already in place before we left the locker room, which is something Dad and Zauri laugh at me about. When they put the gumshield in, they say it turns a switch inside my head and my face completely changes. So they put it in before I walked to the ring. The switch was tripped as the three of us stepped from the tunnel for my final walk to the Olympic ring. Everything else was blanked out. I expected the crowd's reaction and I knew there was going to be a rush of noise. There was and it was a wild, bring-the-roof-down welcome, but I couldn't allow myself to enjoy it. It was tempting to take a quick glance up and say: 'Wow! How great is this!' But I couldn't break my focus like that. I felt energised by the noise. I felt my nerves and the expectation on me, but I was also confident that if I performed to my ability that I could win. Dad was just telling me to relax and stay focused. So there was no other thought in my head except winning as I walked towards the ring.

I never looked up to the crowd. I didn't allow myself become drained or distracted. Other boxers I know glance around and suck up the energy and feed off it, or they smile and wave at everybody, or jump up on the ropes and shake their fists in delight to pump themselves up. That impulse was hanging there, but I ignored it. I ducked under the ropes and was so focused that I really couldn't hear much at all. The only voice I could distinguish was Dad's, which I've learned over the years to pick out. Everything else coming from around the ring was muddled, background noise.

I was entering the ring for my Olympic final, and there was no place in the world I would rather have been. I believed the moment was mine and this was my destiny. It was going to be hard, very hard; I knew I needed to maintain my discipline and make no mistakes. But if I did all of that, I believed I could win. I'd beaten her 11–7 earlier in 2012 to win the World Championship in China, and defeated her 10–5 the previous year to take the European Championship. None of that mattered now; this was a clean slate. The more you box against the same opponent the harder it becomes, you both become familiar with each other. I walked to the centre of the ring towards Ochigava's corner. I touched her glove with mine. I listened to the referee speaking. I thanked God for what He had already given me. I heard the bell and we began to box.

1. From reading this article, what do you think about Katie Taylor?
2. Do you think Katie could influence young people to have more belief in God?
3. Why, do you think, has Katie so much faith in God?
4. Why, do you think, are some people afraid to show their faith?

Religious Faith: A Response to Life's Search for Meaning

The following questions were asked at the start of this section.

- Why are we here?
- What is the purpose of life?
- What gives meaning to our lives?
- What is most important in life?
- What happens when we die?
- Who helps you in times of need?

When you look back at your answers, you may not have mentioned religion or God. However, all of these questions could be answered through a belief in a God. As already mentioned, human beings are created with free will. For people of religious belief, this means that God gave us free will through creation. This God refers to the Jewish God, the Christian God, the Muslim God, etc.

Free will is the ability that most people have to decide between right and wrong. This free will is a cause for some of the evil and suffering that takes place in the world. People who inflict hurt and suffering on others do so through their free will. Regardless of the influences a person may have throughout their life, they are ultimately responsible for their own actions.

For people of religious belief, God plays an important role in their life and in times of suffering they turn to their God to provide answers and comfort. The three monotheistic faiths believe that the purpose of life is closely associated with God and their relationship with Him.

People with a deep faith find comfort and support in their relationship with their God. This relationship plays an integral part in their day to day life. This relationship should not be one-sided. However, at times, the need for God's support may be stronger. For example, in times of bereavement, people draw on the belief that death is not the end and they will see their loved ones again.

Elie Wiesel is one such person who turned to God in his time of adversity. He was sent to Auschwitz during World War II when he was 16. He survived the Holocaust. He has written about his time in the concentration camps in a book entitled *Night*.

'We believed in God, trusted in man, and lived with the illusion that every one of us has been entrusted with a sacred spark.'

'I pray to the God within me that He will give me the strength to ask Him the right questions.'

Elie Wiesel

1 Explain free will in your own words.
2 What do you think of free will?
3 Do you see people using their free will mostly for good or for bad?
4 How might a person find comfort in their God in times of suffering?
5 Comment on the Elie Wiesel quotes. How do they make you feel?

End of Section Summary

- It is part of human nature to ask questions. Each human being may ask questions in their search for meaning throughout their life.
- For some people, the search for meaning is too much at times: they choose to avoid it.
- Contemporary expressions of the search for meaning can include music, film, spirituality, art and literature.
- Symbols help us in our search for meaning, especially at times when words fail us.
- Symbols are also of importance in the religious world.
- Religious symbols are important for remembrance, identification and education.
- Suffering is a part of life.
- Some things that happen in this world are within human control and some are outside of human control.
- All religions have a perspective on suffering, e.g. many Hindus see it as a part of life and accept it, while many Muslims view it as testing of character and/or as the result of sin.
- Spirituality involves 'the deepest centre of the person'.
- Religion can provide answers to people in their search for meaning.

End of Section Activities

1. From your study of this chapter, write a detailed account of what you have learned about the search for meaning.
2. Write an account of one person who has a strong religious faith and explain how they search for meaning in their life.
3. Write an account of one person who is not a member of an organised religion and explain how they search for meaning in their life.
4. From your experience, how relevant are symbols for young people today?
5. Write an essay entitled 'Spirituality and Young People Today'.

- 'Can one escape the search for meaning?'
- 'Spirituality is only for the religious.'
- 'Suffering is necessary.'

1 Find one example of a contemporary expression of the search for meaning and explain why this means something to you.

2 Research the views of the following world religions in relation to suffering: Buddhism, Judaism and Christianity.

3 Explore the topic of spirituality in relation to young people in Ireland today.

Throughout your Leaving Certificate cycle, try to journal regularly about your search for meaning.

Interview three members of a family across three generations. Ask them about the search for meaning in their lives. Pick the main points from your conversation and present your findings to the class.

Films

★ *Into the Wild*
★ *Touching the Void*
★ *Life is Beautiful*
★ *Seven Pounds*
★ *The Family Man*
★ *Castaway*
★ *Tuesdays with Morrie*
★ *Life of Pi*
★ *Viktor and I*
★ *The Boy Whose Skin Fell Off*

Books

★ *Man's Search for Meaning* – Viktor Frankl
★ *Tuesdays with Morrie* – Mitch Albom
★ *Life of Pi* – Yann Martel
★ *The Five People You Meet in Heaven* – Mitch Albom
★ *The Catcher in the Rye* – J.D. Salinger
★ *The Alchemist* – Paulo Coelho
★ *The Kite Runner* – Khaled Hosseini

Websites

★ www.nualadocumentary.com
★ www.jseliger.wordpress.com
Search for 'Why "Man's Search for Meaning" and Viktor Frankl'
★ www.viktorandimovie.com
★ www.beacon.org
Search for Frankl and then under the book 'Man's Search for Meaning' go to the teacher's guide.

Podcasts

★ Listen to an interview between Marian Finucane and Pierce Brosnan on his search for meaning.
Go to www.rte.ie/radio1/ and search for it.

Section 2

Christianity

Context

In this section, we will explore the historical context into which Jesus was born. We will develop an understanding of the message and vision of Jesus. The early Christian communities will also be briefly explored, with particular attention on Thessalonica.

Palestine at the Time of Jesus

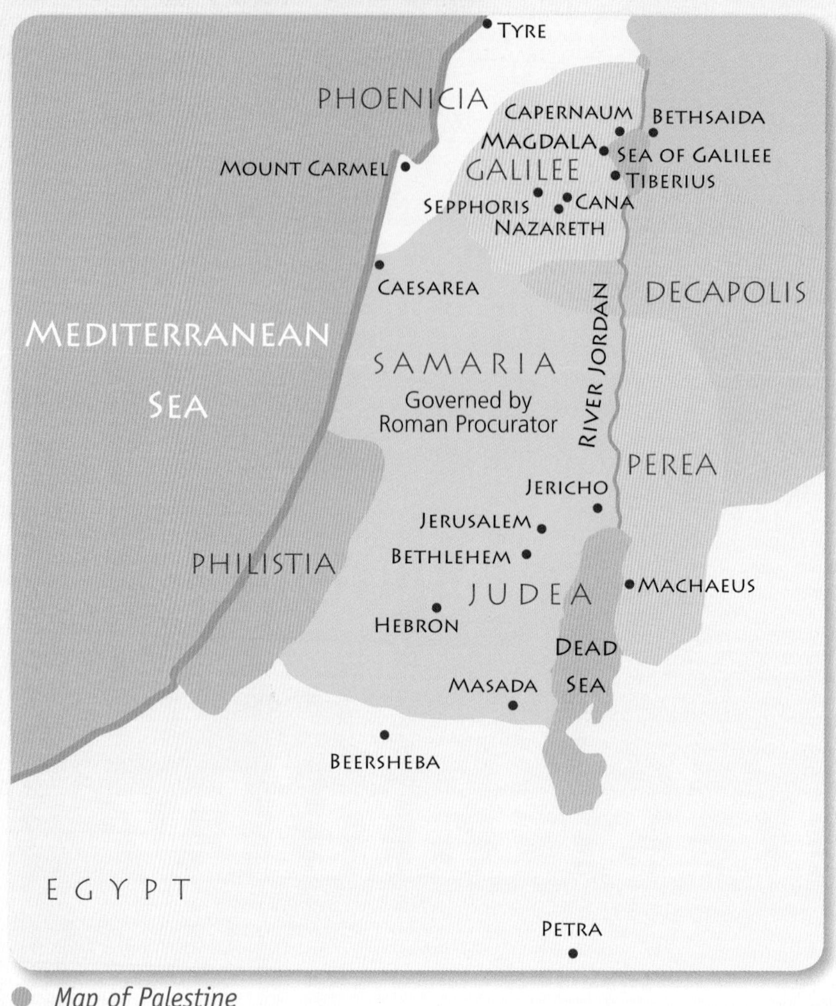

Map of Palestine

Watch the trailer for 'The Greatest Story ever told' on YouTube. It shows the context of Palestine at the time of Jesus.

Political System

In Jesus' time Palestine was part of the Roman Empire. Jesus lived his entire life in Palestine. The Roman Emperor controlled the Roman Empire. He ruled the empire and appointed Governors in each of the areas conquered. When the Romans conquered Palestine they allowed the Jews to practise their own faith. However, all people living in Palestine had to pay taxes for the upkeep of the Roman Empire and they had to follow Roman laws.

The Jewish people held great contempt towards the Romans because of the imposed taxes and laws: they were unwilling subjects. King Herod, the Roman ruler at the time of Jesus, introduced a new law that involved the massacre of all Jewish baby boys. King Herod also placed false idols in the Jewish Temple. Both of these actions caused further anger and resentment towards the Roman Empire.

At the time of Jesus, people living in Palestine were either Jews or Gentiles (non-Jews). These two groups tended not to associate with each other, since they held different beliefs.

Since Jews were allowed to practise their own faith, they had their own Jewish court of law called the Sanhedrin. Here they could punish Jews for not following Jewish laws. However, the Sanhedrin did not have the power to condemn anyone to death. This was the responsibility of the Roman Governor.

The Pharisees and the Sadducees were the religious groups that controlled the Sanhedrin. The Pharisees lived in towns and villages all over Palestine. They controlled the synagogues and had good standing in their communities because of their commitment to and knowledge of their faith. They guided people on the laws that should be followed.

The Sadducees were from wealthy families and lived mainly in Jerusalem. They played a key role in the running of the Temple and they co-operated with the Romans. This co-operation was not popular with the Pharisees.

Religious System

The Jews were monotheistic, with a belief in one God. This belief was very important to them and a lot of the time their lives centred on their faith. Worship on the Sabbath was very important to them. The day began on Friday at sundown and ended at Saturday sundown. Everything done on the Sabbath was in honour of their God. Jews normally attended the synagogue for Sabbath services weekly. They also tried to visit the Temple in Jerusalem at least once a year in order to celebrate one of the Jewish festivals.

The Jews were waiting for a Messiah throughout their history. They believed that this Saviour had been promised to them by God. Their understanding of this Messiah was that he would bring them political freedom from foreign rulers and the opportunity for their faith to be renewed.

1 Do you think the political system at the time of Jesus was fair? Give reasons for your answer.

2 In your opinion, what was it that kept the faith of the Jews so strong as they waited for the Messiah?

1 Investigate the Sabbath laws at the time of Jesus.

2 Research the four main religious groups who lived in Palestine around 1 CE: Pharisees, Sadducees, Zealots and Essenes.

Expectations of the Messiah: Priestly, Davidic and Prophetic

The term 'Messiah' means 'the anointed one' (*Christos* in Greek). Prior to the birth of Jesus the Jewish people were awaiting a Messiah as promised to them by God (Messianic Expectation). This expectation grew stronger in the first century BCE. Among the Jewish people there were different expectations of this Messiah: Priestly, Davidic and Prophetic.

Priestly Expectation came from the second century BCE, when a group of high priests, the Hasmonaean, were both priestly and national leaders. They were also warriors, which was an unexpected role for high priests. This expectation not only brought about the Good News but fought against enemies.

Davidic Expectation was the belief that the Messiah would be like the Jewish King David: he would come and free the Jewish people from Roman rule and restore the Jewish as the rightful leaders of their land. This belief is found in the book of Psalms.

Prophetic Expectation came from prophets, most notably Moses. Moses led the Jewish people to freedom and taught them the importance of following God's laws. This expectation would not only ensure the people would lead a correct lifestyle but also follow God in the right way and try to teach others the value of following the Jewish faith.

The Jewish Understanding of the Kingdom of God

The Jews had come to expect a Messiah who would rule Palestine and require people to become Jewish and to follow Jewish law. As the Jewish people continued to wait, adherence to the law became more important in their daily lives.

Jewish people had a strong faith in the Kingdom of God. They understood the Kingdom of God to be one that was established by God. It would have no end and it would be open to all people. Even though its origins were on earth, it would be a heavenly kingdom.

At the time of Jesus, some Jews believed that the Messiah that they were waiting for was Jesus. However, other Jews did not believe this and they continued waiting for their Messiah to come.

Jesus' teachings on the Kingdom of God were a lot like the prophecies in the Old Testament. Jesus taught people about the Kingdom of God through his telling of parables and his performing of miracles.

Jesus and his followers

The Life of Jesus

The Life of Jesus

Baptised in Jordan River
Baptised by John the Baptist
Holy Spirit descends from heaven
Appears to Saul (later Paul) on the Road to Damascus
Matthew
Luke
Suicide by hanging
Mark
Also called Judas, son of James
Fishermen
John
Judas
Andrew
James
Sons of Zebedee
Betrayed for thirty pieces of silver
Virgin birth
Denied Jesus three times
Thaddeus
Peter
Called twelve disciples
Bartholomew
Born in Bethlehem of Judea
The Zealot
Mother: Mary
Carpenter
Simon
Betrayed at Gethsemane
Thomas
Condemned by Herod
Jesus Christ
Son of God
Father: Joseph
Crucified at Calvary
Faced Pontius Pilate
Family
Fulfilled prophecy
Flogged thirty-nine times
Descendant of King David
Preceded by John the Baptist
Barabbas the Murderer
Called 'King of the Jews'
Promised Messiah
Carried own cross
Sanhendrin
Crown of thorns
Side pierced by spear
Temple veil splits

1 Use the mind map to write a detailed account of the life of Jesus, in your own words. Create a mind map that shows the special times in your own life.

Go to www.lds.org and search for the video of 'The Baptism of Jesus'.

After his baptism Jesus went to the desert for forty days and reflected on the message he would preach. This was the beginning of his public ministry, which lasted three years. During his public ministry he travelled all over Palestine spreading his message. He taught people about the kingdom of God through his telling of parables and his performing of miracles.

The Christian Understanding of the Kingdom of God

'And after John was delivered up, Jesus came into Galilee, preaching the Gospel of the Kingdom of God and saying: "The time is completed, and the Kingdom of God is at hand: repent, and believe in the Gospel."'

Mark 1:14

The good news of the Kingdom of God was always at the centre of Jesus' teachings. Jesus imparted this message to his followers by word (telling parables) and action (performing miracles). Pope John Paul II summarised the Kingdom of God very simply.

'In a word, the Kingdom of God is the manifestation and the realisation of God's plan of salvation in all its fullness.'

Redemptoris Missio #15

1 Explain the *Redemptoris Missio* quote in your own words.
2 Complete the following sentence: 'The Kingdom of God is...'

The Kingdom of God as preached by Jesus was a message of love: love for God and love for others. Jesus had a vision of the perfect world, a world full of love and full of people with compassion for one another. Jesus was aware that this way of life would be a challenge for people but it would result in great rewards for everyone. During his public ministry Jesus spoke about this vision to his followers. He did this through telling everyday stories that people could relate to and that were easy to remember. Each story held a deeper meaning that people could easily understand. Jesus wanted his followers to know that everyone was welcome to become part of the Kingdom of God and he emphasised that there would be a special place for the poor.

Go to godtube.com and search for the Parable of the Lost Sheep animation.

Read the following parables. Then complete the questions below for each parable.

★ Garments and Wineskins (Luke 5:36–39)
★ Good and Bad Fruit (Matthew 7:16–20)
★ Wicked Tenants (Mark 12:1–11)
★ Pharisee and Publican (Luke 18:9–14)
★ The Lost Sheep (Matthew 18:12–13)
★ Lamp on a Stand (Mark 4:21)
★ Strong Man (Matthew 12:29)
★ Closed Door (Luke 13:24–30)

1 Explain the message that Jesus was trying to teach about the Kingdom of God.

2 Relate the meaning of the parable to people's lives today.

As well as telling parables, Jesus also performed miracles. This helped people to believe that he was the Son of God and that he could do great things. There were three types of miracles that Jesus performed: Nature, Healing and Expelling.

Some of these miracles were performed in small groups and at other times there were large groups of witnesses. Jesus made sure to always seek out the outsiders and to help them. Jesus performed around thirty-seven miracles.

Go to godtube.com and search for the '5 loaves & 2 fishes' animation.

Read about the following miracles. Then complete the questions below for each miracle.

★ Jesus Turns Water into Wine (John 2:1–11)
★ Jesus Heals an Official's Son (John 4:43–54)
★ Jesus Drives Out an Evil Spirit (Mark 1:21–27, Luke 4:31–36)
★ Jesus Heals Peter's Mother-in-Law (Matthew 8:14–15, Mark 1:29–31, Luke 4:38–39)
★ Jesus Heals Many Sick at Evening (Matthew 8:16–17, Mark 1:32–34, Luke 4:40–41)
★ First Miraculous Catch of Fish (Luke 5:1–11)
★ Jesus Cleanses a Man With Leprosy (Matthew 8:1–4, Mark 1:40–45, Luke 5:12–14)
★ Jesus Heals a Centurion's Servant (Matthew 8:5–13, Luke 7:1–10)
★ Jesus Heals a Paralytic (Matthew 9:1–8, Mark 2:1–12, Luke 5:17–26)
★ Jesus Heals a Man's Withered Hand (Matthew 12:9–14, Mark 3:1–6, Luke 6:6–11)
★ Jesus Raises a Widow's Son in Nain (Luke 7:11–17)
★ Jesus Calms a Storm (Mark 8:23–27, Matthew 4:35–41, Luke 8:22–25)
★ Jesus Casts Demons into a Herd of Pigs (Matthew 8:28–33, Mark 5:1–20, Luke 8:26–37)
★ Jesus Heals a Woman in the Crowd (Matthew 9:20–22, Mark 5:25–34, Luke 8:42–48)

- ★ Jesus Raises Jairus' Daughter to Life (Matthew 9:18, 23–26, Mark 5:21–24, 35–43)
- ★ Jesus Heals Two Blind Men (Mark 9:27–31)
- ★ Jesus Heals a Man Unable to Speak (Mark 9:32–34)
- ★ Jesus Heals an Invalid at Bethesda (John 5:1–15)
- ★ Jesus Feeds 5,000 (Mark 14:13–21, Mark 6:30–44, Luke 9:10–17, John 6:1–15)
- ★ Jesus Walks on Water (Matthew 14:22–33, Mark 6:45–52, John 6:16–21)
- ★ Jesus Heals Many Sick in Gennesaret (Matthew 14:34–36, Mark 6:53–56)
- ★ Jesus Heals a Gentile Woman's Demon-Possessed Daughter (Matthew 5:21–28, Mark 7:24–30)
- ★ Jesus Heals a Deaf and Dumb Man (Mark 7:31–37)
- ★ Jesus Feeds 4,000 (Matthew 15:32–39, Mark 8:1–13)
- ★ Jesus Heals a Blind Man at Bethsaida (Mark 8:22–26)
- ★ Jesus Heals a Man Born Blind (John 9:1–12)
- ★ Jesus Heals a Boy with a Demon (Matthew 17:14–20, Mark 9:14–29, Luke 9:37–43)
- ★ Miraculous Temple Tax in a Fish's Mouth (Mark 17:24–27)
- ★ Jesus Heals a Blind, Mute Demoniac (Matthew 12:22–23, Luke 11:14–23)
- ★ Jesus Heals a Crippled Woman (Luke 13:10–17)
- ★ Jesus Heals a Man With Dropsy on the Sabbath (Luke 14:1–6)
- ★ Jesus Cleanses Ten Lepers (Luke 17:11–19)
- ★ Jesus Raises Lazarus from the Dead (John 11:1–45)
- ★ Jesus Restores Sight to Bartimaeus (Matthew 20:29–34, Mark 10:46–52, Luke 18:35–43)
- ★ Jesus Withers the Fig Tree (Matthew 21:18–22, Mark 11:12–14)
- ★ Jesus Heals a Servant's Severed Ear (Luke 22:50–51)
- ★ Second Miraculous Catch of Fish (John 21:4–11)

1. Explain the message that Jesus was trying to teach about the Kingdom of God through each of these miracles.
2. Place each miracle in its correct category: Nature, Healing or Expelling.

Jesus as a Threat to the Establishment

During his public ministry, Jesus came into conflict with the religious and political leaders at the time because of his message. He proclaimed the Kingdom of God and support for this message grew quickly. Jesus' message went against some of the upheld teachings of the time. He was seen as a threat to authority, notably when he healed the man and ate from the cornfield on the Sabbath. Both of these actions were seen as working on the Sabbath and consequently breaking Jewish laws, which offended the Pharisees.

The final act that sealed Jesus' fate was when he tried to 'cleanse the Temple'. He was horrified when he saw traders and stallholders illegally trading in the Court of Gentiles.

> *'Jesus began to drive out those who were selling and those who were buying in the temple, and he overturned the tables of the money changers and the seats of those who sold doves; and he would not allow anyone to carry anything through the temple'.*
>
> **Mark 11:15–16**

Jesus thought that this behaviour was disrespectful to his father's home.

'Is it not written my house shall be called a house of prayer for all the nations? But you have made it a den of robbers.'

Mark 11:17

Jesus now became a threat to the religious hierarchy in Jerusalem and his actions in the Temple led to him being arrested. The Temple was of great importance to the Jewish community and to peace in Judea. Jesus was seen as a threat to law and order at the time. Both Jewish and Roman leaders wanted to have Jesus crucified.

Jesus' Trial

Jesus' actions caused controversy and he was arrested in the Garden of Gethsemane when Judas betrayed him, kissing him on the cheek to identify him to the soldiers. The soldiers brought Jesus into the courtyard of the high priest. Peter followed and waited to see what happened. On three occasions Peter denied being a follower of Jesus. Peter wept as he remembered Jesus' prediction of this at the Last Supper.

Jesus was then questioned by Caiaphas, the Chief Priest of the Temple. Caiaphas wanted to get rid of Jesus: he feared that his own position in the temple would be threatened by Jesus.

Jesus was put on trial before the Sanhedrin. Jesus was accused of challenging authority and established laws, giving new meaning to Jewish laws, breaking the Sabbath laws and blasphemy. The accusations of blasphemy brought before Jesus were the most serious aspect of his trial. The Romans feared that Jesus and his followers might start a rebellion. The Jewish authorities feared the outcome of this rebellion.

From the Sanhedrin, Jesus was sent before the Roman Governor Pontius Pilate on the charges of treason. Initially Pilate felt the charges were not strong enough to warrant the crucifixion of Jesus. He suggested an alternative punishment but to no avail. As the crowds in Jerusalem expanded, there was increasing pressure on Pilate to sentence Jesus to death by crucifixion. Since it was the feast of Passover, tradition allowed one prisoner to go free from trial. Pilate asked the crowd if they wanted Jesus to be freed. The crowd rejected this – shouting for Barabbas, a criminal, to be freed instead. Jesus was then sentenced to death by crucifixion.

'Then the governor's soldiers took Jesus into the Praetorium and gathered the whole company of soldiers around him. They stripped him and put a scarlet robe on him, and then twisted together a crown of thorns and set it on his head. They put a staff in his right hand and knelt in front of him and mocked him. "Hail, king of the Jews!" they said. They spit on him, and took the staff and struck him on the head again and again. After they had mocked him, they took off the robe and put his own clothes on him. Then they led him away to crucify him.'

Matthew 27:27–31 (NIV)

1 Explain the reasons why Jesus was seen as a threat to the establishment.
2 Why, do you think, was Jesus so angry at what he saw in the Temple?
3 In your opinion, how much was Pontius Pilate to blame for the crucifixion of Jesus?
4 How do you think Jesus felt when he was sentenced to death by crucifixion?

Go to godtube.com and search for 'The Trial of Jesus' animation.

The Response of Jesus' Followers to His Suffering and Death

'When the centurion and those with him who were guarding Jesus saw the earthquake and all that had happened, they were terrified and exclaimed, "Surely he was the Son of God!"'

Matthew 27:54

Read the following Gospel accounts of the response of Jesus' followers to his suffering and death. Then complete the question below for each account.

- ★ Matthew 26:36–28:20
- ★ Mark 14:32–16:20
- ★ Luke 22:47–24:12
- ★ John 18:1–20:31

1 Write a summary of each Gospel account, using relevant quotations.

Impact of the Resurrection on the Disciples

Read the following Bible references on the impact of the Resurrection on the disciples.

'When the Sabbath was over, Mary Magdalene, and Mary the mother of James, and Salome, bought spices, so that they might come and anoint Him. Very early on the first day of the week, they came to the tomb when the sun had risen. They were saying to one another, "Who will roll away the stone for us from the entrance of the tomb?"'

Mark 16:1–3

'And behold, a severe earthquake had occurred, for an angel of the Lord descended from heaven and came and rolled away the stone and sat upon it. And his appearance was like lightning, and his clothing as white as snow. The guards shook for fear of him and became like dead men.

Matthew 28:2–4

'Looking up, they saw that the stone had been rolled away, although it was extremely large. Entering the tomb, they saw a young man sitting at the right, wearing a white robe; and they were amazed.'

Mark 16:4–5

'The angel said to the women, "Do not be afraid; for I know that you are looking for Jesus who has been crucified."'

Matthew 28:5

"'He is not here, but He has risen. Remember how he spoke to you while he was still in Galilee, saying that the Son of Man must be delivered into the hands of sinful men, and be crucified, and on the third day rise again.'"

Luke 24:6–7

"'Go quickly and tell his disciples that he has risen from the dead; and behold, he is going ahead of you into Galilee, there you will see him; behold, I have told you." And they left the tomb quickly with fear and great joy and ran to report it to his disciples.'

Matthew 28:7–8

'And they remembered his words, and returned from the tomb and reported all these things to the eleven and to all the rest. Now they were Mary Magdalene and Joanna and Mary the mother of James; also the other women with them were telling these things to the apostles. But these words appeared to them as nonsense, and they would not believe them.'

Luke 24:8–11

'So Peter and the other disciple went forth, and they were going to the tomb. The two were running together; and the other disciple ran ahead faster than Peter and came to the tomb first; and stooping and looking in, he saw the linen wrappings lying there; but he did not go in. And so Simon Peter also came, following him, and entered the tomb; and he saw the linen wrappings lying there, and the face-cloth which had been on his head, not lying with the linen wrappings, but rolled up in a place by itself. So the other disciple who had first come to the tomb then also entered, and he saw and believed.'

John 20:3–8

1. Outline how Jesus' death and resurrection impacted on his disciples.
2. Complete the following sentence: 'Jesus' death and resurrection greatly affected his disciples in that...'

Read the following passages of the Bible. Then complete the question below.

- ★ Matthew 28:8
- ★ Mark 15:42–45
- ★ Luke 24:8–9
- ★ Luke 24:6–7
- ★ John 20:3–8
- ★ John 20:24–29
- ★ Matthew 28:7
- ★ John 20:19–20
- ★ Matthew 27:60
- ★ Mark 16:4
- ★ Matthew 28:5
- ★ Matthew 28:2–4
- ★ Luke 24:10–11
- ★ Mark 16:5
- ★ Mark 16:1–3
- ★ John 19:39–41
- ★ Luke 23:54–56

1 Place each Bible passage into one of the following categories:

A Joseph of Arimathaea and Nicodemus anointed the body and placed it in a tomb. Once the Sabbath was over, Mary Magdalene and the other women came to anoint the body properly.

B They expected to find Jesus' body in the tomb but the tomb was empty.

C From the empty tomb, they heard a voice telling them that Jesus had risen from the dead and that they must go and tell the disciples.

D Not everybody believed the women's story. Many looked for evidence to verify what the women had said.

Historical Sources for the Evidence of Jesus

There are two sources that prove the existence of Jesus:

★ Religious sources (Gospels)
★ Historical sources (Tacitus and Pliny the Younger).

There is historical evidence from the first and second centuries that proves that Jesus lived in Palestine. Roman and Jewish historians have written accounts that mention the existence of Jesus. Two such historians are Tacitus and Pliny the Younger.

Tacitus

Tacitus was a Roman historian. He was born around 56 CE into an aristocratic family in Gaul. He was involved in politics, eventually becoming Governor of the Roman Province of Asia. Tacitus stated that Jesus (Christos) suffered the death penalty under the rule of the Emperor Tiberius.

> *'Consequently, to get rid of the report, Nero fastened the guilt and inflicted the most exquisite tortures on a class hated for their abominations, called Christians by the populace. Christus, from whom the name had its origin, suffered the extreme penalty during the reign of Tiberius at the hands of one of our procurators, Pontius Pilatus, and a most mischievous superstition, thus checked for the moment, again broke out not only in Judaea, the first source of the evil, but even in Rome, where all things hideous and shameful from every part of the world find their centre and become popular'.*

The work of Tacitus is held in high regard as being factually correct about the existence of Jesus. Edwin Yamauchi has said that the work of Tacitus is 'probably the most important reference to Jesus outside the New Testament'.

Pliny the Younger

Pliny the Younger was a Roman historian. He was born in 61 CE to a landowner in Comum, Northern Italy. He was Roman Governor of Bithynia in Asia Minor. Pliny the Younger wrote in his letters about the early Christians living in Asia Minor. In one of his letters he outlined the beliefs and practices of people called Christians.

'They were in the habit of meeting on a certain fixed day before it was light, when they sang in alternate verses a hymn to Christ, as to a god, and bound themselves by a solemn oath, not to any wicked deeds, but never to commit any fraud, theft or adultery, never to falsify their word, nor deny a trust when they should be called upon to deliver it up; after which it was their custom to separate, and then reassemble to partake of food – but food of an ordinary and innocent kind.'

The letters of Pliny the Younger prove that Christians did exist and wanted to follow the teachings set down by Jesus. These letters prove that Jesus must have existed and spread his message for people to be his followers after his death.

1 What do the writings of Tacitus and Pliny the Younger prove about Jesus?
2 In your opinion, why did both historians mention Jesus in their work?

Early Christian Communities: Beliefs, Behaviours and Lifestyles

After the Resurrection and Ascension of Jesus, early Christian communities began to form.

Go to vimeo.com and search for 'Pentecost video'.

Before Jesus ascended into heaven he promised the disciples that he would send the Holy Spirit from heaven to help them. This happened ten days after the Ascension; it is known as Pentecost. On this day the first Christian community began in Jerusalem, when Peter and the apostles baptised 3,000 new followers.

Other Christian communities developed throughout Palestine and the Roman Empire as a result of the work of the apostles and the early Christian missionaries.

The lives of the early Christians are explored in a book entitled *We Look For The Kingdom: The Everyday Lives of the Early Christian* by Carl J. Sommer.

Carl J. Sommer

Author

In what ways did the existence of the Roman Empire help or hinder the early Christians?

The Romans aided the spread of Christianity unintentionally, in some very general ways. First of all, the Romans made travel throughout the Mediterranean world relatively safe and easy. They cleared the seas of pirates, suppressed banditry in the countryside and built an excellent system of roads. This made the general spread of ideas possible, and since Christ's message, the Gospel, is the best idea the world has ever encountered, Christianity spread as well.

Secondly, the Romans kept the Mediterranean world at peace throughout most of this period. Granted, it was a rough peace, enforced by the sword sometimes quite brutally, but the absence of open military conflict made it possible for Christianity to spread.

Thirdly, in a strange way, the persecutions helped spread Christianity, since people who were not familiar with the Christian message were exposed to the Gospel and got to see the fortitude of the martyrs. The Romans – particularly Roman soldiers –were very impressed with physical bravery, and they were exposed to many examples of Christian fortitude as a result of the persecutions.

On the other hand, the Romans deliberately did some quite specific things to hinder the spread of Christianity. The persecutions undoubtedly deterred many people from becoming Christians, and not everyone behaved with fortitude under the threat of persecution. We hear about large numbers of lapsi, people who abandoned the faith under the threat of torture, during the persecution of Decius in 251 CE. Many of these lapsi were later readmitted into the Church, but some were lost forever. Beyond the persecutions, the fact that Christianity was illegal presented the Church with other obstacles. The Christians could not have public worship spaces as other religions could, but had to worship in private houses. This meant that passersby could not just walk in to see what was going on. Also, the process of admission into the Church was complicated by the necessity of protecting the bishops, who were the primary targets of the persecutions, from government infiltrators.

In examining how the early Christians lived, what do you think would surprise modernday Catholics the most? What aspects of early Christian worship and liturgy might be most strange or foreign to twenty-first-century Catholics?

In my experience, modern Catholics are most surprised by how much the structure, beliefs, and worship of the early Christians resembles our own. This is particularly true in the case of the liturgy. We have been led to believe, primarily by a flawed interpretation of New Testament evidence, that the worship of the early Church was charismatic and unstructured. But when people see Justin Martyr's description of the liturgy as it was practised in 150 CE, they realise that very early on the Christians were worshipping almost exactly the way we do today. Of course, there was a certain amount of development between the New Testament period and 150 CE, but the basic structure of the liturgy appeared quite soon, and did not change very much.

There are two aspects of early Christian worship that would appear strange to us today: the agape meals and the refrigerium. The agape meals were typically eaten on Sunday evenings, and combined elements of a potluck dinner, where everyone would bring something for the table, and a prayer service. The agape meals had their own prescribed prayers, and typically a bishop or presbyter was the presider. The refrigerium was even stranger, for the early Christians appear to have had the practice of eating meals at the gravesites of prominent Christians. We don't know much about this practice, but archaeologists have found, scattered throughout the empire, martyria, or gravesites of martyrs (there is a beautiful example of this in Hierapolis, the martyrium of Philip). Some of these martyria are complete with recognisable dining areas. We certainly don't have either one of these practices today, though I think that in some ways the Church could benefit from a revival in the practice of agape.

There has been a decent amount of scholarly debate over how much or intensely the early Christians were persecuted. How bad, in fact, was the Roman treatment of Christians, and what would have been the general attitude of the average Roman towards the Christian religion?

Both sides of the debate over persecution have valid points. In the 300-year period of the early Church, there are approximately 1,000 known martyrs. Periods of persecution tended to be intense, savage and local. Notable examples in my book would be the persecutions in Rome from 64–67 CE, the persecution in Lyon in 178 CE, the persecution in North Africa around 205 CE, and the final great persecution that began in 303 CE and was not really ended until Constantine won his great victory at Milvian Bridge. On the other hand, there were long periods of time (including two thirty-year periods in the third century), when the Church was relatively free from persecution. But those who favour the notion that the persecutions were overblown have to realise that until Constantine the threat of martyrdom was constantly present. Some of the most famous martyrs of the early Church – Ignatius of Antioch, Polycarp of Smyrna and Justin Martyr – were martyred under emperors who were disposed to show some lenience to the Christians. Other factors have to be considered as well. There were also some spontaneous persecutions that were brought about by local circumstances. For instance, Tarsicius of Rome was murdered by a mob while he was trying to take the Eucharist to the sick. We will never know exactly how many Christians died in these spontaneous persecutions.

The average Roman tended to see the Christians as dangerously impious. The Romans thought that the Christians' failure to honour the Gods of Rome was likely to lead to famines, floods, earthquakes, military disasters, diseases and a host of other ills. Consequently, every time one of these events occurred (and they occurred often), the Christians were blamed.

1. Write a summary of the main points that Carl J. Sommer makes about the early Christian communities.
2. Did anything surprise you in the interview with Carl J. Sommer?
3. Highlight the main difficulties faced by the early Christian communities.
4. What does the early persecution of these communities tell us about their faith in Jesus?

St Paul

One of the early Christian missionaries was a Jewish man called Saul. God appeared to Saul on the road to Damascus, which brought about a dramatic change in Saul's life. Saul changed from being a persecutor of Christians to being a follower of Christ. He changed his name to the Christian name Paul and went on three religious journeys. Today he is known as one of the most famous Christian missionaries. Paul set up many Christian communities (e.g. Thessalonica) and he kept in contact with the communities through his letters.

St Paul and the Early Christian Community in Thessalonica

Thessalonica existed as far back as 315 BCE and it is located south of Philippi. It was a busy business centre and held a major naval station. It was central to the spread of Christianity. The first letter from St Paul to the Thessalonians was written around 50 BCE. The letter gave an insight into the issues facing the Christian community established there.

While there, St Paul built up a good relationship with the community: 'Like a mother feeding and looking after her children we felt so devoted to you' (1 Thessalonians 2:7). St Paul shared with them his own experiences of God's message and tried to guide and encourage them to have belief in God.

However, not everybody received his message well. He often faced great resistance: 'we had received rough treatment and insults at Philippi' (1 Thessalonians 2:2). The Christian community was only just emerging and there were people who attempted to undermine the authority of Paul, which created tensions.

The early Christians in Thessalonica believed that the second coming of Christ would happen in their lifetime. They listened to St Paul when he told them to reflect on their lifestyles and to live good and holy lives. He instructed that they must not be lazy and that they must keep away from undisciplined people. They must pay for their own food and see the early missionaries as their role models. St Paul told them to 'go on quietly working and earning the food that they eat' (2 Thessalonians 3:12). He instructed them to 'admonish those who are undisciplined, encourage the apprehensive, support the weak and be patient with everyone'. St Paul also asked them to respect the new leaders in the community and he showed an awareness of the cultural diversity that existed in the city at that time. St Paul also encouraged people to refrain from lustful activities and to have respect for their bodies.

St Paul wanted the early Christian community to be an inspiration to other religious communities. He wanted to prevent further tensions between the Christian and Jewish communities. St Paul's hope was that the early Christian communities would be places of love. He felt that the lifestyle, work and faith of the early Christian people should be something that Jews and Gentiles would aspire to. The early Christians endured great hardships but it was their love of

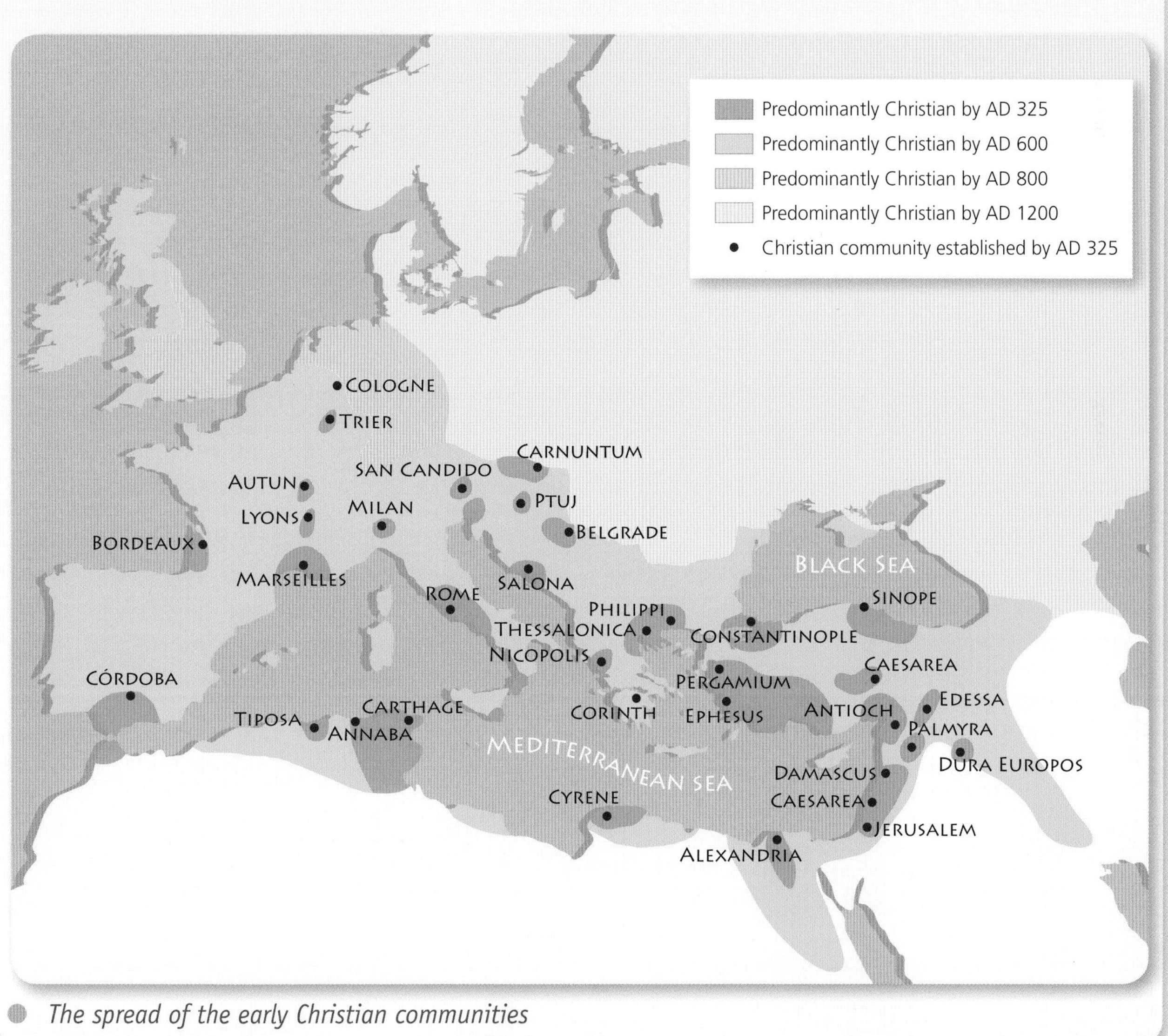

The spread of the early Christian communities

God and their belief in the Holy Spirit that strengthened them. 'Among the churches of God we take special pride in you for your perseverance and faith under all the persecutions and hardships you have to bear' (2 Thessalonians 1:4).

St Paul was mindful that the early Christian communities would face many difficulties: persecution, opposition from detractors, a change in their beliefs and in their lifestyles. So he gave the early Christians advice that they could use when he was not there to guide them: 'We urge you and appeal to you in the Lord Jesus; we instructed you how to live in the way that pleases God, and you are so living; but make more progress still' (1 Thessalonians 4:1).

1. Examine the map of the early Christian communities (p.53). Name the communities set up by St Paul.
2. How do you think the early Christian missionaries brought the message about Jesus to the places shown on the map?

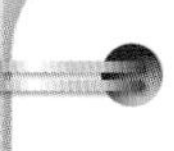

End of Section Summary

- In Jesus' time, Palestine was part of the Roman Empire.
- The Romans allowed the Jews to practise their faith.
- Two historians that wrote about the existence of Jesus were Tacitus and Pliny the Younger.
- The Jews had three different expectations of the Messiah: Priestly, Davidic and Prophetic.
- Christians believed that Jesus was the Messiah; the Jewish people are still waiting for their Messiah.
- The Romans and some Jews were threatened by Jesus' message.
- This led to Jesus' arrest, trial and crucifixion.
- After the Resurrection, the early Christian movement began to spread beyond Palestine.
- Thessalonica was one of the early Christian communities established by St Paul.

End of Section Activities

1. Explain in your own words the steps that led to Jesus' crucifixion.
2. Compare what Tacitus and Pliny the Younger had to say about Jesus.
3. Write an account of what the Jews meant by Messianic Expectation (referring to Priestly, Davidic and Prophetic).
4. What do you think of the message that St Paul gave to the Thessalonians?

- 'Jesus did exist.'
- 'Christianity has lost its way and needs to go back to its original vision.'
- 'Jesus was given a fair trial.'

1 Research what it was like growing up in Palestine at the time of Jesus.

2 Research one of the following early Christian communities: Antioch, Corinth, Ephesus or Rome. Present your findings to the class.

3 Write a comparative account entitled 'Palestine: Then and Now'.

4 Use the map on p.53 to create a timeline that shows the spread of the early Christian communities.

Imagine you are Jesus and journal about the last week of your life. Write entries from your arrival into Jerusalem up to the Resurrection.

Imagine you are Jesus and write out the questions and answers from your time on trial.

Films

★ *The Greatest Story Ever Told*
★ *The Passion of Christ*
★ *The Life of Brian*
★ *Jesus of Nazareth*
★ *The Last Temptation of Christ*
★ *King of Kings*
★ *Jesus Christ Superstar*
★ *The Miracle Maker*

Books

★ *The Da Vinci Code* – Dan Brown
★ *The Passion of Jesus Christ* – John Piper
★ *The Cross of Christ* – John R.W. Scott
★ *Jesus and His Friends* – D.A. Carson

Websites

★ www.godtube.com
★ www.old.reonline.org.uk
★ www.allaboutjesus.com
★ www.jesuscentral.com

Section 3

Morality

Context

Morality is a person's understanding of what is right and wrong in a given situation. It is a key component of the Leaving Certificate Religion programme because it affects each of us in our everyday lives. This section aims to explain what morality is and allows us to explore moral issues that may be faced in life.

Consider the following scenarios.

★ There is something negative written on Facebook about your friend. Your friend is not on Facebook. What do you do?

★ At a friend's party, you are offered an ecstasy tablet. Everyone else is trying it. What do you do?

★ You find a substantial amount of money in a classroom. No one has seen the money except you. Do you take it?

1 Which of these scenarios made you think most about right and wrong?

2 Is each scenario straightforward or is there a grey area with any of them?

3 From this discussion, what do you think it means to be moral?

What is Morality?

Morality is a person's understanding of what is right and wrong in a situation.

- 'Murder is always wrong.'
- 'It is always wrong to steal.'
- 'You should always tell the truth.'
- 'Any wrong action must be punished.'
- 'Most teenagers are selfish.'
- 'Should we buy pet food when there are people dying of hunger in the world?'
- 'Should we always be accountable for our actions?'
- 'People under the influence of alcohol/drugs should not be punished for their actions.'
- 'You should always stand by your friends.'
- 'You should tell lies to get your friends out of trouble.'

Conscience

A human can grow in many ways, e.g. physically, emotionally, spiritually, intellectually and morally. When it comes to morality, humans are born with the ability to develop a conscience. A fully developed conscience is the ability to know what is right or wrong in any given situation by using your own judgment and experience.

Throughout your life many people help to develop your conscience. It starts in childhood with the guidance of parents, teachers and other adults. The next key stage of this development occurs during adolescence when you are first faced with making important moral decisions on your own. These decisions can determine what path you take in life. An informed conscience takes a lot of effort. This effort needs to continue into adulthood if we are to become a morally responsible person.

People describe conscience in different ways. It can be described as a voice in your head that tells you right from wrong. Others say it can be a feeling they get when they make a moral decision: this can be a good feeling when you do the right thing or a guilty feeling when you do something wrong. However, both of these descriptions are too narrow: sometimes that voice or feeling can *mislead* you to do the wrong thing, e.g. take revenge.

Examination of Conscience

1. Have I spoken disrespectfully of others?
2. Have I misbehaved in school?
3. Have I been disrespectful to my parents or teachers?
4. Have I had any arguments with my friends in the last month?
5. Have I made fun of anybody?
6. Have I stolen anything?
7. Have I damaged anyone's property?
8. Have I helped others to do wrong in any way?
9. Have I told lies to get out of trouble?
10. Have I talked behind other people's backs?

Moral Growth

Moral growth is a process that people experience as they go through life. It involves learning right from wrong through guidance from others and your own experiences. This normally occurs in two stages:

★ Moral immaturity is when a person is at the first stage of moral growth. Decisions are usually made with the help and advice from others.
★ Moral maturity is when a person has reached the final stage of moral growth. Decisions are usually made by themselves without any need for guidance from others.

However, people reach different levels of moral maturity. Moral immaturity occurs when:

★ You rely on others to teach you right from wrong
★ You have uninformed notions of morality
★ You do the right/wrong thing to seek approval from others
★ Your conscience is still developing.

Moral maturity occurs when:

★ You rely on your informed conscience to know right from wrong
★ You have informed notions of morality
★ You do not need approval for your actions from others
★ Your conscience is fully developed.

1 How do you think a person goes from moral immaturity to moral maturity?
2 Describe an action where you might seek approval from others.
3 How long do you think it takes to develop to moral maturity?
4 Who might you rely on to help your morality to grow?
5 Why, do you think, do some people do not reach moral maturity?
6 How would you know when you have reached moral maturity?
7 Do you think that morally mature people are capable of immoral acts?
8 Can a person who is morally immature be held responsible for bad moral behaviour?

Principle of Double Effect

When people reach moral maturity the principle of double effect can come into play.

The general principle of Christian moral theology is that the end does not justify the means. If an act is considered wrong in itself, one cannot do it, even if good comes from it.

However, Catholic moral theology uses the principle of double effect when there are two effects. A person can allow the evil to happen so that the good may be achieved, but the evil that comes about must not be directly intended and must be proportionate to the good effect. In other words, the decision must not involve an evil that far outweighs the good that is achieved.

Here are some examples of the double effect principle.

During World War II, Jews were in hiding for fear of being sent to concentration camps. However, some Jewish people were hidden by others during this period. If people were to tell the truth about those hidden, the evil that may come from it may be that many people will die (think of those who hid the Frank family). In this case the wrong that comes about far outweighs any good that would be achieved by telling the truth.

When a woman has an ectopic pregnancy, the baby cannot survive. An operation to remove the baby will mean the woman's life can be saved but the unintended result of the operation is that the child dies. The principle of double effect will allow this, since the result of the baby dying is not intended and the woman's life is saved: a life is equal to a life (proportionate reason).

When someone kills an aggressor in an act of self-defence, then it is justified because the intention of the person was self-defence in order to save a life (their own). The unintended outcome is the death of the aggressor.

In order to understand double effect in any scenario, we must ask: Do I need the bad thing to happen in order to get the good result? For example, if there was a way to save the lives without lying, or a way to save both the baby and the mother, or a way to keep my own life without killing the aggressor, would I do that? If the answer is yes (even though these options may not be available), then the double effect principle is in action.

Double Effect Principle in Action

Consider the following scenarios in terms of the double effect principle.

A pregnant woman finds out that she has cancer of the womb. In order to save herself she needs chemotherapy. An indirect result will be that the baby will die.

What is the right thing to do in this situation?

A man is driving a train and he sees five men on the track in front of him. If he keeps going down the track he is supposed to be on, then he will surely kill the five men (there is no way to warn them in time). The train driver then notices that he could switch tracks and go onto another track but there is one man on the other track (this man is where he is supposed to be).

Should the train driver switch tracks in order to save five lives and take one life?

A white woman is raped by a black man during the African-American Civil Rights Movement. The sheriff knows that if he does not find the perpetrator there will be a race riot. The sheriff has a black homeless man in custody who has already committed a crime. The sheriff has the option to frame this man and prevent a fatal race riot breaking out in his town.

What is the right thing for the sheriff to do?

What were your thoughts on each of these scenarios? The person who believes that the train driver should not switch tracks nor should the sheriff frame the homeless man agrees with the principle of double effect. The person who believes that the train driver should switch tracks and that the sheriff should frame the homeless man agree with the greater good theory. The greater good theory states that the act of saving five lives is better than the act of saving one life.

Moral Dilemmas

Hold a classroom debate about each of the following scenarios.

- ★ You are the captain of a ship that crashes into an iceberg. You and the twenty passengers get into the only lifeboat. The lifeboat can only hold eight people. It is obvious that some passengers will have to leave the lifeboat if anyone is to have a chance at survival. What do you do?
- ★ In *Sophie's Choice* by William Styron a Polish woman and her two children are arrested by the Nazis and sent to Auschwitz. On arrival, Sophie is given a choice: one of her children will be sent to the gas chamber and one will be spared. After great turmoil, Sophie tells the guards that they can take her daughter to the gas chamber. She made this decision because her son was older and stronger and she felt he would be better able to survive in the camp. What would you have done?
- ★ John is a very competent swimmer. On his way to a family wedding, he passes by a deserted pier and notices a teenage boy who has fallen in and cannot swim. John knows he could easily save the boy without any danger to himself but he chooses not to: he does not want to ruin his outfit for the wedding. Was John right to do what he did?
- ★ You are a psychiatrist and your patient has just told you that he intends to kill a woman. You do not know if he is telling the truth or not. Should you report the threat to the police or should you remain silent under the principle of confidentiality?
- ★ It is Sarah's role to hire new staff in her firm. A lot of very qualified people apply. Her friend Jane also applies. Jane has good qualifications but she is not as qualified or experienced as the others. Sarah decides to give the job to Jane. What would you have done?
- ★ A friend tells you that he committed a crime and asks you to promise never to tell. A week later you discover that an innocent person has been arrested for the crime. You beg your friend to confess to the police, but he won't. He also reminds you that you promised not to tell. What should you do?

Abortion

Abortion can be defined as the deliberate termination of a human pregnancy. There are two types of abortion: procured and spontaneous (miscarriage).

1 When you think about abortion, what comes to mind?

2 Define abortion in your own words.

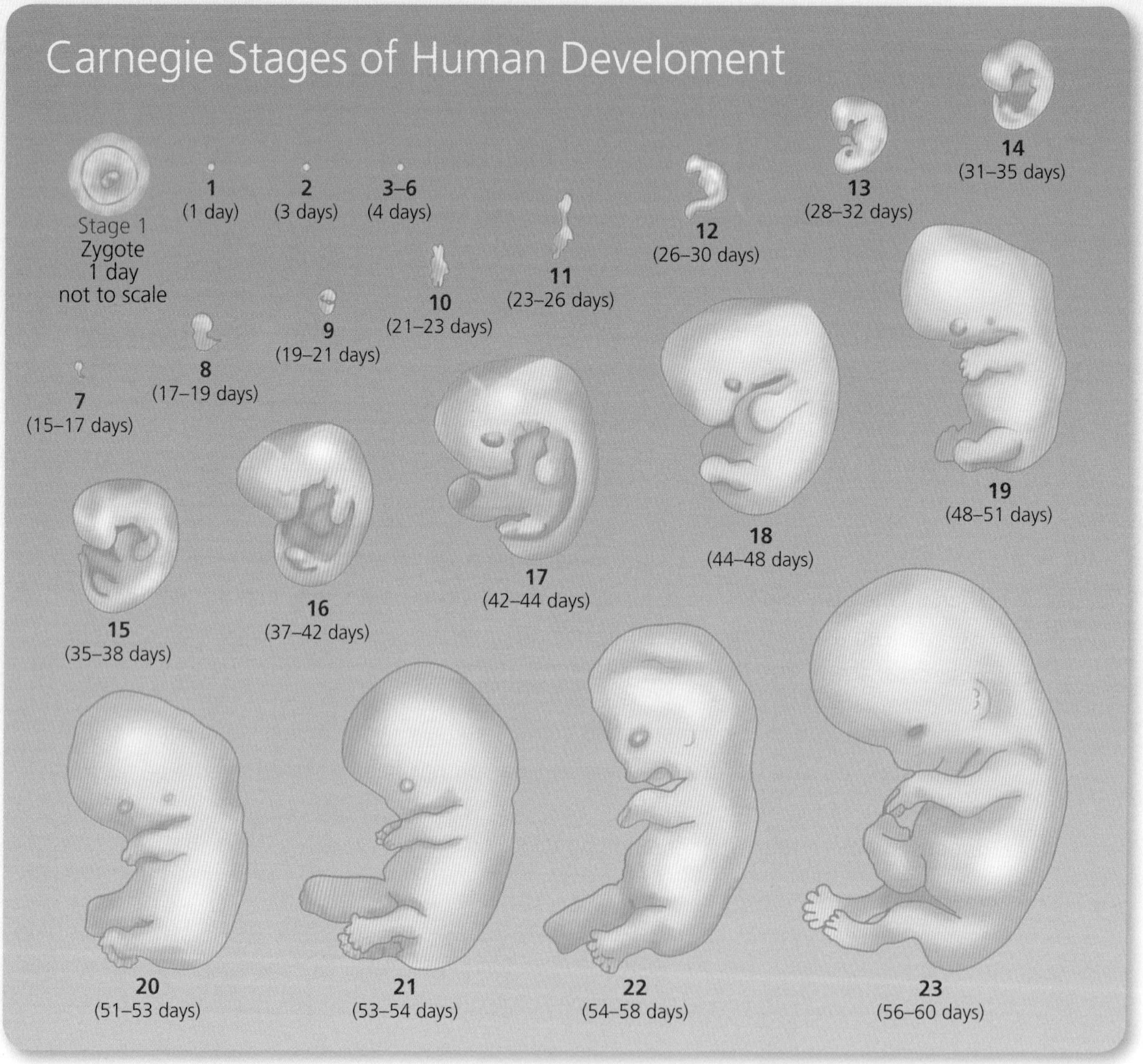

Carnegie Stages of Human Develoment

Stage 1
Zygote
1 day
not to scale

1 (1 day)
2 (3 days)
3–6 (4 days)
7 (15–17 days)
8 (17–19 days)
9 (19–21 days)
10 (21–23 days)
11 (23–26 days)
12 (26–30 days)
13 (28–32 days)
14 (31–35 days)
15 (35–38 days)
16 (37–42 days)
17 (42–44 days)
18 (44–48 days)
19 (48–51 days)
20 (51–53 days)
21 (53–54 days)
22 (54–58 days)
23 (56–60 days)

Examine the chart of Life Before Birth and answer the following questions.

1 Are you surprised at the size of a foetus at image 9? Why/Why not?

2 Looking at the chart, when do you think human life begins?

3 Does anything surprise you at the different stages of behavioural development?

4 Looking at the chart, when do you think the most important stage of development takes place?

5 Write a detailed paragraph on the development of the foetus (growth, behavioural and developmental)

The procedure of abortion can involve some of the following methods.

1 Suction: The foetus is taken from the womb by a powerful suction pump.

The following three procedures are rarely used; they take place after 16 weeks of pregnancy.

2 Sectioning: The foetus is cut into pieces by a surgeon and the pieces are then removed by suction.

3 Hysterotomy: The foetus is taken out of the womb through an abdominal incision.

4 Saline induction: A concentrated salt or glucose solution is injected into the fluid sack in which the baby lives. The foetus will die within 48 hours.

Why Might a Woman Choose Abortion?

There are many different reasons why a woman might choose to have an abortion. Medical reasons include the following:

★ When there is a serious problem with the development of the foetus in the womb

★ When the mother's life is at risk (this could include cancer of the uterus/cervix or mental health issues).

Other reasons include the following:

★ Traumatic personal situations, e.g. rape or incest

★ Pressure from another party, e.g. partner

★ Economic hardship

★ Single parenthood

★ Unplanned pregnancy.

1 In your own words explain the medical reasons that might lead a woman to choose an abortion.

2 Can you think of any other reasons a woman might choose an abortion?

Moral Debate on Abortion

Many people believe that abortion is morally acceptable in certain circumstances. Some of the following arguments have been made.	Many people believe that abortion is never morally acceptable. Some of the following arguments have been made.
★ Every woman has the right to decide what happens to her body. ★ Legalising abortion reduces the number of 'backstreet' abortions that risk the health of the woman. ★ It is wrong to bring unwanted children into the world. ★ If a woman becomes pregnant as a result of rape or incest, they should not be forced to have the baby. ★ Abortion is not murder, since it destroys a collection of cells that can't survive outside of the mother's womb before the 24th week. ★ If the mother's life is at risk, she should be allowed have an abortion.	★ The unborn child is alive from the moment of conception and has the right to life. ★ Abortion could be seen as just another type of contraception, which might encourage casual sex. ★ Many childless couples would adopt unwanted babies. ★ After the abortion there may be mental and physical risks to the woman, which might lead to sterility, guilt and depression. ★ There is no need for an abortion if the woman is lacking emotional and/or financial support that can be sought from outside support networks. ★ The United Nations declaration says children have a right to protection before, during and after birth.

1 Summarise in your own words the ethical debate surrounding abortion.

2 Can you think of any other aspects that should be included in the debate about abortion?

3 In your opinion, which of the arguments is strongest?

Abortion Law in Ireland (a brief history)

★ In 1983 there was an amendment made to the Constitution of Ireland that prevented abortion being legalised in the future. The following statement was inserted into the Constitution:

> *'The State acknowledges the right to life of the unborn and, with due regard to the equal right to life of the mother, guarantees in its laws to respect, and, as far as practicable, by its laws to defend and vindicate that right.'* (Article 40.3.3)

- In February 1992 the High Court issued a ruling that prevented a 14-year-old girl from travelling to England to have an abortion. This girl had been raped. The High Court made its ruling based on Article 40.3.3. The girl travelled to England with her parents and they contacted the Gardaí before the abortion in order to seek advice on DNA evidence. The Gardaí contacted the Attorney General who in turn prevented the girl from having the abortion, since it was in breach of Article 40.3.3. The case was then brought to the Supreme Court who ruled in favour of the girl on the grounds of suicidal tendencies as a result of the pregnancy. Based on this ruling the girl was allowed to travel to England to have the procedure. This case became known as 'the X case'. The girl remained unnamed so that her identity could be protected.

  The Supreme Court ruling in the X case meant that any pregnant woman could seek to have a legal abortion on the grounds of suicidal tendencies. The abortion could take place in Ireland, if a doctor was willing to conduct the procedure.
- In 1992 there was a referendum on abortion, which centred around three issues. The outcome of this referendum was as follows: the first two issues regarding information on abortions and the right to travel for an abortion were both passed. However, the third issue regarding the legalisation of abortion in Ireland was rejected by 64 per cent.
- In 1997 a second case was brought to public attention. This time it involved a 13-year-old girl from the Travelling community, who was raped and became pregnant as a result. The girl was in the custody of the Eastern Health Board (EHB) when she found out she was pregnant. She stated that she had suicidal tendencies as a result of the pregnancy. The EHB sought to bring the girl to England to have an abortion, as they were in fear for her life. The girl's parents were against their daughter having this procedure. The Children's Court ruled in favour of allowing the girl to travel to England to have an abortion. The High Court upheld this ruling. The case was known as 'the C case'.
- In 2002 there was another referendum on abortion. The Irish people rejected the 25th Amendment of the Constitution (Protection of Human Life in Pregnancy) Bill 2002. The vote decided that the threat of suicide was not grounds for abortion.
- In 2010 a case was brought before the European Court of Human Rights (*ABC v Ireland*). Three Irish women challenged the position of the Irish Constitution on the issue of abortion. These three women had travelled to England to have abortions and felt that they were put under undue stress and pressure as a result of Ireland's legislation on abortion. They claimed that Ireland's legal position on abortion goes against Article 8 of the European Convention of Human Rights: 'The right to respect for private and family life'.
- July 2013
  - President Michael D. Higgins signs the 'Protection of Life During Pregnancy Act' into law.
  - The Act states that two doctors must confirm there is a physical threat to the life of the woman.
  - Where the threat arises because of suicidal risk, three doctors must agree that the woman's life is at risk.

The X Case and the Letter of the Law

Linda Kelly

Twenty years ago, the Supreme Court ruled a suicidal pregnant teenager had the right to an abortion. So why are we still in a legal quagmire without relevant legislation, asks Linda Kelly.

Where were you on 23 February 1992? Celebrating the departure of Charles Haughey as Taoiseach? Maybe you had retired or had started college? Maybe you were a newlywed or maybe you were welcoming another child into your family? Or maybe you were like me, still at school and blissfully unaware of the court case that was rocking the nation. The X case, as it became known, divided the country in 1992, but does it still divide us in 2012?

It's hard to believe it's two decades since the details of the case, a tragic story of one Irish family, gripped the nation. Newspapers related the heart-breaking tale of the 14-year-old girl abused by a neighbour. In late 1985, he raped her and she became pregnant. In January of 1986, she told her parents about the abuse, as well as her suicidal thoughts as a result of the pregnancy. They reported the rape to the Gardaí and organised an appointment in England for an abortion. Before going, the family asked the Gardaí if DNA from the abortion would be admissible as evidence as the neighbour was denying the charges (the man was tried, jailed, had his sentence reduced on appeal, was released, whereupon he attacked a 15-year-old girl in 1999, was convicted, and imprisoned again for three and a half years.) The Gardaí contacted the Director of Public Prosecutions about the case, who contacted the Attorney General, Harry Whelehan.

Whelehan sought a temporary injunction to stop the girl from obtaining an abortion under article 40.3.3 of the Constitution. The injunction was granted by the High Court and the family, in England, was informed. The girl returned home without having the abortion. A few days later, an application was made for a permanent injunction against her and this was granted by the High Court — effectively imprisoning the girl in Ireland until the birth of the child.

During the High Court hearing, the story broke on the front page of *The Irish Times*, bringing it into the public spotlight, where it would remain for many months. The girl's parents appealed the decision of the High Court to the Supreme Court and on 26 February 1992, the Supreme Court found in favour of 'X' (the girl) in a majority verdict of four to one, and overturned the injunction. She was now free to travel to England to access abortion services. While in England, waiting for the procedure, she suffered a miscarriage.

The decision of the Supreme Court was released in March and made it clear they believed, in line with the Constitution, that a woman has a right to access an abortion in Ireland if there is a 'real and substantial risk' to her life and that this included a risk to her life from the possibility of suicide. It was then — and still remains — up to the

Government to create legislation to give effect to the Supreme Court decision. Twenty years later, successive Irish governments have failed to legislate for the X case.

In the immediate aftermath of the case, the Government put three referenda to the Irish people — these were known as the 12th, 13th and 14th proposed amendments to the Constitution.

The 12th amendment asked to remove suicide as grounds for abortion, the 13th amendment asked that women should have the right to travel outside the State for abortion, and the 14th amendment asked that information about abortion should be available in the State.

Now, if Ireland is as opposed to abortion as is suggested in certain quarters, you would expect that the 12th amendment would have passed and the 13th and 14th amendments would have failed. The opposite is actually true. In a majority of 2:1, Irish people voted to reject the 12th amendment, thereby endorsing the Supreme Court's decision on X. They also voted to allow women the right to travel for abortion and the right to information about abortion to be made available in Ireland.

In doing this, a majority of the Irish people demonstrated their support for abortion in line with the X case.

Despite the results of these referenda, the political system did not act on the Supreme Court decision, and, in 1997, history repeated itself with the C case. Again, the court found the girl in question had the right to travel for an abortion.

Instead of tackling the issue then, the government engaged in delay tactics, commissioning reports and expert committees and this continued until 2002. A decade after the original case, then Taoiseach Bertie Ahern held another referendum, asking pretty much the same question as the failed referendum in 1992 — to remove the threat of suicide as a ground for abortion.

The Irish people gave the same answer — no. They voted to support the X case decision.

After this second vote, legislation was still not forthcoming and in 2007 another woman, known as Miss D, took a case to allow her to leave Ireland for an abortion for her anencephalic pregnancy. As with the previous case, the court ruled she had the right to travel.

Niall Behan, chief executive at the Irish Family Planning Association (IFPA), says it's clear that it's not just the judiciary that supports access to abortion in the limited circumstances of the X case. Behan points to a variety of opinion polls, from the 2010 YouGov PLC poll to the Red C/Irish Examiner Poll in 2009 to TNS/MRBI Opinion Poll in 2007, all of which found a large majority in favour of allowing access to abortion where the life of the mother is in danger.

The issue came to the fore again last year, when the European Court of Human Rights found in favour of a woman, C, finding that her rights had been violated because the Government has failed to legislate for the X case.

Speaking about this most recent case, Stephanie Lord, of Choice Ireland, a group which is part of the newly formed Action on X Alliance, says 'Successive governments have neglected this issue for far too long. It is clear from the judgment in this case that the Government must now legislate for abortion in cases where it is already legal — that is, under the terms of the X case. The failure to legislate for X has been a damning indictment of governmental attitudes to women's health.'

Lord is not the only person with strong feelings on the topic. Sandra McAvoy, a campaigner in Cork, says 'the X case judgment established a woman's right to have an abortion in Ireland when there was a real and substantial risk to her life. By continuing to ban abortion, we do not prevent it; we just export it, disguise it and deny it, instead of addressing these women's genuine needs.'

The Government has now established an 'expert group' to address the issue. The group has until the end of June to propose a way forward for Enda Kenny and his Cabinet colleagues and the 'expert group' has begun its work, meeting for the first time a few weeks ago, at the end of January. They will be closely watched to see if, twenty years and six months after the infamous X case, a resolution can finally be found.

Judge Jails C Case Rapist For 'Dreadful Evil Act'

Tomas Mac Ruairi

The rapist at the centre of the C case has been sentenced to twelve years in prison by Mr Justice John Quirke at the Central Criminal Court. Simon McGinley (now 25), a married man and father of three children from Dowdalshill, Dundalk, Co. Louth, had pleaded guilty at an earlier hearing in October to raping the 13-year-old girl on 27 August 1997.

Mr Justice Quirke told him he had to pay a heavy penalty for what was a particularly abhorrent rape. Not only had he violated an innocent girl but his action had also led to the death of a child through abortion. His victim was only 13 and the effect on her had been devastating. She had endured much not only from the rape but from what followed.

'You have deprived her of some of her childhood and all of her adolescence. You do not seem to appreciate the enormity of what you have done.' The judge continued: 'You are not a demon, though some less responsible sections of the media have attempted to demonise you. You are a human being who did a dreadful, evil thing which has left this young woman heavily psychologically scarred for the rest of her life.'

The effect on her would probably have followed even if she had consented to have sex with him because she was only a child. The judge said he was sure McGinley should be conscious of that because he had a daughter himself who would soon be 13.

Mr Justice Quirke said he took into account McGinley's previous good character, the fact that he was a responsible husband and good provider for his family and that he had pleaded guilty even though that was after a jury had been sworn in to try the case.

However, his plea had spared his victim having to relive her terrible experience in evidence. He suspended the final four years of the sentence on condition that McGinley undergo therapy in prison.

Detective Sergeant Gerard Kelly told prosecuting counsel Anthony Sammon SC the victim and accused were members of the Travelling community. He came from one of the largest Travelling clans and had no previous convictions.

The victim had been babysitting in a Dublin suburb for McGinley on the night of the rape and he offered afterwards to leave her home. But he drove past her halting site and when she queried this he said he was going to buy cigarettes. He stopped his Hiace van at a council site entrance, leaned over to her, punched her in the face, dragged off her clothes including her underwear, dragged her into the rear and, after undressing, raped her.

Detective Sergeant Kelly said that while they were both still in the back of the van, McGinley's wife came looking for him and banged on it. He looked out, pushed her away and while totally naked drove off for about half a mile.

The girl dressed herself while he was driving and after some time he stopped to put on his own clothes. She decided to make a run for it but he caught her and punched her again before pulling her back into the van. McGinley then drove her home and threatened her he would cut her up if she reported what happened.

Detective Sergeant Kelly said the girl's mother was out when she got home and was in fact with McGinley's wife searching for him. Her family was also threatened not to report the rape but it was reported 18 hours later to Gardaí by a third party who was also a Traveller.

McGinley's identity as the culprit was known to the Gardaí from the start but by then he had left the area. Gardaí searched areas of Waterford, Tipperary and Louth but failed to locate him until 21 November 1997 in Dundalk.

During the intense media interest surrounding the 'Miss C' abortion issue in the courts, McGinley's father approached a detective he knew and went with him to Dundalk where McGinley presented himself, drove to Dublin and was arrested.

McGinley claimed in his initial admissions the girl seduced him and consented to sex. Michael Durack, for McGinley, said his client was contrite for his crime, which seemed to have been 'an aberration' committed after a combination of about 10 pints and cannabis.

Counsel also submitted that some of the matters referred to in the victim impact report arose from the events which followed the court appearances, something the defendant had no control over.

A Sorry Saga for Pregnant Teen Victim

On 27 August last year the teenage Traveller at the centre of the C case controversy was brutally raped. At the time the tragic youngster must have thought that things could not get any worse. But the 13-year-old had no way of knowing that her horrific ordeal would subsequently plunge her into a new nightmare as a pawn in Ireland's bitter abortion debate.

The sorry saga began when she went to babysit the children of a 24-year-old male Traveller in Balgaddy, west Dublin. When she returned to the two squalid roadside caravans in nearby Clondalkin which were home to her, her parents and 11 siblings a huge crisis broke.

She told her parents she had been raped by the man and was taken to Crumlin Children's Hospital where she was examined. Although she was given the morning after pill to prevent pregnancy, the treatment failed.

'Sickened'

Within a week the girl was taken into the care of the Eastern Health Board after the family, who already had their fair share of problems, received threats apparently for having reported the rape. Six weeks after she went into care, the girl's parents were given the devastating news by a social worker that their daughter was pregnant.

According to Garda sources, the girl was naturally 'totally sickened' by the attack and wanted an abortion and, in two court sittings in early November to discuss the child's future care, her parents raised the possibility of an abortion. It was her father who broke the news of the pregnancy to a newspaper and spoke of his support for his daughter's decision to terminate the pregnancy.

U-Turn

'What we really want to do is get our daughter to England, to have an abortion for her own safety,' her father said in one radio interview. Then, in a dramatic U-turn following the intervention of anti-abortion groups, her parents went to the Children's Court to tell the Eastern Health Board they were opposed to an abortion and wanted their child back.

They were accompanied to the court by members of two pressure groups, Youth Defence and Family and Life, who were providing taxis, accommodation and legal advice for them. Not since the 1992 X case had the anti-abortion groups had such a high profile and they made the most of the opportunity.

The crusade to force the girl to continue with her pregnancy was deemed crude by many people, and there were accusations that the impoverished family were being blinded by promises of money and support.

In the ensuing public rows, a psychiatrist's report concluding the girl was at risk of suicide if forced to continue with the pregnancy. As the furore raged, the Eastern Health Board came in for a barrage of criticism from anti-abortion campaigners amid claims the parents were being denied access to their daughter, a claim the board strenuously denied.

As total strangers squabbled over her fate, the child, who was being cared for by a foster family in the Midlands, is reported to have said: 'I will kill myself if I have a child... because it is not my child.'

When the Children's Court ruled in favour of allowing the girl to travel to Britain for an abortion, her parents, backed by Youth Defence, appealed to the High Court which upheld the order.

In early December the teenager travelled to Britain in the company of her foster mother and social workers and her pregnancy was terminated.

In October this year the girl was given her only chance in more than 12 months to have her say when she addressed the Central Criminal Court by video link after her rapist pleaded guilty. Now aged 14, she told the court: 'I hope he gets locked up for life.'

1 Compare and contrast the X and C cases from the newspaper articles above and the newspaper articles below.

Has your opinion of abortion changed in any way since completing this chapter?

Roman Catholic Teaching on Abortion

The Roman Catholic Church has always maintained that abortion is morally wrong. This teaching goes back as far as first-century Christian writers, with the most recent from Pope John Paul II in his papal encyclical *Evangelium Vitae* (The Gospel of Life).

> *'I declare that direct abortion, that is, abortion willed as an end or as a means, always constitutes a grave moral disorder, since it is the deliberate killing of an innocent human being.'*
>
> ***Pope John Paul II, Evangelium Vitae, 1995***

The above teaching is also clearly outlined in the Catechism of the Catholic Church (CCC).

> *'Human life must be respected and protected absolutely from the moment of conception. From the first moment of his existence, a human being must be recognised as having the rights of a person — among which is the inviolable right of every innocent being to life.'*
>
> ***CCC 2270***

> *'Since the first century the Church has affirmed the moral evil of every procured abortion. This teaching has not changed and remains unchangeable. Direct abortion, that is to say, abortion willed either as an end or a means, is gravely contrary to the moral law...'*
>
> ***CCC 2271***

Abortion and World Religions

Christianity teaches that every human being has a right to life from the moment of conception. The Church holds that every abortion is a grave moral evil. However, within the different denominations there are some variations regarding the risk to the life of the mother.

Islam forbids abortion except when the mother's life is in danger. Muslims consider human life to begin from the moment of implantation. They believe this egg has the potential to reach its full formation. Human life is so sacred that even in the case of a pregnant woman who is found guilty of a capital crime will not face punishment while she is carrying another human life.

Hinduism encompasses scriptures and traditions that have always been against the practice of abortion, except when the life of the mother is in danger. Hinduism teaches that the foetus is a living person in need of protection. Hindu scriptures refer to abortion as 'garha-batta' (womb killing) and 'bhroona hathya' (killing the undeveloped soul).

Buddhism teaches against abortion. Buddhists believe that a foetus has consciousness and this is when human life begins. Therefore they condemn abortion.

Judaism teaches that the foetus is part of a woman's body and so does not have the same individual rights as the mother. However, it is taught that a woman should not abort a foetus since this would mean voluntarily harming her body and this is not condoned within Judaism. There is only one instance where abortion is permitted: this is when the woman's life is at risk and her life must take priority over the unborn child.

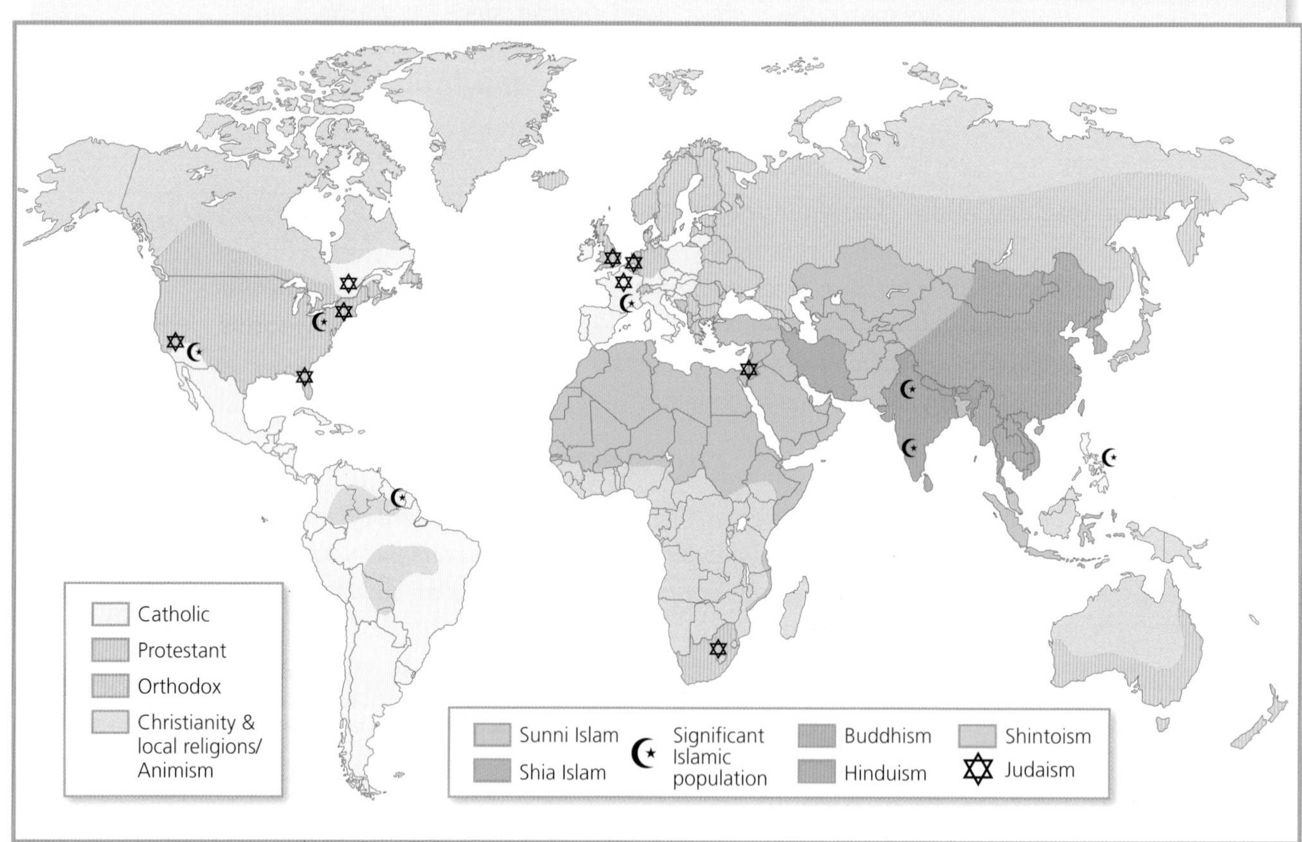

A world view – world faiths

Euthanasia

Euthanasia can be defined as the painless killing of a patient suffering from an incurable and painful disease or in an irreversible coma.

Some people interpret euthanasia as the practice of ending a life in a painless manner. In the majority of countries euthanasia or assisted suicide is against the law.

There are two main types of euthanasia: voluntary and involuntary.

Voluntary euthanasia is euthanasia conducted with consent. Since 2009 voluntary euthanasia has been legal in Belgium, Luxembourg, the Netherlands, Switzerland, and two American states (Oregon and Washington).

Involuntary euthanasia is euthanasia conducted without consent. The decision is made by another person because the patient is incapable of doing so.

Euthanasia can be carried out in two ways: passive or active. Passive euthanasia occurs when life-sustaining treatments are withheld. This might mean that a doctor gives medication or treatments in order to ease the pain of a patient but not to prolong his or her life.

Active euthanasia occurs when actions are taken by medical staff to actually end the patient's life. The intent is to cause the patient's death in a single act. Some people refer to this practice as a 'mercy killing'.

1 Write down your definition of euthanasia.

2 What is the difference between voluntary and involuntary euthanasia?

3 What is the difference between active and passive euthanasia?

Moral Debate on Euthanasia

Many people believe that euthanasia is morally acceptable in certain circumstances. Some of the following arguments have been made:	Many people believe that euthanasia is never morally acceptable. Some of the following arguments have been made.
★ Every person has the right to decide when they want to die. ★ It is wrong to use extraordinary means to keep a person alive, e.g. life support machine. ★ People should be given the choice to die with dignity when they are facing an incurable illness. ★ Relatives should be spared the upset of watching their loved ones suffer a slow, lingering death. ★ Humans should not have to endure a painful existence if they know that there is no chance of recovery.	★ Involuntary euthanasia could be abused. ★ Against all odds people may recover: doctors' diagnoses might be wrong. ★ Hippocratic oath: 'I will give no deadly medicine to anyone if asked, nor suggest such counsel.' ★ Patients who are terminally ill may be vulnerable and not thinking straight. ★ Older people may feel that they are a burden on their families and might choose euthanasia for that reason.

1. In your opinion, which of the arguments is strongest?
2. Can you think of any other aspects that should be included in the debate about euthanasia?
3. Comment on any options as an alternative to euthanasia.

Marie Fleming Partner Says He Would Be Willing To Help Her Die

Ruadhán Mac Cormaic

The partner of Marie Fleming, the terminally ill 59-year-old who today lost her landmark challenge to the blanket ban on assisted suicide, has indicated he would help her to die if she made that decision.

Tom Curran said he and Ms Fleming, who is in the final stages of multiple sclerosis, were 'very disappointed' after the Supreme Court rejected her appeal against the High Court's refusal to grant orders that would allow her to be lawfully helped to end her life at a time of her choice.

'It's very difficult to understand how a person with a disability can be deprived of something that's legally available to everybody else, every able-bodied person,' Mr

Curran said at the Four Courts after the judgment this morning. 'And for that not to be discriminatory under the Constitution. That's something we fail to understand. The Constitution is there to protect people like Marie and to give them solace that they will be looked after.'

The seven-judge Supreme Court ruled there was no Constitutional right which the State, including the courts, must protect and vindicate, either to die by suicide or to arrange for the termination of one's own life at a time of one's choosing. The principle of equal treatment also did not confer on Ms Fleming, as a disabled person, the right to be assisted in taking her own life, the court ruled.

Mr Curran said: 'The court has ruled on Marie's future, as far as they're concerned, and we will now go back to Wicklow and live our lives until such time as Marie makes up her mind that she has had enough. And in that case the court will have an opportunity to decide on my future.'

Asked whether that meant he would help his partner to die, Mr Curran replied: 'That will only come up if Marie makes the decision herself.'

The Chief Justice, Mrs Justice Susan Denham, stressed nothing in the court's judgment 'should be taken as necessarily implying it would not be open to the State, in the event the Oireachtas were satisfied that measures with appropriate safeguards could be introduced, to deal with a case such as that of Ms Fleming's'.

Ms Fleming was not well enough to attend today's brief court hearing. Mr Curran, who was in court with other family members, said his partner was 'very disappointed' she could not attend. She was suffering from 'what could have been a fatal chest infection,' he added. 'As you probably know, it has been a very difficult situation, both emotionally and physically, for Marie to bring this case here – to ask for help to die.'

Ms Fleming had claimed the absolute ban on assisted suicide in Section 2.2 of the Criminal Law Suicide Act 1993, in her particular circumstances as a severely disabled person unable to take her own life unaided, disproportionately infringed her personal autonomy rights under the Constitution and European Convention on Human Rights. She claimed the ban was discriminatory in that an able-bodied person may take their own life lawfully, but she could not be lawfully helped to do the same.

Ms Fleming had not appealed against the High Court's refusal to direct the DPP to issue guidelines as to what factors would be taken into account in considering whether to prosecute cases of assisted suicide.

Last January, the High Court ruled the absolute ban is fully justified under the Constitution to protect the most vulnerable in society, and cannot be diluted even in the 'harrowing' case of Ms Fleming.

However, the court said it was 'sure' the DPP would act in a 'humane and sensitive' way in considering whether or not to prosecute any assisted suicide of Ms Fleming.

Marie Fleming passed away in December 2013.

Journal your response to the ruling that was made in the Fleming case.

Roman Catholic Teaching on Euthanasia

The teaching on euthanasia in the Roman Catholic Church is one of compassion. They are against the practice of euthanasia, since human life is sacred, but they acknowledge that a person may seek euthanasia in times of suffering. However, they feel these people need extra support and love to help them through their pain and suffering.

In *Evangelium Vitae*, Pope John Paul II stated the following.

> *'Euthanasia is a grave violation of the law of God, since it is the deliberate and morally unacceptable killing of a human person.'*
>
> *'True compassion leads to sharing another's pain; it does not kill the person whose suffering we cannot bear.'*

Pope John Paul II spoke out against what he called a 'culture of death' in modern society, and said that 'human beings should always prefer the way of life to the way of death'.

The Catechism of the Catholic Church also states that Euthanasia is morally wrong.

> *'Whatever its motives and means, direct euthanasia consists in putting an end to the lives of handicapped, sick, or dying persons. It is morally unacceptable.'*
>
> *CCC 2277*

> *'Intentional euthanasia, whatever its forms or motives, is murder. It is gravely contrary to the dignity of the human person and to the respect due to the living God, his Creator...'*
>
> *CCC 2324*

Euthanasia and World Religions

Christianity mainly teaches against euthanasia. Christians believe that life is given by God. They also believe that human beings are made in God's image. Some churches also emphasise the importance of not interfering with the natural process of death.

Islam teaches against euthanasia. Muslims believe that all human life is sacred. They believe that life is given by Allah and, therefore, Allah chooses how long each person should live. Human beings should not interfere with this.

Hinduism in general would teach that a doctor should not accept a patient's request for euthanasia since this will cause the soul and body to be separated at an unnatural time. It is believed that doing this will damage the karma of each person involved, i.e. doctor and patient. Some Hindus believe that euthanasia cannot be allowed because it breaches the teaching of ahimsa (doing no harm). However, some Hindus say that by helping to end a painful life a person is performing a good deed. In Hinduism, good deeds are an important moral obligation.

Buddhism is not unanimous in its view of euthanasia. The Buddha made no particular teachings on the subject of euthanasia; however, most Buddhists are against involuntary euthanasia. Their position on voluntary euthanasia is less clear.

Judaism regards the preservation of human life as one of its supreme moral values and forbids doing anything that might shorten life. However, this does not involve prolonging the patient's suffering.

Experimentation with Life

Experimentation with life has become more common in recent years with the advancements in research and medical science in this area. Adoption and/or childlessness are no longer the only answers to people's struggles with infertility. For couples who may have difficulty conceiving naturally, there are now many options. Artificial insemination, intro-vitro fertilisation, surrogacy and genetic engineering are some options open to childless couples to enable conception. Despite the common practice of these procedures around the world, they are still controversial from a moral point of view. This section will allow students to become more aware of the issues surrounding the medical advancements in these areas and also in research involving human embryos.

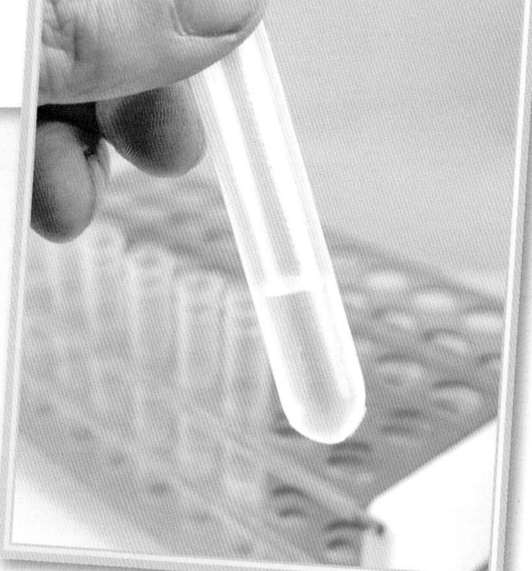

Artificial Insemination (AI)

Artificial insemination is used by couples when there is a problem with conceiving naturally. It was first practised on animals and then the procedure developed so that it could be used by humans.

The procedure of AI involves the following steps:

1. Sperm is collected in a specimen cup; it is washed to remove any impurities. This ensures the sperm sample is as healthy as possible.
2. An instrument called the speculum is inserted into the woman's vagina in order to keep the walls open for semen insertion.
3. A catheter is then placed inside the vagina and guided into the womb.

4 The sperm sample is passed through the catheter and into the womb.
5 This is a short procedure – it usually takes 10 minutes.

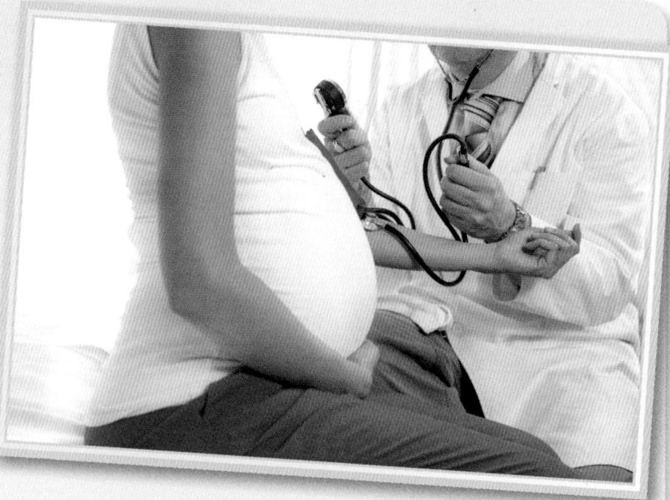

In the case of male infertility a donor's sperm can be used in the above procedure. The decision of using a donor sperm may be a difficult one for the couple. It may require a lot of consideration due to the sensitive nature of infertility. If a couple decide to use donor sperm, the procedure used is the same as above. The couple can be assured that all sperm has been carefully screened for any infections, genetic and hereditary disorders that could affect the health of the child. The couple can also access information on the physical characteristics of the sperm donor if required.

1 What is infertility?
2 In your own words explain what is involved in the AI procedure.
3 In your opinion, why do people donate sperm?
4 Why, do you think, might AI be a difficult decision for a couple to make?
5 Would knowing the information on the physical characteristics of the donor be important? Explain why/why not.

In-Vitro Fertilisation (IVF)

IVF is another method used by couples who cannot conceive naturally. This procedure was first called test-tube fertilisation. The procedure of IVF involves the following steps.

1 The woman is given drugs to stop her natural cycle for about two weeks.
2 When the woman's cycle is stopped, a fertility hormone called FSH (follicle stimulating hormone) is taken for around twelve days. This hormone increases the number of eggs produced, which boosts the egg supply for the procedure.
3 The woman is monitored carefully throughout the treatment. An injection is given 34–38 hours before the eggs are collected to help them mature.
4 A needle collects the eggs from the ovary. The needle is inserted through the vagina and into each ovary.

5 The woman's eggs are mixed with the sperm of her partner or donor and cultured in the laboratory for 16–20 hours. After this time the eggs are examined and the most fertilised embryos are grown in the laboratory incubator for 1–4 days. The best embryos will be chosen for transfer into the woman's womb.

6 The healthiest embryos are transferred into the woman's womb. The number of embryos being transferred is restricted because of the risks associated with multiple births.

IVF is not something that a couple enters into lightly. It requires great commitment from the couple, since it is normally a procedure that is used when other methods have failed. For some couples it is seen as their last chance to have their own child. IVF is not recommended for women over the age of 42 due to reduced chances of success.

1 Why might a couple chose IVF?
2 Do you think this procedure would be difficult for a couple?
3 In your own words summarise or explain the procedure of IVF.
4 What do you think happens to the embryos that are not transferred to the womb?
5 Why would this procedure involve great commitment from the couple?

Surrogacy

A surrogate is someone who acts as a substitute for somebody else. In relation to this topic, a surrogate is a woman who is willing to carry a child for another couple who are having difficulties with infertility. There are two types of surrogacy: traditional and gestational.

Traditional surrogacy uses artificial insemination. This involves the surrogate mother being inseminated with the biological father's sperm. This means that the surrogate mother would have a biological connection to the child.

Gestational surrogacy uses IVF. The surrogate mother is prepared to have a fertilised egg implanted into her womb and to carry the child to full term. The egg can come from the intended mother or a donor egg and the sperm from the intended father or the sperm donor.

Both of the types of surrogacy can cause legal complications. Currently 44 of the 50 states in America have legislation to protect all parties involved in surrogacy. However, in Ireland and Europe such

legislation has not yet been put in place. This leaves the practice of surrogacy open to debate when it comes to the question of parental rights and citizenship, especially when couples choose to go abroad.

1 Explain surrogacy in your own words.
2 Summarise the difference between traditional and gestational surrogacy.
3 Why might there be legal issues surrounding surrogacy?

The Long Road Home for Surrogate Babies

Carl O'Brien

Susan Cooper's baby boy, Alex, is the talk of the town. 'Everyone here in Youghal has been fantastic,' she says. 'People come up to me and say, "He looks the head off his father" or "He has your colour". He's adorable. After everything we've been through, I'm just enjoying time with him.'

Alex was born via a surrogate mother in India last August. While still considered a novelty, it's a route being chosen by more and more would-be parents who aren't able conceive on their own. But it's also a process which can be riven with legal uncertainty. 'My newborn son and I had to remain in India for five weeks while my husband returned to Ireland to go through the court system, having being directed there by a government department,' says Ms Cooper. 'As you can imagine, this was devastating for my husband and I. All we ever wanted was a family, and at only a few days old it was ripped apart thanks to the indifference of the Irish Government.'

It is estimated there are several hundred children living in Irish families who were born abroad to surrogate mothers but whose legal status under Irish law may be uncertain. However, passport officials in Ireland say they have only been officially notified of between 35 and 40 births, suggesting that many are deliberately avoiding telling the authorities.

There is no specific law for surrogacy in Ireland. This means surrogate children born to parents who have difficulty meeting strict legal requirements relating to parenthood and guardianship can be left in a legal limbo, without a passport or citizenship of any kind. Legislation was recommended in a report from the Commission on Assisted Human Reproduction, published seven years ago, but has never been produced by successive governments.

Minister for Justice Alan Shatter recently published new guidelines giving information to commissioning parents on practical and legal considerations. He also insisted it was incorrect that parents would need to leave a newborn child abroad while they returned to Ireland to obtain court orders to get a passport for their child.

His comments, however, have angered many parents who have found themselves unable to get clear answers from State authorities and who have spent weeks – and in some cases months – waiting to get passports for their children.

For the Coopers, it was their last chance to have a child. Susan, a factory worker, and her husband Anthony, a carpenter, were both in their mid-40s. They hadn't been able to have a child naturally. They were at an age at which many IVF clinics stop providing services. The international adoption route was, in effect, blocked off as a result of new restrictions. Surrogacy was the only option.

'People think that surrogacy is for rich couples; that you wait on a sun-lounger sipping a cocktail, while another woman has the child. It's not like that. 'It's very, very tough and stressful. You need to be a strong couple to get through it. With adoption, you know the baby is coming. There is a defined process. With surrogacy, there is so much uncertainty, which is made worse by the lack of legislation over here.'

A key obstacle for many couples is getting a passport for the child. Mr Shatter says Irish authorities may issue an emergency travel certificate to enable a child to enter the State. In the case of the Coopers, this was easier said than done. When they went looking for such a certificate, they were told it was issued only in 'exceptional cases of genuine emergency'. After getting a court order for a passport – which entailed DNA tests and evidence relating to parentage and guardianship – they said they had to wait another week to get the passport itself. In all, it took five weeks of toing and froing. It was also hugely expensive.

'We were lucky with the judge we got. He dealt with it very quickly, but we're aware of cases where that hasn't been the case,' says Ms Cooper.

The case of Robyn Maye-Coffey has been the subject of considerable media attention. In this case, her parents fought for 18 months to get citizenship and a passport. 'We ended up bringing our lives and that of our daughter into the public domain to highlight the lack of legislation,' says Catherine Maye. Her daughter's case was finally resolved in the High Court in recent days. However, the couple are bound to a confidentiality agreement.

Senior officials involved in the process of issuing passports – speaking on condition of anonymity – point out that they are obliged to work within the confines of the law, which is in place to prevent abduction and protect the best interests of children.

'The passport is not a magic bullet – parents need to establish citizenship and guardianship for the welfare of the child. When that is established, that's where we come in and issue a passport,' a senior official said.

What everyone agrees on is that legislation is needed to make the process easier and faster and to give much-needed legal certainty. Mr Shatter says officials are working on this. In the meantime, he urges those considering arranging a surrogate birth outside the State to obtain detailed legal advice beforehand.

Susan Cooper is continuing to live amid another form of uncertainty and invisibility in the eyes of the law. She's not legally entitled to maternity leave – though her employer has been very good to her – and she is not the legal mother of Alex.

'My name isn't on the birth cert. I can't sign any official forms for him. I worry about something terrible happening to my husband. What would happen then? The only route for me is to adopt my own child, which seems very unfair. This is an area the Government must address and deal with urgently.'

Surrogacy by the Numbers

35	The number of surrogate children born abroad to Irish parents that authorities know about, though the real figure is likely to be in the hundreds
€2 billion	The estimated worth of the surrogacy industry in India next year
20,000	The typical overall cost of a surrogacy in India
$85,000	The typical overall cost of surrogacy in the United States
€4,000	The typical payment to an Indian surrogate mother for carrying a baby
$25,000	The typical payment to a US surrogate mother for carrying a baby

Exploring Surrogacy

The Legal Situation in Ireland

Mothers and Babies Magazine

Surrogacy in Ireland is an area that is still somewhat under the radar, receiving less attention than the likes of IVF and adoption. Many people, therefore, don't have a huge understanding of what exactly is involved, particularly on the legal side, both for the child and parents.

With IVF the embryo, fertilised externally, is transferred back into its natural mother's womb for gestation and delivery. However, in the case of surrogacy, it is transferred into the womb of another woman.

The surrogate mother will not usually be genetically related to the child she is carrying, although in traditional surrogacy (still practised in some countries), the surrogate mother is also the biological mother. Surrogacy can also involve anonymous sperm and egg donors, making it even more complicated. In surrogacy, a legal contract is entered into between the biological parents and the surrogate mother, and a fee is agreed.

But while surrogacy here doesn't garner major headlines, it has been in the news lately, not least because Minister for Justice Alan Shatter recently published new guidelines giving information to so-called 'commissioning parents' on practical and legal considerations.

This was done because currently there is no specific law for surrogacy in Ireland, which means people are going overseas to go down this route and therefore surrogate children and indeed their parents can be left in a legal limbo, often without a passport or citizenship of any kind.

Launching the guidelines earlier this year, Minister Shatter said their purpose was to provide information to prospective commissioning parents on the steps necessary to ensure that a child born abroad through a surrogacy arrangement may enter and reside in the State and to secure the best interests of the child.

'The law relating to parenthood and guardianship rights in the context of surrogacy is complex. I intend to develop legislative proposals in this area in collaboration with the Department of Health, taking into account developments in the law of other jurisdictions, and practical experience in dealing with surrogacy cases,' he added.

Legislation, however, was recommended in a report from the Commission on Assisted Human Reproduction, published seven years ago, but it has never been produced.

Legal Advice

The guidelines do give some direction to people thinking about surrogacy. They stress that those intending to make surrogacy arrangements for the birth of a child should obtain expert legal advice in Ireland first. They also note that establishing whether an intended parent is a legal parent of a child, whether the child is an Irish citizen and whether the consent of the child's guardians has been obtained will all take time and may involve more than one application to an Irish court.

Marion Campbell is a solicitor in Dublin who specialises in the area of surrogacy. She believes that legislation should be brought in to deal with the whole issue of surrogacy/ assisted human reproduction as soon as possible.

'Because of the lack of legislation, both parents and children born by way of surrogacy are in a legal minefield and serious issues arise regarding custody, maintenance, Succession Act rights and entitlements. I am aware that there are talks taking place within various government departments regarding this legislation but am not at all certain as to when legislation will be brought in.

'The guidelines published were extremely helpful insofar as they clarified issues for people who travel abroad to have children born by way of surrogacy. They set out clearly both the procedures and documentation required by the courts in terms of applications for guardianship and travel documents.'

Campbell believes there is an increasing number of couples here looking at surrogacy as an option.

'I see an average of four couples a month in relation to surrogacy queries. They are from all parts of the country. With the majority of them, the woman is not in a position to have children. Adoption is extremely long drawn out and even at the end of that process, there is no guarantee that there will be a child available to be adopted.

'The other very strong decision-making factor for couples who decide to go the surrogacy route is that there is a biological connection with the child, generally through the father.'

Irish people seeking a surrogate have been going to countries such as India and Ukraine; however, Campbell says Ukraine is more popular.

'Most clients view India with some doubt because of concerns for ethical issues arising. If people can afford it, then they are going to the US as a child born by way of surrogacy there is a US citizen and acquires a US passport. Difficulties then in relation to travel do not arise.

'A child born in Ukraine has to establish a connection with Ireland; an application has to be made for an Irish passport to allow the child be removed from Ukraine back to this jurisdiction.'

Until the Government decides to introduce legislation on surrogacy in Ireland it remains a problematic area that is best pursued abroad.

'Surrogacy is not illegal in Ireland,' explains Campbell. 'However if a child is born by way of surrogacy the birth mother is the mother in Irish law and has all the rights in respect of that child. Her name is on the birth certificate.

'If the birth mother is married, then her husband is presumed to be the birth father of that child. If the birth mother is unmarried, then she has sole rights of guardianship and custody over that child. I would advise against any couple in this country having a baby by way of surrogacy. Surrogacy contracts are unenforceable.'

Journal your response to the above articles.

Genetic Engineering

Go to howthingswork.com and search for videos on genetic engineering.

Genetic engineering has given humans the power to change the foundation of life on earth. All living organisms have genes. It is genes that contain all the information, like the instruction manual, on how to build a person or another living organism. These genes can be controlled and manipulated using science with the intent of changing the organism in some way, allowing it to perform new functions or to make new substances. Genetic engineering can be used in plants, animals and now human cells.

★ 'Genetic engineering has few limits.'

Cloning

The aim of human cloning is to copy the genes of a person so that an identical being is created. Human cloning became a real possibility after Dolly the sheep was cloned by Scottish scientists in 1996. Dolly was the first mammal to be cloned from adult DNA. When Dolly was introduced to the world in

1997, her cloning created worldwide headlines due to the ethical implications of cloning. Up until then cloning was practised only in the industries of food and agriculture.

Go to www.dnatube.com and search for 'How did they clone Dolly the Sheep'.

There are three types of cloning.

1 DNA Cloning: The use of DNA manipulation procedures to produce multiple copies of a single gene or segment of DNA. This technique is often used by scientists today to study a particular gene they are interested in.

2 Reproductive: This is human cloning with the aim of creating a new human being, as explained above.

3 Therapeutic cloning or 'embryo cloning': This is the generation of human embryos for use in medical research. The aim of this is to find cures of diseases and illnesses primarily by using stem cells found in the early stages of embryo development.

In most countries it is illegal to attempt to produce a cloned human being (reproductive cloning). Some countries, however, allow researchers to pursue therapeutic cloning for research in very specific circumstances.

Moral Debate on Cloning

Many people believe that cloning is morally acceptable in certain circumstances. Some of the following arguments have been made.	Many people believe that cloning is never morally acceptable. Some of the following arguments have been made.
★ Cloning can save lives, e.g. organ cloning. ★ Infertility issues can be overcome by cloning, e.g. embryo development. ★ Cloning is important in terms of genetic research, e.g. hereditary illnesses. ★ Cloning can help with the curing of disease. ★ Science must always improve: we should clone because we can.	★ Cloning could lead to the abuse of medical authority. ★ Cloning devalues humankind and natural process. ★ Cloning undermines the value of human life. ★ Embryos are discarded during cloning. ★ Cloning could lead to unrealistic expectations in society.

1 Can you think of any more aspects that should be included in the debate about cloning?
2 In your opinion, which of the arguments is strongest?
3 What is the biggest moral issue with cloning?
4 Do you expect that world religions would be in favour of cloning?

Potential Dangers of Human Cloning

Gary Wickman

Some folks consider human cloning as the biggest breakthrough of the century, while others consider it a living nightmare. As such, human cloning means creating an identical human being with the aid of recent technology and genes of the donor. While the cloned individual will look like a carbon copy of the donor in terms of appearance, the personality of the two individuals could be world-apart from each other.

While outward appearance can be cloned, the personality of an individual cannot be cloned. After all, every person out there builds a unique personality for himself based on real life experiences and knowledge gained with growing age. It's believed that the potential dangers linked with human cloning outweigh the advantages associated with human cloning, which is why human cloning is banned in most countries out there. Let's have a look at the potential dangers of human cloning.

Medical Issues

Human cloning can give rise to certain medical issues. Technically, human gene grows older with age. It's feared that the cloned individual would retain the age of the donor's genes. Imagine what will happen if a 40-year-old gene is manifested into a newborn baby.

Social Hiccups

There is a possibility that cloned individuals might not receive their due share of respect and acceptance in the society. It's believed that there will be unsettled opinions about the rights granted to a clone. Also, the real beauty of humanity lies in the differences we witness amongst each other. Cloning would kill the surprise element over here.

Health Concerns

The health risks involved with human cloning is something that cannot be sidelined on all accounts. There is a possibility that the cloned individual might carry certain abnormalities, and may die sooner than the standard life expectancy.

Moral Issues

Technological abuse is one aspect that can come into the picture once human cloning becomes a prominent feature. Imagine what a corrupt guy will do after cloning himself. There will always be someone or the other who will try to abuse this technological advancement to the extreme. In some cases, the clone might also turn out to be better than the donor.

Since a clone can conduct almost every activity an average individual can perform such as eating, drinking, bathing, etc., it won't come as surprise to learn that human clones will be illegally traded for personal gains. Needless to say, trade of human beings is illegal and against all morals.

Ethical Concerns

Ethical concerns will also be raised on human cloning. There will be loads of protest from various groups, if human cloning is to be legalised in the near future. The whole idea of human cloning is already hurting the sentiments of truckloads of people out there. Some believe that human cloning is playing around with God's rules. The million dollar question that really needs our attention is whether we can create a human being at our will and wish?

Legal Issues

Human cloning laws are said to be very complicated in nature, and they vary from one country to another. The fact that the laws are divided on such a sensitive issue is a certain feature of potential trouble. There have been decent attempts made in the past to pass federal law to ban human cloning completely, but there is no definite law passed as yet that bans all human cloning.

As such, the twentieth century hasn't seen much progress on human cloning as one might have expected, considering the fact that the technological advancement has seen robust growth in the last few decades or so.

Considering all the above said disadvantages linked with human cloning, one can only be happy that the development of human cloning has not seen the day of light as yet. The first mammalian clone was a sheep called Dolly. Although the successful cloning of Dolly was a significant step in this matter, Dolly died young due to a rare disease, which is usually not seen in the sheep of her age group.

Journal your response to the Gary Wickman article on cloning.

Designer Babies

This is a general term that can be used to describe an embryo that, for medical reasons, was screened and selected from other embryos to ensure the baby would be free of fatal genetic diseases. This is already in practice by some doctors today.

The term 'designer babies' also refers to the more controversial potential future use of genetic engineering, which would allow parents to choose particular physical or intellectual attributes for their children as well as good health.

1 In your own words describe a designer baby.
2 What is your opinion on designer babies?
3 List possible advantages and/or disadvantages of designer babies.

Go to cbsnews.com and search for the video on 'Designer Babies'.

Designer Babies: Ethical? Inevitable?

A baby born in England recently was chosen in the embryonic stage to be free of a gene linked with certain types of cancer.

'This little girl will not face the specter of developing this genetic form of breast cancer or ovarian cancer in her adult life,' said Paul Serhal, medical director of the assisted conception unit at University College Hospital, London. The case is not the first of its kind.

In the United States, a man with an 50 per cent chance of passing on a gene for deadly colon cancer used the technique, too. He and his wife had embryos screened prior to implanting one in her womb, resulting in a daughter that won't get the disease.

The British woman, who has remained anonymous, made the decision in June to undergo screening of eleven embryos, each three days old, because her husband's female relatives suffered cancers, according to *The Guardian*. 'We felt that, if there was a possibility of eliminating this for our children, then that was a route we had to go down,' she said at the time.

The same genetic testing, called pre-implantation genetic diagnosis (PGD), has been used to test for inherited disorders such as cystic fibrosis and Huntington's disease, life-shortening diseases known to be certainly acquired by those carrying a single gene. What's new in this case is that the gene tested for, called BRCA1, does not inevitably lead to cancer in someone who carries it and if the cancers do develop they are potentially treatable.

Women who carry the BRCA1 gene have an 80 per cent chance of developing breast cancer and a 60 per cent chance of developing ovarian cancer during their lifetime. They also have a 50 per cent chance of passing the gene on to each of their children.

The events might presage other screenings designed to create designer babies based on gender, IQ or athletic ability, some ethicists fear.

'There are many complex issues to take into account and the decision will finally come down to an individual's personal ethics,' said Kath McLachlan, a clinical nurse specialist at the charity Breast Cancer Care.

Some fear the worst if laws are not crafted to corral the burgeoning field of 'reprogenetics', as it is called — combining reproductive technologies with genetic screening.

'If misapplied, [these technologies] would exacerbate existing inequalities and reinforce existing modes of discrimination...the development and commercial marketing of human genetic modification would likely spark a techno-eugenic rat-race,' says Richard Hayes, executive director of the Center for Genetics and Society. 'Even parents opposed to manipulating their children's genes would feel compelled to participate in this race, lest their offspring be left behind.'

The polar opposite argument is made by Dartmouth College ethics professor Ronald M. Green, who envisions a nearly disease-free future in which the information gleaned from reprogenetics allows genes to be tweaked, producing healthier humans without discarding embryos. 'Why not improve our genome?' Green asks.

A report last year in the journal *Nature* predicted a host of changes to human fertility technology in thirty years' time: Artificial wombs and experiments on human embryos grown in the lab will be commonplace, several scientists said. With embryos grown in labs, mutations could be corrected and improvements could be engineered. The same researcher said there would be no designer babies, however, because no single gene is that predictive of a perfect child.

Meanwhile, the British mother and daughter are said to be doing well.

Journal your response to this article on designer babies.

Stem Cell Research

Watch the TED-Ed 'What are Stem Cells?' video on YouTube.

The following types of stem cells are being used in current clinical trials:

- ★ Embryonic stem cells (ESCs)
- ★ Tissue stem cells, e.g. skin, blood
- ★ Umbilical cord blood stem cells (which is a type of tissue stem cell)
- ★ Mesenchymal stem cells (a type of tissue stem cell obtained from bone marrow).

Embryonic stem cells can produce all the different types of cells in the body and can self-renew (copy themselves) almost forever, so large supplies can be made. Embryonic stem cell research poses a moral dilemma. It forces us to choose between two moral principles: the duty to prevent or alleviate suffering and the duty to respect the value of human life. In some countries embryonic stem cell research is illegal or is very limited; however, there is no specific legislation dealing with stem cell research in Ireland.

Tissue stem cells can only make the types of cells that belong in their own tissue. For example, skin stem cells make types of skin cells only: they do not make brain or blood cells. Since they are already partially specialised, this makes it more straightforward to obtain the particular specialised cell type required, but this also limits their use. Tissue stem cells used in treatments for blood diseases, severe burns and some types of corneal damage have been proven; no other treatments are yet proven, since tissues must be 'matched' or come from the patient's own body.

Claims that stem cells from the bone marrow can produce new heart cells have been proved wrong, but research is ongoing to investigate other possible beneficial effects of these cells on the heart and other tissues.

Research what is involved in these trials:

★ Umbilical cord blood stem cells

★ Mesenchymal stem cells.

Roman Catholic Teaching on Experimentation with Life

In *Human Life is Sacred* (HLS) the Irish bishops discuss the dangers involved with the experimentation of life.

> *'The only totally secure barrier for man against attacks upon his right to life is the absolute principle that innocent human life is sacred, and that every human being has its right to life directly from God, and not from any human authority.'*
>
> **HLS, p.48**

The papal encyclical *Donum Vitae* (The Gift of Life) further outlines the position of the Catholic Church on experimentation with life. In this document, the church's moral position on this issue is put forward.

> *'Attempts to obtain a human being without any connection with sexuality through "twin fission", cloning or parthenogenesis are to be considered contrary to the moral law.'*
>
> *'Although the manner in which human conception is achieved with IVF and ET cannot be approved, every child which comes into the world must in any case be accepted as a living gift of the divine Goodness and must be brought up with love.'*
>
> **Donum Vitae**

It is clear from the above teaching that the Catholic Church is against all forms of experimentation with life. From their position, human life is sacred and it should be given the utmost respect.

Addiction

In this section we will define addiction and explore the different types of addiction. We will become better informed on the different types of drugs so that we can increase our awareness of the dangers involved. Addiction is a moral issue, since human beings are free to make their own decisions when it comes to substance abuse.

Addiction can be defined as the fact or condition of being addicted to a particular substance or activity.

When a person is addicted, the substance or activity they are addicted to becomes their main priority. They tend to show little regard for any possible negative consequence to their health, state of mind, family, job or relationships with others. Addiction comes in many forms, including drugs, alcohol, nicotine, gambling, shopping and eating disorders.

Drug Abuse

A drug can be defined as a chemical substance that affects the processes of the mind or body. Not all drugs are bad for us. For example, when we are sick we may go to the doctor and he or she may prescribe drugs to make us feel better. We go to a chemist and the pharmacist will dispense the drugs to us. We then take the drugs in order to help us to get better. However, a problem occurs when we choose to take legal or illegal drugs that are not prescribed by a doctor in order to make ourselves 'better'. This type of self-medication can lead to drug abuse. Drug abuse can be defined as habitual use of drugs to alter our mood, emotion or state of consciousness. Drug abuse can lead to drug addiction. There are two types of drug addiction: physical and psychological.

Physical drug addiction occurs when the body cannot function as it normally would without the use of the drug. The person may experience physical discomfort from withdrawal of the drug.

Psychological drug addiction occurs when the mind cannot function as it normally would without the use of the drug. The mind is completely fixated on acquiring the drug and there is a deep longing for the feeling that comes from taking the drug.

There are many different types of drugs.

- ★ Stimulant: produces an increase in mental and physical activity
- ★ Hallucinogenic: may distort reality and cause hallucinations
- ★ Sedative/depressant: reduces feelings of anxiety and tension
- ★ Opiate: pain relieving drugs derived from the opium poppy.

Stimulant		Hallucinogenic	Sedative/Depressant	Opiate
Mild:	Nicotine	LSD	Alcohol	Heroin
	Caffeine	Inhalants	Sleeping tablets	Morphine
Strong:	Cocaine	Solvents	Tranquilisers	Codeine
	Amphetamines	Magic Mushrooms	Anti-Depressants	Opium
	Ecstasy	Ecstasy	Cannabis	Cannabis

Source: *HSE*

1. Why do some people abuse drugs?
2. Are young people more likely to abuse drugs, compared to adults? Explain your answer.
3. Which addiction do you think might be stronger: physical or psychological?
4. Study the table (above) and answer the following questions.
   (i) Which stimulant is most commonly used?
   (ii) Why are ecstasy and cannabis in two group types?
   (iii) Why is alcohol in the sedative group?

(iv) Which two substances in the opiates group can be prescribed by doctors to relieve pain?

5 What famous people have died from abusing drugs?

6 What do you think are the consequences of drug abuse?

<table>
<tr><th colspan="2">COCAINE</th></tr>
<tr><td colspan="2">Category: Stimulants</td></tr>
<tr><td colspan="2">Also called: snow, C, charlie, coke, rock, dust, white.</td></tr>
<tr><td colspan="2">How it's used: Cocaine is a strong but short acting stimulant drug ('upper') which comes in a white powder. You can divide it into lines and snort up the nose with a rolled up bank note or straw. You can also smoke it or make into a solution to inject.</td></tr>
<tr><td>Short-term effects
• Effects of cocaine start quickly but only last for up to 30 minutes
• You may feel more alert, energetic, exhilarated and confident
• Your heart and pulse rate speed up suddenly
• Hyperactivity, dilated pupils, dry mouth, sweating and loss of appetite
• Higher doses can make you feel very anxious and panicky
• Increased sex drive</td><td>Long-term effects
• Tightness in chest, insomnia, exhaustion and unable to relax
• Dry mouth, sweating, mood swings and loss of appetite
• You may become aggressive or even violent
• You may feel depressed and run down
• Damage to nose tissue
• Digestive disorders, dehydration and anorexia
• Kidney damage
• If you use it often you may lose your sex drive
• Injecting may cause abscesses
• Smoking may cause breathing problems
• Anxiety, paranoia and hallucinations, if you use a lot
• Restlessness, nausea, hyperactivity, insomnia and weight loss</td></tr>
<tr><td colspan="2">Addictive
• Cocaine is very psychologically addictive so you find it hard to live without it. Your tolerance increases over time so you have to keep taking more to get the same buzz.</td></tr>
<tr><td colspan="2">Withdrawal
• You may feel tired, panicky, exhausted and unable to sleep, which can cause you extreme emotional and physical distress. This distress can lead to symptoms such as diarrhoea, vomiting, the shakes, insomnia and sweating. You may have long-term effects such as anorexia and depression. Once you stop using, you will have an intense craving for more.</td></tr>
<tr><td colspan="2">How long does it stay in your system?
• Cocaine shows up in a urine test for 2–4 days.</td></tr>
</table>

CANNABIS

Category: Hallucinogens/Sedatives

Also called: hash, hashish, blow, pot, ganja, marijuana, grass, joint, THC, bhang, black, blast, blunts, Bob Hope, bush, dope, draw, hemp, herb, puff, northern lights, resin, sensi, smoke, soap, spliff, wacky backy, zero, afghan, moroccan.
Skunk is called: sinsemilla, homegrown, buds, tops, nederwiet or netherweed.

How it's used: Cannabis usually comes as a dried resin (hash) or dried leaves (grass or weed). You can smoke it with tobacco in a joint, inhale through a pipe or bong or make into a tea or food. Skunk is herbal cannabis which is much stronger than regular hash or grass.

Short-term effects

- You may feel sedated, chilled out and happy
- Some people feel sick
- You may get 'the munchies' or feel hungry
- Your pulse rate speeds up and blood pressure goes down
- Bloodshot eyes, dry mouth
- Tiredness

Long-term effects

- May damage your lungs and lead to breathing problems
- Has been linked with mental health problems, such as depression and schizophrenia
- May lower sperm count and suppresses ovulation so you may have problems getting pregnant
- Regular use may affect your memory, mood, motivation and ability to learn
- May cause anxiety and paranoia
- May affect your coordination and reactions so you are more at risk of accidents, especially if you also drink alcohol

Addictive

- You can get psychologically addicted to cannabis; in this case, you might find it hard to cope without it. If you smoke it with tobacco you may get physically addicted to tobacco.

Withdrawal

- Anxiety, irritability
- Urge or cravings to smoke
- Sleep problems, restlessness
- Loss of appetite.

How long does it stay in your system?

- Cannabis will show up in a urine test for 2–28 days.

HEROIN

Category: Opioids

Also called: gear, H, smack, skag, junk, brown, horse, china white, dragon.

How it's used: Heroin is an opiate with strong sedative ('downer') and painkilling effects. It comes in powder form which varies in colour from brown to white. You can inject it, sniff it or smoke it on foil or in a tobacco-based joint.

Short-term effects

- Effects can start quickly and last for several hours; this depends on how much of the drug you use and how you take it
- Makes you feel warm and relaxed with a hazy feeling of security
- Pinpoint pupils
- Pain relief
- You can have nausea and vomiting the first time you use it
- Dramatic mood swings
- Your breathing and heart rate slow down
- Higher doses cause drowsiness – 'goofing off'

Long-term effects

- You build tolerance, so you need to take more to get the same buzz
- Chronic constipation
- Irregular periods in women
- High doses can cause you to feel drowsy all the time, fall into a coma or die from breathing failure
- If you smoke heroin, you risk lung and heart disease
- You may stop eating properly and not look after yourself

Addictive

- Heroin is highly addictive, both physically and psychologically, so your body craves it and you feel you can't cope without it. If you use it regularly for 2 to 3 weeks you will build tolerance so you need to keep taking more to get the same buzz.

Withdrawal

- You may start to experience withdrawal after several weeks on high, frequent doses of heroin. Withdrawals start 8–12 hours after your last use and include aches, shakes, sweating, chills, sneezing and yawning and muscle spasms. These fade after about a week and are not life threatening.

How long does it stay in your system?

- A urine test will detect heroin for 3–8 days. (The length of time depends on the test used, the amount you take, if you have other medical conditions and your own metabolism. This figure is a guide only.)

ECSTASY	
Category: Hallucinogens/Sedatives/Stimulants	
Also called: E, disco biscuits, hug drug, mitsubishi, rolex, dolphins, XTC, yokes, love doves, MDMA, brownies, M and Ms, sweeties, tulips, X.	
How it's used: Ecstasy is a stimulant drug ('upper') that also produces mild hallucinogenic effects. Ecstasy tablets come in a variety of colours and shapes and often have a logo or design.	
Short-term effects • Effects can start after 20 to 60 minutes and last for several hours • Your pupils dilate and your jaw tightens • You may have nausea, sweating, loss of appetite, dry mouth and throat • You can have epileptic fits and paranoia for the first time • Your body temperature, blood pressure and heart rate go up • You may feel intense emotions and love for people around you • Anxiety, panic attacks and confusion	**Long-term effects** • Weight loss • Loss of interest in work • You may get flashbacks • Sleep problems, lack of energy and dietary problems • Bouts of depression, personality change and memory loss
Addictive • You won't become physically addicted to ecstasy but there is a risk of psychological addiction, when you feel you can't enjoy yourself without it. You may build tolerance to it so you have to keep taking more to get the same buzz.	
Withdrawal • If you use regularly, you may feel tired and depressed when you withdraw from ecstasy.	
How long does it stay in your system? • Ecstasy shows up in urine tests for 3–8 days.	

1 Summarise the information on drugs in the tables above and present this information to the class.

Redemption Story – Girl With the Arms

John Spain

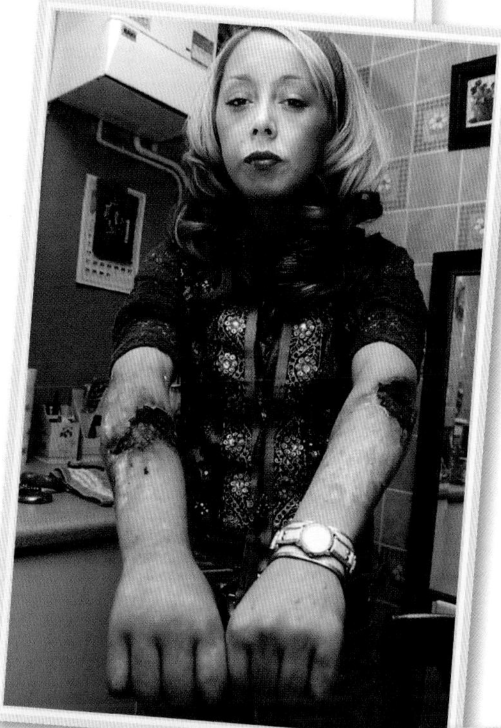

The picture on the cover of Rachael Keogh's book is truly shocking. But then it's meant to be. That picture of the rotting sores in her arms saved her life ... and she is now hoping that the image will help save other junkies as well.

Published this week, Rachael's book is a real life horror story of growing up in Ballymun, of being on the booze at 11, hash at 12, Es at 13, heroin at 14, in prison at 15, a prostitute at 16. Ten years later, 26, and a hopeless junkie, she was at death's door with arms so bad that doctors were warning that they might have to be amputated.

That was in 2006. But the main picture of Rachael you see here, a beautiful young woman, was taken this year. She is now 29, a college student, a mother of a baby boy, happy, healthy, optimistic about the future.

So although this story is horrific in places, fundamentally it is a story of redemption. It is the story of how one remarkable young woman went through hell and then somehow found her way back. It is a story told with dignity because even at her lowest point, degraded by what she had to do to get drugs, Rachael always retained a sense of her own worth as a human being. And that is what saved her.

The way back began when, as she puts it herself, she became 'the girl with the arms'. Her mother was beside herself with worry. Rachael was down to seven stone, constantly overdosing and in and out of casualty. It was clear time was running out yet her mother could not get her long-term treatment.

In desperation she contacted the *Irish Independent* and this paper ran a story about Rachael with the shocking picture of her arms exposed. At that point she became 'the girl with the arms' and in the frenzy that followed, Rachael appeared on Sky News.

When asked by the reporter, Rachael rolled up her sleeves and explained the damage that shooting up had done, how her veins were blocked and the heroin had burned her flesh. The blackness was necrosis, the medical term for dead flesh caused when tissue is starved of blood, and which can end up as gangrene and require amputation.

'The doctors told me that if I continue to use, they will have to amputate both my arms,' Rachael told the reporter and even though she was determined not to cry, the tears flowed. But she could not stop using not without help, and none was available.

The TV appearance played an important part in saving her. But before the book gets to that part, it goes through the years of addiction.

It begins with the family background in Ballymun. Her mother was one of five children. She was only 15 when Rachael was born and so Rachael was raised mainly by her grandparents in a house where drink and violence created problems. Her grandfather, she recalls, had 'hands like big shovels', was moody and unpredictable.

Her own father was a young junkie, who her grandparents would not let into the house. When her mother eventually went to live with him, the violence continued. One of Rachael's first memories is of an incident when her father pushed her mother's head inside the oven when the grill was on. 'I could see that the bars on the inside were scorching red…her high-pitched screams paralysed me,' she says.

But the main problem for Rachael was that when her mother got a new boyfriend, she abandoned Rachael (who was then 7). Rachael's granny was working fulltime so by the time Rachael was approaching her teens she was alone most of the day.

She was free to mitch from school and hang out around the drug-infested towers.

The description of her descent into this hell over several chapters is a unique insight into what life was like for many kids in Ballymun at the time. The towers were known as 'The Devil's Playground', with gangs of feral kids in abandoned flats shooting up.

But her book is also a revealing insight into the mind of the addict. You realise that her family was not as uncaring as she thinks.

They made endless attempts to help her, even as she turned their lives into a nightmare – lying, robbing, bringing her grandparents to the edge of a complete breakdown. The extraordinary efforts by the extended family to help her included bringing her abroad three times for treatment. But she frustrated all efforts, relapsing again and again in a messy cycle of detox and overdose that went on for years and must have been heart-breaking for those around her.

And all the time she blamed her internal hurt and despair on being abandoned by her mother. All the time she saw the world through the skewed, self-centred, self-pitying vision of the junkie. The reality is that her mother was not perfect, but it was not all her fault and she was there for Rachael in the end. It is to Rachael's credit that she shows this clearly in the book.

This is the best book by far about the drugs explosion in Dublin, about the inadequacy of treatment facilities and about the mindset of a young junkie. It's only by managing to come out the other end, by becoming 'the girl with the arms', that Rachael Keogh has managed to stay around to write it. Many of her peers were not so lucky.

After the media frenzy generated by her picture and TV appearance, Rachael was back in court on an outstanding warrant for shoplifting and back in prison. By then there was widespread awareness of her plight, no doubt helped by the media coverage of her case. It took months, but eventually she got a place first in the Cuan Dara detox unit in Cherry Orchard Hospital and then in Keltoi, the recovery facility in the Phoenix Park. She was clean and on her way…and full of gratitude for those all the people who helped her, whom she names.

She is still clean. She is now in college studying psychotherapy. Her arms still bear the scars…but they have healed. The arms that saved her.

1 Looking at the picture of Rachael today, are you surprised at her story?
2 What did you find the most disturbing about her story?
3 Comment on the type of life Rachael had from the ages of 11 to 16.
4 How important was the role of the media in helping Rachael to recover? List all of the people and organisations that have helped Rachael in becoming the woman she is today.
5 What does this story tell you about the power of addiction?

Go to drugs.ie and watch Rachael's video 'My Heroin Hell' under Resources/Multimedia/Documentaries.

If Cocaine Was Legal, Katy French Might Still Be Alive

Louis Jacob

So what's all the fuss about Katy French? So say the smart-asses in the media. I want to give them a few answers they won't like.

First, it is a long time since I felt so completely deflated as when I learned of Katy French's untimely death last Thursday week. It is impossible for the people of her generation not to feel a kinship with her. You see, Katy's story, warts and all, is all of our stories.

Second, I suppose the most natural question to ask would be: Why would a beautiful, young, intelligent girl with a bright future jeopardise everything by snorting cocaine? The thing is that this question is redundant. The real question is, why wouldn't she?

You see, teenagers and young adults have no problems coming up with answers to questions, but the one sure thing is that at some stage in their lives, they will find themselves in a situation where they have to decide 'do I or don't I?' and when that time comes, what they need is a head equipped with 'legitimate' reasons why they shouldn't.

What are the reasons that their parents would give?

Because drugs kill? But everyone knows that bar a few unfortunate exceptions that they don't. Every week in this country, thousands of young people take class A drugs casually. The prospect of it being fatal is not an issue. No wonder young people think: 'It will never happen to me'. Death is as remote as Pluto.

Because they jeopardise your future? But Ireland is now one of the richest countries in the world and we have one of the most alarming drug habits. Everyone knows someone who is successful, has it all and takes drugs casually at the weekends. 'Everybody takes drugs.' This may sound like flippant generalisation but it is an argument that I have heard a million times and from a million people. There is no point in highlighting for them the 'worst possible case scenario' because they see it as just that.

Because it's illegal? So is driving on an L-plate without a fully licensed driver with you. Come on, everyone does it and anyway the Gardaí are after the dealers.

Because I said so? If there is one thing that is clear in a teenager's mind, it's that their parents 'don't know shit'. If anything, saying this is an incentive to do the opposite.

Because your older sister never took drugs? Because it's too expensive? Because what would the neighbours think???

The thing is this: young people are optimists. They are still dreaming about their futures without the obstacles of hindsight and regret. They still have a very idealistic belief in their decision making. Their minds are open to mythologies that mature adults shy away from. Adolescents want to explore. Only with experience and the onset of fear do people strive to make things taboo.

There is no point in trying to make them stay away from so-and-so, the town junkie, because the world is full of so-and-sos. And unless you keep your kids locked up under the stairs, they are going to run into another so-and-so every time they go to a club or a party. It sounds funny but that it is the stone cold truth of it.

The thing is this too: taking drugs or not is not a question of good vs evil. It is a lifestyle decision, like whether to join a gym or the debating society, whether to work in advertising or volunteer for some charity work. Taking drugs defines how a young person sees themselves. Drugs are hip and dangerous (in the glamorous sense). They have somehow become a symbol of freedom.

Bill Clinton, the great hero of middle Ireland, smoked dope. George Bush is widely believed to have taken coke. And where did it get them? Only to be President of the United States. Then there are the Beatles, Jim Jarmusch, Liam Gallagher and the countless Irish success stories who shall remain nameless. Even movies that show the hard side of drug abuse manage, somehow, to romanticise it. Who wouldn't want to be a young Jim Morrison? You see, the decision is theirs and theirs alone. In every aspect of life these days, young people are encouraged to make their own decisions. We spend fortunes in time and money trying to make sure that they have every last piece of information, every angle, before allowing them to make rational educated decisions for themselves.

If young people are being empowered to make their own decisions in every walk of life, then it should follow that they would empower themselves to make their own decision on drugs and this is what's happening. Whether we like it or not, it is a decision that they will have to make themselves and when faced with the decision on whether or not to take drugs, they simply don't have the necessary information to draw on.

We live in a virtual world where we put all kinds of efforts into stimulating the senses into making people feel that they have experienced something that they have not. We have video games where people travel through space, reality TV shows where people live on tropical islands for months on end, *The Lord of the Rings*; nine hours of believing in a world of hobbits and wizards. People feel the themes and emotions, even though they haven't experienced the reality.

Can't these techniques somehow be used to let teenagers experience the dark side of drug use; before they have to make the decision on whether it's something they need in their lives. We need to educate with hard medical facts but we also need to somehow simulate the depression, despair and anxiety which exist, not just in the worst case scenarios, but in the very lives that young people aspire to, and which are the real reasons to say 'no'.

The setting up of centres and drug awareness programmes certainly has its place, but this is a problem that needs to be brought right into the centre of the mainstream. It needs to be demystified, turned into something that everyone is a qualified expert on. I often wonder if Ireland has the stomach to face its problems and to ask the hard questions.

At least the Taoiseach, by sending his aide de camp to Katy French's funeral showed that he's not unaware that these tragedies matter to my generation. Isn't the problem grave enough that it merits two or three school hours a week and to do this consistently, not as some Micky-Mouse side show? Might it be a good idea to have a Leaving Cert paper on it, complete with the carrot of 100 points for an A1? It is surely as relevant in today's Ireland as Home Economics or Business Organisation was twenty years ago.

It all boils down to this. It is impossible to protect young people from exposure to drugs. There is no dynamic – socially, mentally or otherwise. So when the time comes and they are asking themselves *Why wouldn't I?* we need to make sure that they are looking at this lifestyle decision from every angle.

So let me ask again. What's all the fuss about Katy French? Because Katy French's death told us that the time has come to take our heads out of the sand and stop lying to ourselves.

Why was there such an outpouring of grief? I can tell you right now. Because the nation is as guilty as sin.

Katy French was not so much a victim of drugs, but a victim of a system which sees drug users forced to consort with criminals. She was also a victim of our refusal to face the thing we fear the most – coming up with a coherent drugs policy. Above all, she was a victim of our distaste for thinking things through.

Here's the truth. As long as drugs are illegal, the crime lords will continue to make massive profits and to murder at will. Meanwhile, the guardians of morality say, *We will never legalise drugs, no matter what. No sirree* and every dealer in the country says, *Hallelujah. Long live the Free Market. Now I'll be able to afford that new gun.*

Alcohol Abuse

Alcohol Worksheet

Please answer true or false to the following statements by putting **T** or **F** in each box.

1	A person over 16 can buy alcohol in a shop.	☐
2	Children under 15 are allowed in a pub after 7pm.	☐
3	Alcohol gives you energy.	☐
4	It is illegal for a person under 18 to try to purchase alcohol in a pub.	☐
5	If the Gardaí stop a person under 18 and find that the person is carrying alcohol, the Gardaí can confiscate the alcohol.	☐
6	It is illegal to cycle a bike if you are drunk.	☐
7	More alcohol is consumed in Ireland than in any other country in Europe.	☐
8	The effect of alcoholic drink can be noticed within 10 minutes.	☐
9	One unit of alcohol is equal to a pint of beer.	☐
10	Alcohol makes you more likely to do things you normally would not.	☐
11	Men can cope with alcohol better than women can.	☐
12	If a woman drinks during pregnancy it can affect her baby.	☐
13	The younger you start to drink, the more chance you will have of developing a problem with alcohol in later years.	☐
14	Alcohol is the oldest drug in the world.	☐
15	Alcohol alters your mood.	☐

Alcohol

Alcohol is a legal drug that anyone over the age of 18 can buy in Ireland. The component that makes people intoxicated is called ethanol or ethyl alcohol. Many people can enjoy this drug if they consume it sensibly. The Department of Health has outlined what is a safe amount of alcohol to drink for both women and men. Currently for women it is 14 units per week and for men it is 21 units per week. It is important to note that units must be spread out over the course of the week and not be saved for one night, i.e. binge drinking.

A unit is equal to:
2 units
A pint of beer or cider is 2 units
Small glass of wine
Glass of sherry
Shot of spirit

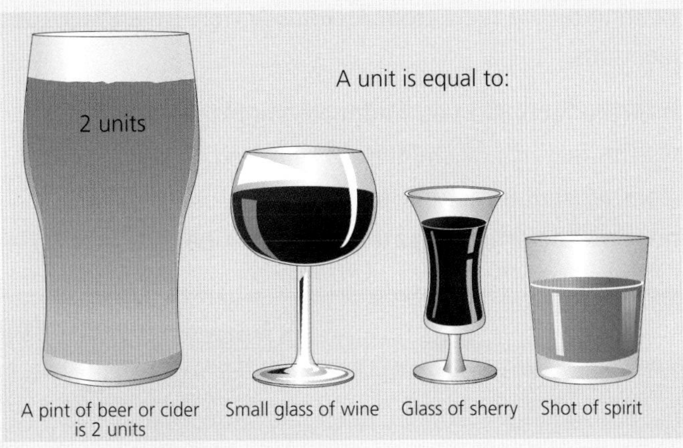

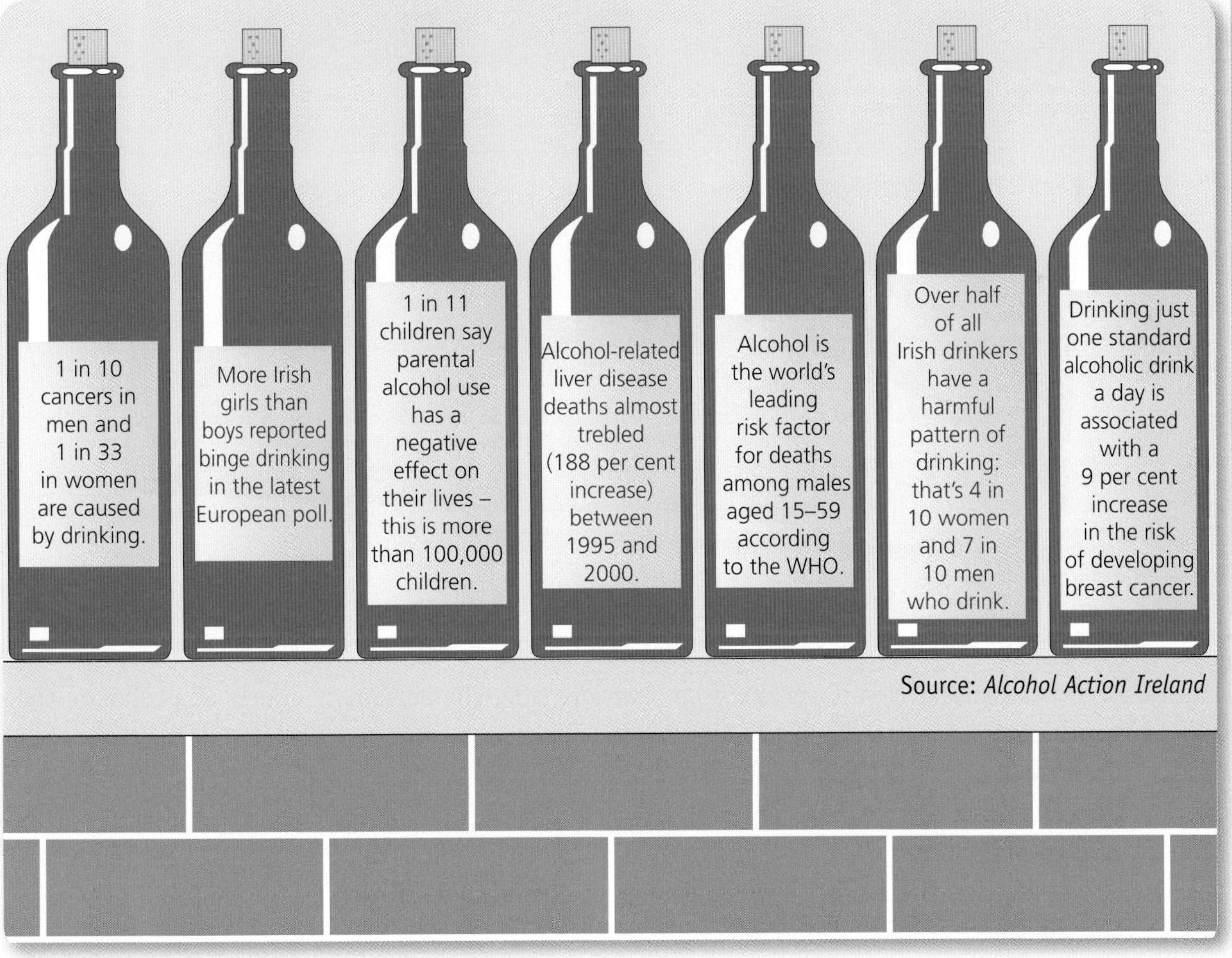

1 in 10 cancers in men and 1 in 33 in women are caused by drinking.
More Irish girls than boys reported binge drinking in the latest European poll.
1 in 11 children say parental alcohol use has a negative effect on their lives – this is more than 100,000 children.
Alcohol-related liver disease deaths almost trebled (188 per cent increase) between 1995 and 2000.
Alcohol is the world's leading risk factor for deaths among males aged 15–59 according to the WHO.
Over half of all Irish drinkers have a harmful pattern of drinking: that's 4 in 10 women and 7 in 10 men who drink.
Drinking just one standard alcoholic drink a day is associated with a 9 per cent increase in the risk of developing breast cancer.

Source: *Alcohol Action Ireland*

1 What do you think about the HSE recommendations on the safe amount of units to drink per week?

2 Comment on the contents of one unit.

3 In your opinion, why do people binge drink?

4 Why, do you think, does the HSE ask people not to binge drink?

5 From your reading of the facts from Alcohol Action Ireland (p.109), answer the following questions.

   (i) Which of the facts did you find most shocking? Why?
   (ii) Discuss the feelings of children as reported in this research.
   (iii) How does alcohol affect one's health?
   (iv) Comment on the drinking patterns of Irish people.

Below is some information on alcohol from www.drugs.ie. The immediate effects of alcohol on the body include:

- Drowsiness
- Loss of balance
- Poor co-ordination
- Slower reaction times (critical when driving or operating machinery)
- Slurred speech

★ Slowed thought processes
★ Nausea and vomiting.

As more alcohol is consumed, there may be a possibility of the following:
★ Unconsciousness
★ Inhibition of normal breathing: This may be fatal, particularly as the person may vomit and can suffocate if the vomit is inhaled.

Potential long-term effects of Ethanol

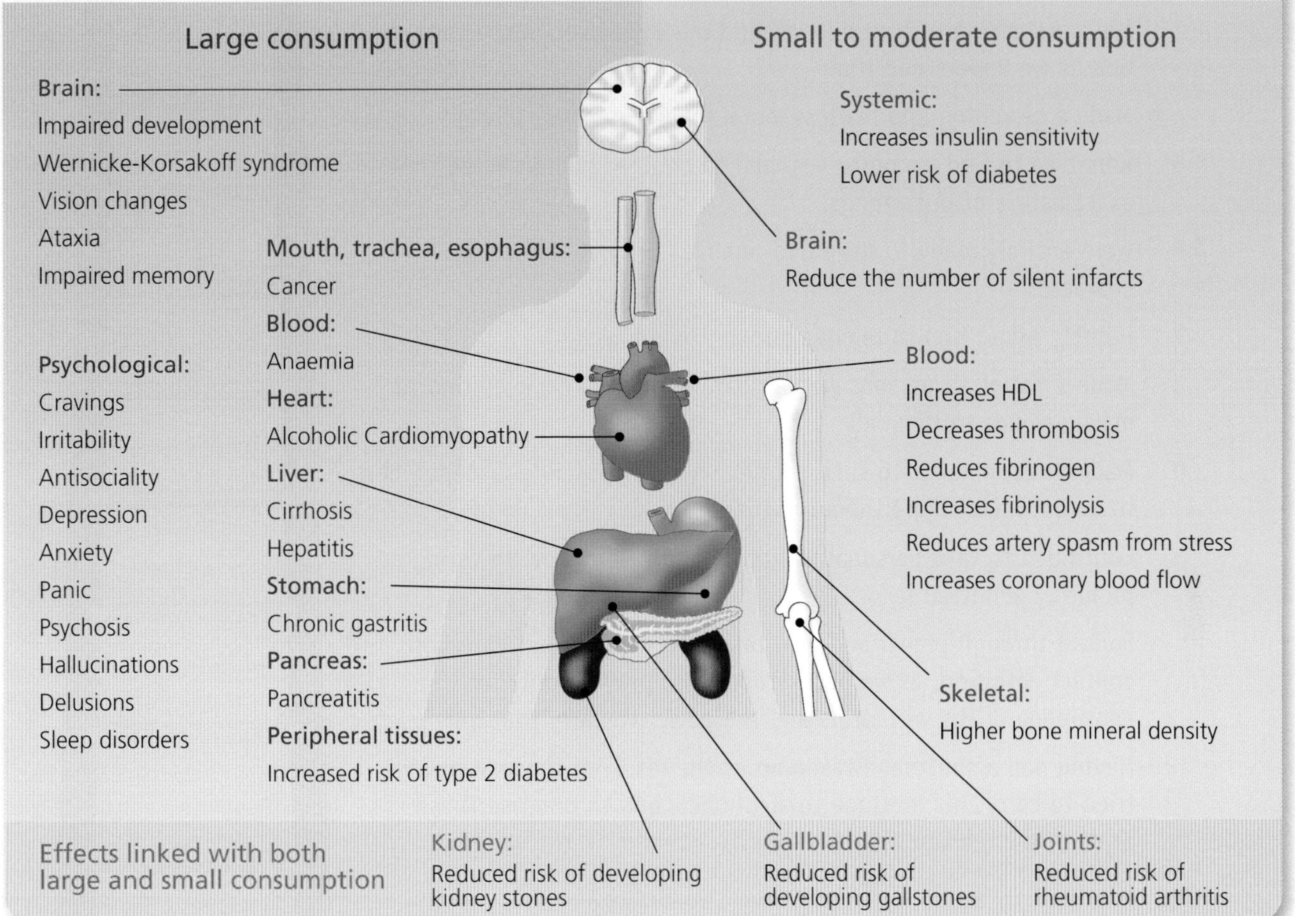

Treatment for Alcoholism

Alcoholism is a treatable disease. However, the alcoholic must first realise that he or she has an addiction, and they must want to seek help. There are various forms of treatment available but the most common is Alcoholics Anonymous (AA).

AA was founded in 1935 by Bill Wilson. It works on the idea that only an alcoholic can help a fellow alcoholic overcome their addiction. It is a self-run and self-funded organisation that prides itself on complete anonymity for all who attend. Alcoholics must attend regular meetings and talk about their addiction and the problems it has caused in their lives. One of the key mottos is: 'What you say here, what you hear here, let it stay here when you leave here.'

Participants of AA must follow twelve steps, which include looking at their problem, trying to find a solution, empowering themselves and maintaining sobriety.

Alcoholics Anonymous Twelve-step Programme

1 We admitted we were powerless over alcohol – that our lives had become unmanageable.

2 Came to believe that a Power greater than ourselves could restore us tosanity.

3 Made a decision to turn our will and our lives over to the care of God as we understood Him.

4 Made a searching and fearless moral inventory of ourselves.

5 Admitted to God, to ourselves, and to another human being the exact nature of our wrongs.

6 Were entirely ready to have God remove all these defects of character.

7 Humbly asked Him to remove our shortcomings.

8 Made a list of all persons we had harmed, and became willing to make amends to them all.

9 Made direct amends to such people wherever possible, except when to do so would injure them or others.

10 Continued to take personal inventory and when we were wrong promptly admitted it.

11 Sought through prayer and meditation to improve our conscious contact with God, as we understood Him, praying only for knowledge of His will for us and the power to carry that out.

12 Having had a spiritual awakening as the result of these Steps, we tried to carry this message to alcoholics, and to practise these principles in all our affairs.

1 What is alcoholism?

2 What factors do you think influence a person's drinking?

3 How would you know if you had a problem with alcohol?

4 What do you think of the service Alcoholics Anonymous provides?

5 Summarise the Twelve-step Programme in your own words.

'I'm Trying to Fight a Winning Battle But I'm Nearly Certain I'm Not Winning'

Vincent Hogan

Paul McGrath peers out across his perfectly manicured lawn to the closed electric gates that, simultaneously, comfort and imprison him.

A high sun dusts Monageer in wan, honeyed light and the view from his living room is all sweeping fields and rippling foliage. We are maybe an hour into the interview and I have just asked him maybe the only pertinent question remaining in the story of a 50-year-old grandfather still running from himself.

Do you understand why people fear where this will end, Paul?

'I worry myself,' he sighs quietly after a pause. 'I think of Alex (Higgins) and, obviously, George (Best). I even think of Paul Gascoigne. Because I do wonder to myself how long more I'm going to get through this.

'When I close those gates, I sometimes think that I may as well be in prison. For me, it's like being trapped. But it's a trap I've set myself. Now I'm saying to myself: "The amount of damage that you've done outside."

'Then again, in other ways, I've loved closing those gates behind me…'

A set of dumb-bells glistens on the table as a kind of vain, redemptive statement. Upstairs, there is a bench-press for the days he's not feeling ruined. Visually, he looks well but Paul's appearance can – routinely – be a lie. Just climbing the stairs, he says, thieves his breath now. Often in the interview, he talks of not having 'the energy' of old.

Chaos

His honesty reaches into deep recesses of chaos and dysfunction. Recently, he stood in court listening to the jigsaw of a black, drunken night being pieced together. The case resulted in him losing his driving licence for three years, a wholly compassionate penalty in the circumstances.

Only the kindness of a neighbour probably separated Paul from a custodial sentence. Two days after the incident, the 65-year-old victim had called to McGrath's house saying he would not press charges on the worst of what had occurred to him that evening. Then he added something that cut Paul to the very core. 'You know you were one of my heroes!'

Later this week, Paul will be in Dublin to launch a warts-and-all DVD of his story, *Paul McGrath, My Life and Football*. There is a moment in it where he admits that he has been to 'something like 13 or 14 rehabs' but that 'a lot of times, within weeks, I'm drinking again'.

And, ostensibly, it is hard to escape a sense of fecklessness in the alcoholic who lapses so habitually and easily. McGrath understands why people might think that way. Repetition eventually wears away all sympathy.

'Look, I've lost patience with myself,' he sighs now. 'Because I haven't really got the energy to do this anymore. I know people will say: "Well just stop drinking! Don't pick it up. Hold your head high and do your walks."

'Of course people are going to lose patience. But it just doesn't seem that easy for me. Even walking out that door now, I feel so self-conscious about some of the things that I've done. These people have really rallied round me, but I've tormented them up and down this road.

'I'm amazed they're still so supportive, but I could understand them thinking: "Paul, enough is enough." I basically knacker things up every time I come out.'

He continues: 'I know that I can't do too many more (rehabs). A lot of the fight is gone out of me. I seem forever drawn to this thing of "I'll just get one last bottle from somewhere and that'll be it…"

'Then I'll take one tablet too many or a drink on a tablet too many and I lose the plot. That's what's hurting me at the moment. Because I was told that this is what could happen. But I never thought I'd be up in front of a court for assaulting someone or taking a car.

'Drunk and disorderly maybe. But that? In all the scrapes I've had, I ended up on the floor most times. And when this man had the kindness to come up to my house and say the things he said, I just thought: "This can't be right anymore…"'

Tiring

'It's very tiring and I honestly don't know where it's going to end up. But that incident threw me completely. I can only thank God he was so decent about it. I'm sure a lot of people are judging me now, wondering how I could have turned into "that thing". People, I suppose, will either understand or they won't.'

It is four years since we collaborated on his autobiography, *Back from the Brink*, a publication that would prove the most successful Irish sports book in history. Paul's candour astonished many at the time and, in the months immediately after its success, he would describe doing *Back from the Brink* as a cathartic experience.

Yet there has been little resolution since to any of the issues that made the book such a remarkable read. If anything, McGrath's life continues to lurch and wheel with increasingly destructive force. And he doesn't much like what he sees himself becoming.

'Something snapped in me that night that led to the court case,' he says. 'And I'm very concerned about that. Very much so. I mean I've been warned so many times in rehab that this doesn't get better. It gets worse. And here I am now, knowing that it is getting worse.

'When I did the book, everything felt hunky dory. But the last two years probably, I haven't been great. I have felt that I'm slipping back into my old ways.

'I don't like the way I've been acting lately. I'm becoming a person that I don't like. I'm upsetting people. Someone offers you "a swift one" and, suddenly, you're in a group for the night.

'You don't know them and, to be fair, they don't know the likely consequences. Maybe they get their photograph taken with you. They don't know what I've become. It's why I like to stay behind the gates now. You might notice the garden's looking okay!'

Eight weeks ago, the birth of Talia conferred grandparent status on McGrath. He describes the little daughter of his eldest boy, Chris, as 'absolutely gorgeous' and is looking forward to their first visit. 'I want to be around to see her growing up,' he says. Yet an inevitable anxiety lingers over how she will come to know her Irish grandfather.

'I'm genuinely trying to fight a winning battle,' he reflects, 'but I'm nearly certain I'm not winning it. People ask me will I go for a game of golf and I'll always go: "Yeah, yeah, Jesus, love to..." and I know for a fact that I won't go 'cos I think to myself, that's out among the public again.

'If I'm being honest about it, I've never been that comfortable in people's company. And that hasn't changed. If anything, it is escalating. Something is not computing too well in my brain, I feel.

'And I've been taking things for so long that my brain is so used to the chemicals, I feel I almost can't function without them. The problem I have, I suppose, is that 80 per cent of the time I can carry it off.

'People who are close to me will know immediately if I've taken something. But most people would look at me with the suit on and be thinking: "He's not doing too bad..."

'I'm getting fed up with that. But mostly I'm fed up of being sick. I mean, I never believed drinking was an illness. I always thought it was just a weak person who couldn't say no, who wanted the bottle rather than look after his kids. Who wanted it to help him get through a game.

'I never believed that I couldn't beat it at some stage. I always thought there'd be a certain point where I'd just say: "That's it, I've had it with this!" because my body, obviously, has taken a hammering.

'But then, in my mind, it's like I'm taking on the challenge too. I've got this good angel, bad angel on the shoulder type of thing. Bad angel saying: "You're still a strong lad, you can carry this off. Pop a pill, have a quick drink. You'll dress up nice and neat."

'That's all very well for the first hour or hour and a half. But then...'

He once went 14 months clean with the help of the late Dr Patrick Nugent and recalls those months as 'the best time of my life'. Yet, he is loathe to use Patrick's death as any glib justification for his recidivism since.

'Look, I've been given every opportunity to make a decent life for myself,' he says, intolerant of the very thought. 'And, to be fair, I have found one or two people since Patrick died who have been a huge help.'

His last spell in rehab ended the week before his annual golf tournament in aid of Cystic Fibrosis last July. He was professionally advised to give the occasion a wide berth but felt his obligations to the event were simply too personal to retreat from it. So he immediately immersed himself back in the organisation and, true to form, lapsed.

Without access to a car now, he has considered the idea of moving back to Dublin, though he has no intention of selling the house in Wexford. He will be at the Aviva for Friday night's European Championship qualifier with Russia and continues to get sporadic coaching work from the FAI.

'They have been brilliant to me,' he says. 'The girls in the FAI often ring asking if I need anything. John Delaney has been a different class.'

Yet, Paul knows the only help that – ultimately – saves an addict is self-help. 'I hate spoofing to people,' he acknowledges. 'When you're an alcoholic and you wake up after one of these benders, especially when you've taken other stuff as well, you feel absolutely rotten.

'It's bad. But I've been doing it now for twenty-odd years. I get out of bed in the morning and I walk like an old man. And I'm saying to myself: "You're not strong enough to do this anymore."'

I finish the interview with a simple question. Where does Paul McGrath see himself at 60?

'Well the Chelsea job should be opened up by then!' he smiles a little weakly. 'Ah no, seriously, I want to see myself sitting on this couch with my granddaughter, watching TV. I'd love to be just someone who potters around his garden, goes for walks, plays a bit of golf, has a few friends.

'I suppose I'd just love to be around, to be here. That would be a God-send. To be still around and for all my kids to be healthy.'

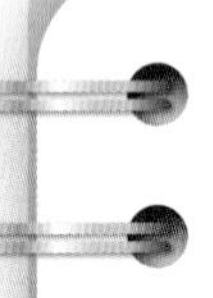

End of Section Summary

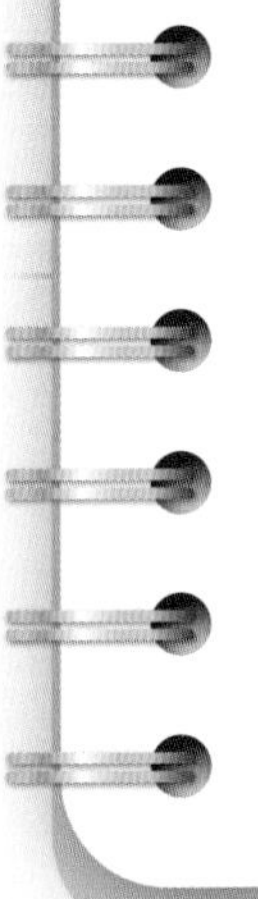

- Morality refers to a person's understanding of what is right and wrong.
- Conscience is a person's ability to decide between right and wrong.
- Moral growth is a process that people experience as they go through life: learning right from wrong.
- A morally mature person is someone who knows the difference between right and wrong and chooses right.
- Abortion can be defined as the deliberate termination of a human pregnancy.
- Euthanasia can be defined as the painless killing of a patient suffering from an incurable and painful disease or in an irreversible coma.
- Experimentation with life involves using medical advancements in research involving human embryos.
- Addiction can be defined as the fact or condition of being addicted to a particular substance or activity.

End of Section Activities

1. Describe the factors that lead one to become a morally mature person.
2. Explain the law on abortion in Ireland from 1983 to present.
3. In your own words, sum up the arguments for and against euthanasia.
4. Describe the three types of genetic engineering.
5. Write two paragraphs on the power of addiction: one in relation to drug addiction and one in relation to alcohol addiction.

- ★ 'Abortion should be legal in Ireland.'
- ★ 'Cloning is unethical.'
- ★ 'Addiction is unbeatable.'

1. Research the demand for 'designer babies' around the world.
2. In relation to abortion, compare and contrast the X case and the C case.
3. Research one illegal substance and present your findings to the class.

Journal your response to each of these topics: morality, addiction and experimentation with life.

- ★ Compile a list of questions for an interview that you could have with someone who has an addiction.
- ★ Compile a list of questions you could ask a doctor who supports experimentation with life.

Films

- ★ *Gone Baby Gone*
- ★ *12 Angry Men*
- ★ *A Few Good Men*
- ★ *The Reader*
- ★ *The Shawshank Redemption*
- ★ *High Fidelity*
- ★ *The Cider House Rules*
- ★ *Vera Drake*
- ★ *Juno*
- ★ *Circle of Friends*
- ★ *Riding in Cars with Boys*
- ★ *You Don't Know Jack*
- ★ *Million Dollar Baby*
- ★ *The Sea Inside*
- ★ *The Hours*
- ★ *The English Patient*
- ★ *It's My Party*
- ★ *A.I. Artificial Intelligence*
- ★ *My Sister's Keeper*
- ★ *Seven Pounds*
- ★ *Never Let Me Go*

Documentaries

- ★ *A Time to Die*
- ★ *The Hospice*
- ★ *The Asylum*
- ★ *I See a Darkness*

Websites

Each of these websites contain information on the moral issues mentioned in this section. Use the site's search engine to find the relevant material.

- ★ www.bbc.co.uk
- ★ www.tes.co.uk
- ★ www.reonline.org.uk

Podcasts

- ★ Go to the podcast section of todayfm.com and search for 'Abortion Email' and listen to the relevant Ray D'Arcy Show episode.

Section 4

A Living Faith: Doing Justice

Context

This section focuses on human rights issues and abuses that take place around the world today. It aims to increase our awareness of our responsibilities as human beings. As we grow and mature into adulthood it is important that we are aware of the onus that is on each of us to make a difference.

What is Justice?

Justice is based on the principles of fairness and equality. Justice is essential in any society that aims to function properly. Justice is always needed if people are to feel equal. In order to be a just person, one must be fair and reasonable.

Justice can be understood from a secular and from a religious point of view. Secular justice is the view that people have an instinctive ability to know the difference between right and wrong and to act in a just and fair manner towards others.

Religious justice is based on secular justice with an added dimension that comes from the teachings found within the sacred texts. In these sacred texts, people of faith can find a detailed understanding of what their religion teaches on the issue of justice.

1 Explain what you understand by the term 'justice'?
2 Explain the difference between secular and religious justice.
3 From your own life experiences, give examples of times when you felt you were treated unjustly.

Justice and World Religions

Christianity teaches love in the commandments. 'Love the Lord your God with all your heart and with all your soul and with all your mind' is the first and greatest commandment. The second commandment is similar: 'Love your neighbour as yourself.' In Christianity, there is a special place for the poor. In terms of justice, nobody is an outsider: everyone is welcome.

Islam teaches that the purpose of sending messengers (prophets) to earth was to end injustice in the world. In Islam, justice means giving everyone their due. You cannot act in an unjust way even when you are dealing with the enemy.

> *'We sent aforetime our messengers with clear Signs and sent down with them the Book and the Balance, that men may stand forth in Justice.'*
>
> **Al-Hadeed 57:25**

Hinduism teaches that love for all beings is of the utmost importance. Leaders of political, social and religious institutions must strive to treat people of all religions, races and classes equally and must ensure that all beliefs and practices are respected. All forms of life are worshiped, since they are expressions of the Hindu Gods. Parents and the elderly must be treated with respect and children must be raised to have good self-esteem and to have respect for human values.

> *'May there be peace in the whole world. May the wicked become peaceful and gentle. Let all people pray with their hearts for peace and mutual wellbeing. May our minds resort only to that which is auspicious and good. May our thought be fixed on Lord Vishnu without any selfish motive.'*
>
> **Shrimad Bhagavatam 5–18–9**

Buddhism teaches that humans are born with free will and, therefore, their destinies are in their own hands. The Buddha stressed the importance of understanding that every person is equal and that each person has the potential to reach their highest truth. Buddhist teachings say that noble and charitable actions are what define people's goodness. They believe that people become outsiders by wrongful deeds.

> *'Oneself is one's own refuge; what other refuge can there be?'*
>
> **Buddha**

> *'Purity and impurity depend on oneself. No one can purify another.'*
>
> **Buddha**

Judaism teaches that God and everything that comes from God is just (Deuteronomy 32:4). In the Jewish faith it is believed that God teaches humans how to be just. God believes that just behaviour will be rewarded (Proverbs 21:21) and God has given responsibility to people to establish and maintain justice in the world.

1 Compare and contrast what each world faith says on the issue of justice.

Justice and Peace

A Level Playing Field with Israel?

Jan Benvie

Ten days ago, I was reminded of the story about Christmas Day in the trenches of World War I. The story tells about enemy soldiers coming together, as human beings, in no-man's land to celebrate Christmas and play football (soccer.) I glimpsed such a moment on 20 July 2007.

Regular readers of our updates may recall the establishment of an Old City Football Team in February of this year, a joint venture between CPT, our neighbor Zleekha Muhtaseb and a Palestinian NGO. It has been difficult to find a safe and suitable place to play, so, Zleekha suggested playing in the street outside the CPT apartment. Closures, curfews, and military occupation have driven all of the residents away; only CPT and Zleekha live here now. The street ends with a high metal fence, designed to prevent access from the Old City to Shuhada Street, where some Israeli settlers live. It seemed an ideal flat, open space where the children could train and play. There were some problems with settler children throwing stones over the fence, but we thought that finally we had a 'home ground' for our football team.

It was disappointing, therefore, when a patrol of soldiers came into the street on 20 July and said that the children, including older youths who were helping train the younger, could not play football there. The soldiers cited the two recent fires in the street, close to their military base, as a reason for banning the street football.

We protested, saying that children are less likely to set fires if they are involved in worthwhile activities like the football team. 'You accuse us of teaching children terrorism. Here we are teaching them football, and you stop us!' Zleekha told the patrol leader.

The soldiers insisted they had their orders and suggested another area nearby. We continued to protest – the other area is smaller and sloping, not an even playing field. The soldiers told us, 'The boys are willing to move.'

I thought, 'It is not an even playing field with heavily armed Israeli soldiers "suggesting" to unarmed, teenage Palestinians that they move.'

Then the Palestinian boys suggested a novel resolution: a football game between themselves and the Israeli soldiers. Already a few soldiers were kicking the ball around, laughing and jostling with the Palestinians teenagers who, after all, are only a few years younger than they are.

And, there it was. That brief moment when supposed enemies met as human beings.

The commander, looking down from the occupied rooftop above, refused to allow the match to go ahead, but, perhaps intrigued by what was happening below, came down to talk.

And so, a compromise was reached. The commander, who gave his name as Israel, agreed that the children can play football in the street from 4.00–7.00 each afternoon and the soldiers will prevent settler children from throwing stones.

It felt a little more like a level playing field.

1 Find the link between justice and peace in this story.

2 Can you think of other examples of justice and peace at work in the world today?

Visions of Peace

Peace and justice are at work in the world today. The two can work simultaneously. Peace can come about as a result of people acting in a just way, as one can see in the story above involving the young boys and the soldiers. Justice prevailed when the young boys were allowed to play soccer from 4pm until 7pm. However, this just act also brought about peace between the two sides: a compromise was reached and the violence ended.

'If you succumb to the temptation of using violence in the struggle, unborn generations will be the recipients of a long and desolate night of bitterness and your chief legacy to the future will be an endless reign of meaningless chaos.'
Martin Luther King, Jr

'It is the enemy who can truly teach us to practise the virtues of compassion and tolerance.'
Dalai Lama

'Is not peace, in the last analysis, basically a matter of human rights – the right to live out our lives without fear of devastation – the right to breathe air as nature provided – the right of future generations to a healthy existence?'
John F. Kennedy

1. Which quote is most similar to your vision of peace?
2. What do you think John F. Kennedy is trying to say in his quote?
3. Create your own quotation for your vision of peace.
4. Find one other quote from a world leader on the topic of peace.

For the achievement of peace, we need a firm determination to respect the dignity of other people, along with a deliberate practice of 'love of neighbour'. Sometimes, for many reasons, this practice is not followed – and war is often the outcome.

War may be defined as armed hostilities between two opposing groups, in which each side puts people forward to fight and to kill one another. Christians believe that it is their vocation to seek to establish peace in the world. They believe that they should try to achieve peace by removing injustices that lead to war.

Pacifism

Christianity teaches that people can choose between two options in the event of war:

★ Pacifism
★ Just War theory.

A pacifist is a person who believes that violence is always wrong and would never condone or support a war effort. Pacifists believe that the participation in any type of violent military action is never just. They also feel that governments who spend money on war should try and redirect this money in order to help the poor and vulnerable in society. In the case of conflict, passive resistance is the only method that should be considered.

1 Explain pacifism.

2 Is pacifism achievable in today's society?

3 Name an issue you feel strongly about. Would you make a peaceful protest for that issue?

Just War Theory

The Just War theory originated with the Greeks and the early philosophers. It was later developed by Christian theologians such as St Thomas Aquinas in order to outline what was deemed acceptable in the case of war.

Today the Just War theory outlines what are acceptable reasons for going to war (*jus ad bellum*) and the right actions to take while in the war (*jus in bello*). The Just War theory is needed because at times there can be a moral justification for going to war and certain guidelines must be followed. Due to the devastating effects that come about as a result of war, the Christian Church puts forward this teaching in order to protect peace and justice for those involved in the war and civilians who are not.

In the likelihood that the difficult decision regarding war has to be made, the Christian Church would ideally hope for compliance with the conditions below. The decision to go to war *cannot* be taken lightly and the Just War theory provides a guide to assess the justice of the decision. The guidelines below must all be satisfied before a war could be called 'just' by the Christian Church.

Jus ad Bellum

Jus ad bellum refers to just reasons for going to war. According to Just War theory, the conditions for going to war include the following.

- ★ There must be an aggressor who is a threat to the nation and its safety.
- ★ Every attempt has been made to solve the conflict – to no avail.
- ★ There must be a chance that you will have success in the war.
- ★ The damage caused in war cannot outweigh the damage that would have come without war.
- ★ It must be remembered that it is only the governing bodies of a country that have the authority to declare war.

Jus in Bello

Jus in bello refers to fair conditions while in wartime. The Catholic Church has put guidelines in place on how a war should be conducted in an ethical way, once war has broken out.

> *'The Church and human reason both assert the permanent validity of the moral law during armed conflict. The mere fact that war has regrettably broken out does not mean that everything becomes licit between the warring parties.'*
>
> **CCC 2312**

In a war effort excessive means must not be used when dealing with the enemy. The welfare of civilians, as much as possible, must be upheld during a war effort.

> *'Non-combatants, wounded soldiers, and prisoners must be respected and treated humanely. Actions deliberately contrary to the law of nations and to its universal principles are crimes, as are the orders that command such actions. Blind obedience does not suffice to excuse those who carry them out. Thus the extermination of a people, nation, or ethnic minority must be condemned as a mortal sin. One is morally bound to resist orders that command genocide.'*
>
> **CCC 2313**

Peace and justice are achievable goals once each human respects the rights of others. All human rights are outlined in the UN Declaration of Human Rights. This document was put together after World War II to prevent the 'scourge of war' and to 'secure justice and advancements for all peoples'.

1. Explain the Just War theory in your own words.
2. Why is the Just War theory needed?
3. Do you think it is followed today by world leaders?
4. Are you surprised that the Christian Church supports war through this theory?

World leaders discussing important matters

Below are pictures of soldiers before, during and after war.

Before	During	After

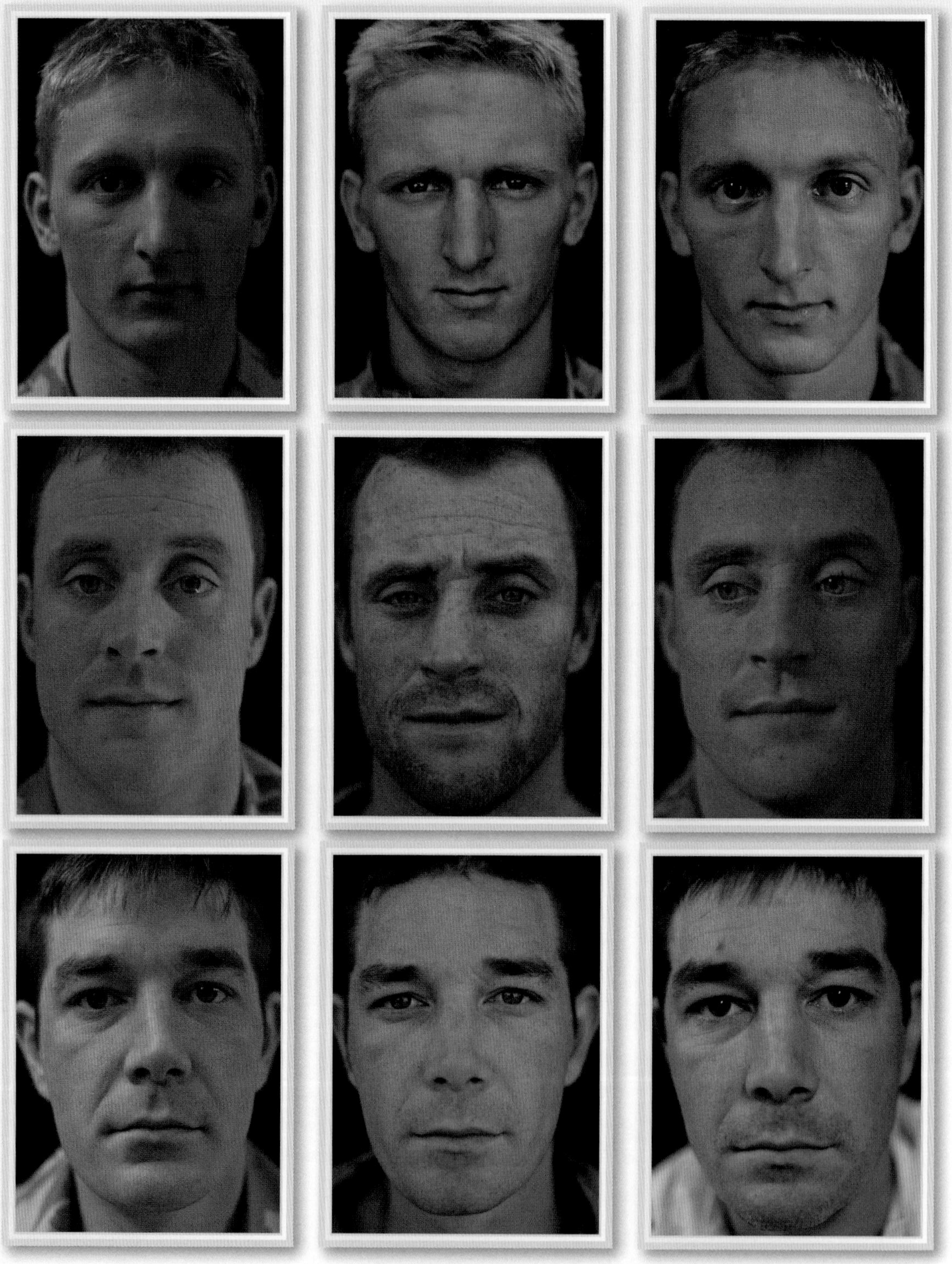

1 Discuss the photos (above) and comment on what you think these soldiers went through during the war.

Watch the following documentary on female soldiers and their visible and invisible wounds.
www.servicethefilm.com

Go to podbay.fm and listen to 'Writing on War in the 21st Century'.

Journal your response to the following question: Does war ever serve a purpose?

Human Rights

1. What makes humans unique?
2. What are rights?
3. What are human rights?

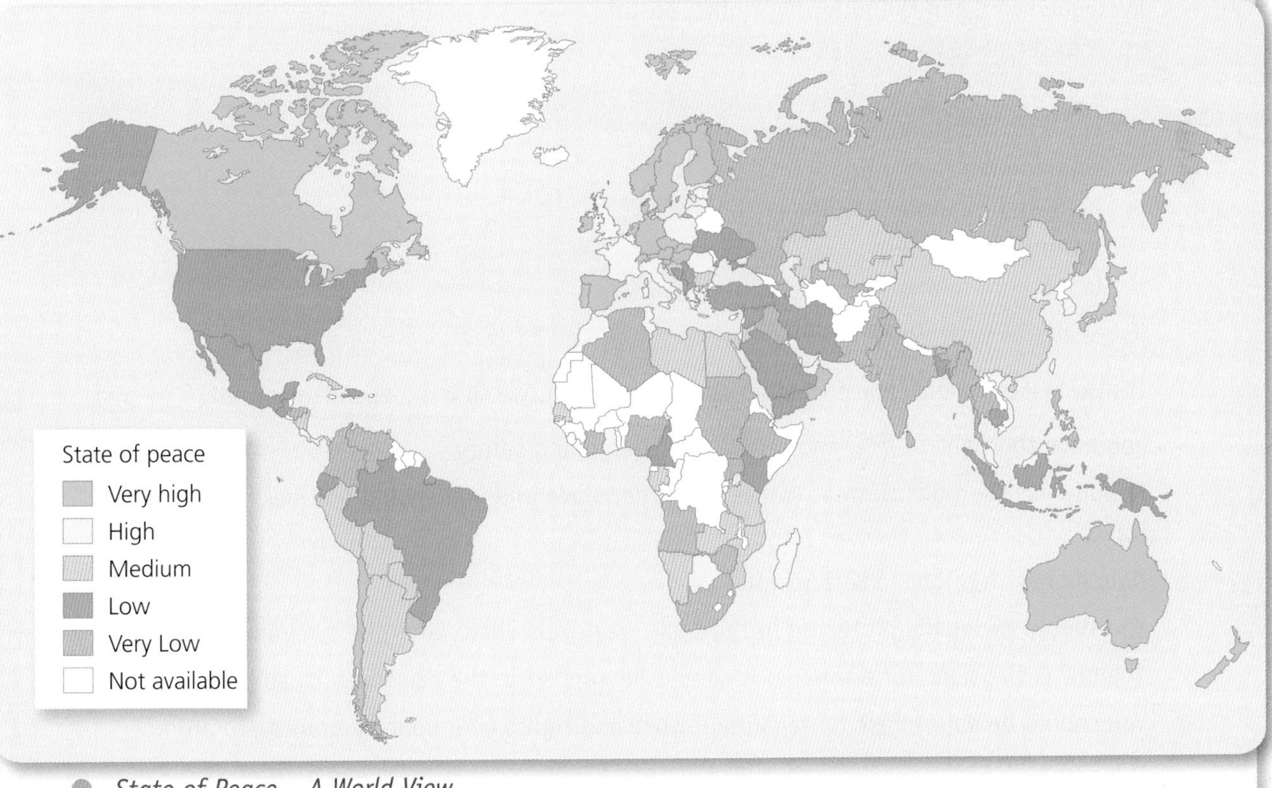

State of Peace – A World View

Answer the following questions based on the map on page 129.

1 List the countries with a very high state of peace.
2 Give some reasons as to why you think they have a very high state of peace.
3 List the countries with a low level of peace.
4 Why do you think these countries have a low level of peace?
5 Looking at the map as a whole, do you think the world today is a peaceful place? Give reasons for your answer.

Declarations of the United Nations

The United Nations (UN) was formed in 1945, after World War II, in order to prevent future generations from experiencing war on such a scale again. In 1948 the UN put together the Universal Declaration of Human Rights (UDHR). There are thirty articles within the UDHR. Articles 1–28 focus on the rights that every human has. Articles 29 and 30 refer to the responsibilities that each of us has towards other humans.

Universal Declaration of Human Rights

1 When children are born, they are free and each should be treated in the same way. They have reason and conscience and should act towards one another in a friendly manner.

2 Everyone can claim the following rights, despite
   - ★ a different sex
   - ★ a different skin colour
   - ★ speaking a different language
   - ★ thinking different things
   - ★ believing in another religion
   - ★ owning more or less
   - ★ being born in another social group
   - ★ coming from another country.

   It also makes no difference whether the country you live in is independent or not.

3 You have the right to live, and to live in freedom and safety.

4 Nobody has the right to treat you as his or her slave and you should not make anyone your slave.

5 Nobody has the right to torture you.

6 You should be legally protected in the same way everywhere, and like everyone else.

7 The law is the same for everyone; it should be applied in the same way to all.

8 You should be able to ask for legal help when the rights your country grants you are not respected.

9 Nobody has the right to put you in prison, to keep you there, or to send you away from your country unjustly, or without good reason.

10 If you go on trial this should be done in public. The people who try you should not let themselves be influenced by others.

11 You should be considered innocent until it can be proved that you are guilty. If you are accused of a crime, you should always have the right to defend yourself. Nobody has the right to condemn you and punish you for something you have not done.

12 You have the right to ask to be protected if someone tries to harm your good name, enter your house, open your letters, or bother you or your family without a good reason.

13 You have the right to come and go as you wish within your country. You have the right to leave your country to go to another one; and you should be able to return to your country if you want.

14 If someone hurts you, you have the right to go to another country and ask it to protect you. You lose this right if you have killed someone and if you, yourself, do not respect what is written here.

15 You have the right to belong to a country and nobody can prevent you, without a good reason, from belonging to a country if you wish.

16 As soon as a person is legally entitled, he or she has the right to marry and have a family. In doing this, neither the colour of your skin, the country you come from nor your religion should be impediments. Men and women have the same rights when they are married and also when they are separated.

Nobody should force a person to marry.

The government of your country should protect you and the members of your family.

17 You have the right to own things and nobody has the right to take these from you without a good reason.

18 You have the right to profess your religion freely, to change it, and to practise it either on your own or with other people.

19 You have the right to think what you want, to say what you like, and nobody should forbid you from doing so. You should be able to share your ideas also – with people from any other country.

20 You have the right to organise peaceful meetings or to take part in meetings in a peaceful way. It is wrong to force someone to belong to a group.

21 You have the right to take part in your country's political affairs either by belonging to the government yourself or by choosing politicians who have the same ideas as you. Governments should be voted for regularly and voting should be secret. You should get a vote and all votes should be equal. You also have the same right to join the public service as anyone else.

22 The society in which you live should help you to develop and to make the most of all the advantages (culture, work, social welfare) which are offered to you and to all the men and women in your country.

23 You have the right to work, to be free to choose your work, to get a salary which allows you to support your family. If a man and a woman do the same work, they should get the same pay. All people who work have the right to join together to defend their interests.

24 Each work day should not be too long, since everyone has the right to rest and should be able to take regular paid holidays.

25 You have the right to have whatever you need so that you and your family: do not fall ill or go hungry; have clothes and a house; and are helped if you are out of work, if you are ill, if you are old, if your wife or husband is dead, or if you do not earn a living for any other reason you cannot help. Mothers and their children are entitled to special care. All children have the same rights to be protected, whether or not their mother was married when they were born.

26 You have the right to go to school and everyone should go to school. Primary schooling should be free. You should be able to learn a profession or continue your studies as far as you wish. At school, you should be able to develop all your talents and you should be taught to get on with others, whatever their race, religion or the country they come from. Your parents have the right to choose how and what you will be taught at school.

27 You have the right to share in your community's arts and sciences, and any good they do. Your works as an artist, writer, or a scientist should be protected, and you should be able to benefit from them.

28 So that your rights will be respected, there must be an 'order' which can protect them. This 'order' should be local and worldwide.

29 You have duties towards the community within which your personality can only fully develop. The law should guarantee human rights. It should allow everyone to respect others and to be respected.

30 In all parts of the world, no society, no human being, should take it upon her or himself to act in such a way as to destroy the rights which you have just been reading about.

1. In your own words, summarise each UDHR article.
2. Reorder the articles, with Number One being the one you find most important.
3. Looking at articles 9–11, why might they be of utmost importance?
4. Can you think of a situation where article 14 would be important to you if you were seeking asylum in another country?
5. Article 18 is about your religious freedom. Explain why this is important.
6. Identify how the final two articles are different from the rest.

Even though the Declaration of Human Rights has existed since 1948, human rights abuses still occur around the world today. They are many and varied; some are encountered by adults and others by children. Due to the fact that children are so vulnerable and abuses against them are so widespread, the UN put together a further declaration specifically for the rights of the child, some of which can be found below.

UN Convention of the Rights of the Child

- ★ The right to **life**
- ★ The right to **be with their parents or with those who will care for them best**
- ★ The right to **have ideas and say what they think**
- ★ The right to **practice their religion**
- ★ The right to **get information they need**
- ★ The right to **special care, education, and training, if needed**
- ★ The right to **enough food and clean water**
- ★ The right to **play**
- ★ The right to **free education**
- ★ The right to **learn about and enjoy their own culture**
- ★ The right not to **be used as a cheap worker**
- ★ The right not to **be hurt or neglected**
- ★ The right not to **be used as a soldier in wars**
- ★ The right to **know about their rights and responsibilities**
- ★ The right to **be protected from danger**
- ★ The right to **speak their own language**
- ★ The right to **health care**
- ★ The right to **meet with other children**
- ★ The right to **a name and nationality**

The child-friendly (unofficial) text of the United Nations Convention on the Rights of the Child was developed by, and provided with, the permission of the Canadian UNICEF Committee.

The rest of these rights can be found online at www.childrensrights.ie

1 Identify the differences between the UDHR and the UNCRC.
2 Explain why there was a need to have a separate declaration for children.

Watch the documentary *Class Dismissed* about a girl's story of her school being shut down by the Taliban at *www.nytimes.com*

Journal your response to the documentary.

Child soldier

Homeless teenager

Human rights abuses take place all around the world and include:

- ★ Third world debt
- ★ Child soldiers, e.g. Uganda
- ★ Homelessness, e.g. Ireland.

All of these human rights issues are in breach of the UDHR and the UNCRC. Each human being in the world has a duty to respect and uphold the rights stated in these UN declarations. Regardless of whether a person practises a religious faith or not, each person has a moral obligation to do the right thing.

Third World Debt

Third world debt is the money that the developing world countries owe to countries in the developed world. This problem stems back to the 1970s, when the price of oil increased. Countries rich with oil resources became very wealthy and invested their money in foreign banks. These banks then decided to lend money to the developing world countries in order to make more profit. Some of this money was mismanaged and given on loan to developing countries, including many African countries. This money could have been used well by governments in developing countries. However, it was spent carelessly by the leaders of those countries. The borrowed money was spent on oil, arms and foreign capital, which left these countries with very little money to spend on education and health. In the 1980s interest rates increased and the foreign banks were now looking for the money to be paid back. It soon became clear that these countries were unable to pay back both the lump sum and the interest. Most of the leaders who had borrowed the money were no longer in power. The International Monetary Fund (IMF) stepped in and helped these countries with repayment plans. They introduced a structural adjustment programme for Africa.

Its terms included the following.

- Wage freezes were put in place, despite inflation.
- The best crops had to be used for cash crops (crops for exports).
- No tariffs were placed on exports.
- Economic policies opened these countries to foreign investment.
- Cheap imports were allowed.
- Government spending on health and education was severely cut.

This debt led to further poverty for the people of Africa and, consequently, more human rights abuses occurred. In recent years there have been numerous campaigns to end this debt. Unfortunately, the legacy and burden of this debt continues to be a cause for human suffering and poverty for millions of people daily. The majority of Africans will never get the chance to receive an education, adequate health care or the opportunity to understand or exercise their basic human rights.

1 In your own words, explain third world debt.

2 Who do you think is to blame for the debt: the leaders of these countries or the banks? Explain your thoughts.

3 What do you think of the structural adjustment programme that the IMF put in place?

4 Do you know any recent campaigns that have taken place to alleviate the debt?

5 Why, do you think, might many people in Africa be unaware of their rights?

Child Soldiers

Watch the lecture on Child Soldiers by Adam Wozniak as an introduction to the topic of Child Soldiers at *www.vimeo.com*

A child soldier can be defined as any child from the ages of 5–17 who is engaged in armed conflict, either directly or indirectly as part of a regular or irregular army. There are approximately 500,000 children involved in child soldiering. Girls are often used as sex slaves or given as wives to successful soldiers.

There are many reasons why children are used in war. They can fit into confined spaces and use modern light-weight weapons. They need less feeding and are easier to transport. They can be an unexpected aggressor towards the enemy. As children, they are more easily manipulated and controlled by fear than adults would be, and their ideas of right and wrong have not fully developed. Child soldiers are used mostly in Sub-Saharan Africa, as well as in parts of Asia and in Burma.

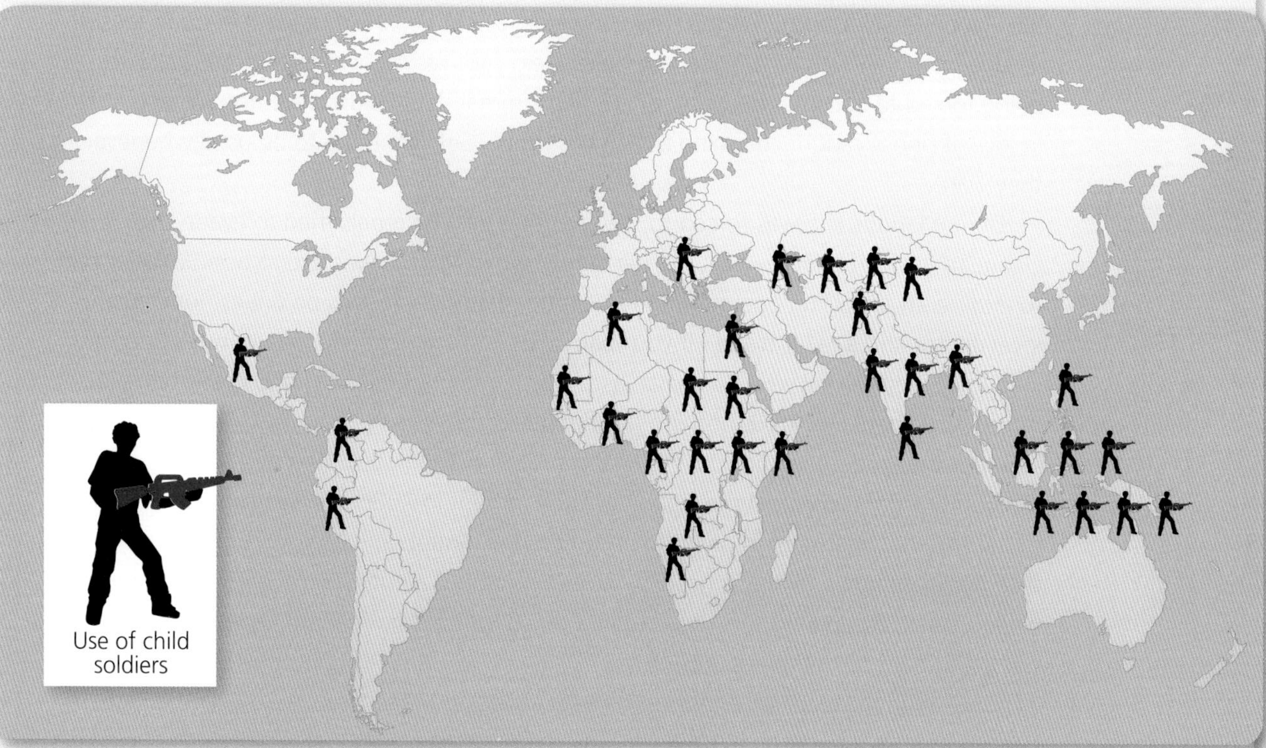

Use of child soldiers in the world

Child soldiers can be involved directly in war as frontline combatants, land mine detectors, decoys, spies, saboteurs, etc. Child soldiers can be involved indirectly, as cooks, porters or sex slaves.

Many child soldiers have weak family structures or no families at all. They may not have any identification papers. Many of them have been abducted from refugee camps or orphanages.

Children become involved in wars due to many reasons. Sometimes they wish to avenge the death of a family member. They might work as soldiers because they see this as a route out of poverty when they have so few opportunities available to them. They may also be influenced by a sense of loyalty to their tribe or clan.

1 What do you know about child soldiers?
2 Why are child soldiers used?
3 In which countries are child soldiers most used?
4 What do child soldiers do in war?
5 Why are children especially vulnerable when they get involved in conflict?
6 Why might a child decide to become a soldier?

Story From a Child Soldier: Juliet's Journey

www.warchild.org.uk

Juliet's unborn baby turned out to be her saviour. Kidnapped by Lord's Resistance Army (LRA) rebels in Northern Uganda when she was just 12 years old, Juliet had no means of escape from the bush where she was being held captive. At 16 she fell pregnant after being forced to become the 'wife' of a rebel commander. 'Soldiers are not allowed to fall in love. If one is caught charming a girl he is killed. Girls are there to be used whenever they want.'

During labour, she was forced to walk for miles as the rebels tried to evade the Ugandan army. The journey caused her son to die before he was even born. So Juliet had to endure an agonising operation to remove the baby. There was no anaesthetic, just a local doctor and a razor blade. 'If your baby dies you are not supposed to mourn for it. If you do, they will kill you. You have just to go somewhere secretly and cry. When you return, you should look like nothing has happened.'

After the crude operation Juliet's health rapidly deteriorated. However, during peace talks between the LRA and the Ugandan Government in 2006 she was given the chance to get hospital treatment in neighbouring Kenya – though an LRA escort had to stay with her at all times. While in hospital Juliet befriended a nurse who heard her story and helped her to escape. 'When I was packing my bags I felt no fear. All I knew is that I was not going back to that place.'

Juliet, with the assistance of the Ugandan Embassy, was then able to board a flight back to the Ugandan capital, Kampala. Juliet now attends a school in Northern Uganda created especially for girls who have missed out on education because of the conflict. She is working hard to catch up on the years of schooling she missed while in captivity with the LRA.

'When I came back I really wanted to go back to school. Although a terrible thing happened to me when my baby died, it led me to get the chance to escape. It shows that something positive can come from something terrible. If you are not educated, you are nothing.'

Juliet

Juliet now hopes to continue her studies at university and qualify as a lawyer so that she can bring those who have recruited and abused girls to justice. As she points out: 'Many girls have been through hardship like me, they are denied an education.' To help Juliet get her voice heard and her plight understood, we brought her to London for a week. We supported her to campaign on behalf of the thousands of girls in northern Uganda who are still being denied an education. She delivered a personal letter and video message to the Prime Minister, appeared on TV and radio, lobbied politicians and inspired school students with her incredible story and compassionate, positive outlook.

Juliet's letter received a personal response from David Cameron and she was mentioned in a debate in the House of Lords by Lord Alton after meeting him. Audiences across CNN, BBC Radio 4, the BBC World Service and beyond heard her incredible story, and she made a real impact on the lives of the young people she met in the two schools she visited while she was here.

Hundreds of school students wrote and signed letters in support of Juliet, and we used those to lobby politicians as part of the Global Campaign for Education and the Millennium Development Goals summit meeting in New York in September. Juliet hopes her journey – from abducted child soldier to global campaigner – will demonstrate the power of education not only in transforming the lives of individuals but also conflict-affected countries as a whole. As Juliet says, 'Children who experience terrible things can also achieve great things in life – if they are given an education.'

'I feel like I've changed a lot having met you, and I really am going to strive towards my goals the way you have. You had nothing and yet you fought so hard to gain what you now have and that sense of achievement must be absolutely amazing so I truly hope that I can be as successful as you have been.'

Catherine, a 15-year-old student from Calthorpe Park School who met Juliet.

1 How did Juliet become a child soldier?
2 How did she become pregnant?
3 How was she able to escape the Lord's Resistance Army?
4 Why is education important to Juliet?
5 Outline what Juliet has achieved since she started her global campaign.

Watch the documentary on the rescue of Joseph Kony's child soldiers at *www.cultureunplugged.com*

Journal your response to the documentary.

Homelessness

Think about your own home. Journal the thoughts, feelings and emotions that come to mind.

Every person is entitled to have a place to call home: it is a basic human right. Homelessness is when a person finds themselves with no place to call home. This could mean living on the streets, staying in temporary accommodation or sleeping on a friend's couch. Homelessness affects people all over the world. In Ireland there are currently over 5,000 people living without a home.

1 In relation to the journaling exercise on p.140, discuss your thoughts on home life.
2 What do you think it would be like to be homeless?
3 What does your home mean to you?
4 Why is homelessness a human rights issue?
5 What is your own experience of this human rights abuse in Ireland?
6 Name two organisations that help the homeless in Ireland.

Homeless People: Rebecca's Story

Dominic Mapstone

In her own words this is our friend Rebecca's story...

Two things happened when I turned 12: my father, who used to beat the hell out of us, left home and the other thing that happened is I started using drugs... One of my friends said 'Here try this it will make you feel better', and it did.

When I turned 13, my Mum found a new partner who lived at home with us. He raped me regularly and abused my younger sisters as well. I was only 13. He also used to beat Mum up and it was hell on earth. For about a year I suffered through it but when I was 14 I couldn't take it anymore, so I said to Mum 'You have to get rid of this guy; either he goes or I go.' Mum chose him and I landed on the streets.

Initially I stayed with friends, and then slept with guys from the neighbourhood to keep a roof over my head. Eventually I had to leave the suburbs for the city streets. Sleeping in abandoned houses and buildings, I lived on the streets with other young people who were like me.

The cuts all up my arm are from slashing up. I slash myself to turn emotional pain into controllable physical pain. It's not usually to kill myself, just to help cope with the pain of the past.

I don't do it much, but if I'm having a shocker week I might just sit there and slash till I reach one hundred cuts.

If the only thing that happens to you in your life is you just keep getting hurt, you end up saying, 'No, this isn't going to happen to me, I'm not going to let myself get hurt anymore, I can't handle the reality of life, I can't handle any of it. Why not end it all? Then I know that I don't have to deal with any of it.'

The last time I tried to kill myself I only had a syringe to slash up with so I was hacking at myself trying to get myself bleeding properly. Then I sniffed paint until I blacked out.

I wanted to bleed to death but it didn't work because someone found me lying in the alley and called an ambulance.

You just give up, that's it: it's the end. As soon as you get to that stage where you don't care if you live or die you end up so upset, so depressed, so hurt with everything that you just can't handle even the day in front of you.

In the end it's a matter of: 'Well, if I get through the day, then great; if I don't, doesn't matter; no big deal. It's not like anyone's going to miss whether I'm here or not.'

To have the confidence to actually do something about where you are is especially hard because you have to build up that confidence.

By the end of the time you come on the streets you've lost all confidence in yourself and you think: 'I can't do it; even if I try, I'm not going to be able to do it.'

Just to know that someone cares is the main thing I guess. Most of the people on the street don't have anyone. We end up with no one when we come out here and you think that no one cares, no one worries about you and no one's willing to listen to what goes on in your life… what problems you have.

Then I meet Dominic and Gerry and the volunteers. They are willing to give up their time to come and see you and worry about you personally and take the time out to listen to what you have to say; it's great.

That's what people need is someone to actually be there and to talk with, to listen, to care; someone to trust.

Knowing that there is someone there to care even if they aren't there 24/7. When they do come out you really know it's someone who accepts you the way you are and they are ready to listen.

They care about me and they miss me if I don't turn up and that really makes me feel really special, well at least to someone.

1 Explain how Rebecca ended up homeless.
2 Describe Rebecca's experience of being homeless.
3 How did Rebecca's situation improve?

Journal your thoughts on the following statement: 'Homelessness is a human rights issue.'

Crime and Punishment

When studying justice, one must look at the issues of crime and punishment. While the majority of people follow the law and understand its necessity, there are others who choose not to. In this section, we are introduced to the idea of 'crime and punishment' and the origins of capital punishment as a form of deterrent. We will explore the moral debate surrounding the death penalty and we will examine case studies on capital punishment.

Crime can be defined as unlawful/illegal activity or a serious offence, especially one in violation of morality (common good). Crime has many different causes. Social and economic factors affect crime rates and social decay invites criminal activity. Sometimes genetic factors may also cause a tendency towards criminal behaviour. Criminal behaviour is linked to a lack of morals. Criminal behaviour is not linked to a lack of religion.

There are many different types of crimes in our society today: domestic violence, homicide, animal abuse, kidnapping, torture, terrorism, sexual crimes, computer and internet crimes, fraud, genocide, white-collared crime, theft, stalking, motoring crimes (speeding, drunk driving), abuse of the elderly or the disabled, arson, etc.

It is clear that crime is on the increase in our society, especially violent crime. This leads to an increasing fear of crime. People wonder what criminal justice measures can be used in order to prevent crime. Tougher laws and the imprisonment of more criminals can help to prevent crime. Community policing strategies are very important. The rehabilitation of criminals is vital in the prevention of crime.

Juvenile crime is another issue in our society. Punishments and crime intervention programmes are necessary in order to prevent juvenile crime. Violence prevention programs are vital, since harsh punishments for juveniles are not justified.

1 What causes crime?
2 What types of crimes exist in our society today?
3 Do you think crime is on the increase?
4 Can stronger criminal justice measures prevent crime?
5 How can juvenile crime be prevented?

Raising Domestic Violence Awareness: Why Talking About Chris Brown Isn't Enough

Nico Lang

There's a lot that troubles me about the ongoing Chris Brown–Rihanna saga. It's now been over three years since photos surfaced on TMZ showing the wounds that Brown inflicted on Rihanna, a physical assault that not only destroyed their relationship but also left an indelible imprint on the popular consciousness. The very image of Rihanna's abuse was inescapable and continues to be so. In fact, just this week, a school in New York re-enacted that night (in blackface!) for a pep rally and an audience of spectators that didn't seem to mind that the students involved re-enacted a woman's brutal abuse for laughs at a school assembly. When the school apologised for the students' skit, they mentioned the racist element of the proceedings (which was also beyond effed up), but not the assault aspect. Luckily, Jezebel was there to remind America that abuse isn't funny. Because guess what? Abuse is never ever funny. Ever. Ever. Ever.

But what troubles me just as much as the students' behaviour is the ongoing discursive tabloid space that their embattled relationship occupies. In the media's obsession with Chris Brown and Rihanna, the abuse element has always been front and centre, forcing us to remember her trauma and relive it, when Rihanna has publicly expressed her desire to move on. People who continue to bring it up say that they want the best for her and to empower her to make good choices, but where is the agency here? For the most part, the coverage isn't about empowerment or raising awareness about the horrors of domestic abuse, which Rihanna has shown she doesn't want to be a poster child for. It's about headlines. When Millionaire Matchmaker Patti Stanger sounded off on her advice for Rihanna should she get back together with Chris Brown (which is much rumoured these days) and put herself in that situation again, do you think it was out of personal concern for Rihanna? No, because who cares what Patti Stanger thinks? It was about getting her name in *People* magazine and promoting herself.

Luckily for Stanger and others, their relationship has proved itself absurdly marketable in a tabloid-obsessed media as a way to generate easy press and pre-packaged controversy. However, the press coverage has focused less on Rihanna than Chris Brown, who will be forever associated with this scandal. Brown can't move without the media reminding us that 'this man beats women' – as a recent group in the UK did by slapping labels with that title all over his albums. Earlier in the year, a critic all but refused to review his most recent album, F.A.M.E., awarding it 'no stars ever'. I don't listen to his music these days because (a) I don't like supporting abusers and (b) it's terrible music. However, we have to ask ourselves what we seek to accomplish when we focus that kind of media attention on Brown. Are we calling him out for being an abuser for the right reasons? Will it help raise awareness about domestic violence, or does it just bully a bully? Does targeting Chris Brown really help anyone?

Until recently, I'd always shrugged off any line of discussion or argument that even sounded a little like it might defend Chris Brown – because, as the child of a domestic abuse survivor, it's a sensitive subject. It's been easier to go, 'La-la-la-la-la-la! Not listening!' than ever broach that topic. However, I was discussing the media's depictions of abuse with a friend the other day, and they mentioned that Sean Penn was convicted of domestic violence during his marriage to Madonna. According to *The Daily Mail*, 'Once, he tied her to a chair and beat her. Another time, he hit her with a baseball bat. He threatened to shave her head. He chased her out of their hotel room.' I had never heard about this before, and as a film nerd, I was a little in shock. This man won two Oscars, one for playing a gay civil rights leader, and I never heard it brought up once. No one questioned a former abuser's right to play Harvey Milk in a movie, and yet there's an app to block Chris Brown from the entire internet. How is that possible?

And Penn is not alone. Michael Fassbender, Nicolas Cage, Sean Bean, Sean Connery, Mel Gibson, Alec Baldwin, Josh Brolin, Mickey Rourke, Matthew Fox and Gary Oldman (who was cleared of all charges) have all been alleged or convicted of abuse in the past, and hardly anyone ever mentions it. Matthew Fox is billed as the co-lead of the new Alex Cross movie this weekend, and despite his history of assault allegations, no one questioned his right to be in the film – in the same way that Brown has faced constant opposition. Fox was even allowed to dodge a question about his past on *Ellen* last week. In contrast, remember that time that Chris Brown appeared at the Grammys and everyone freaked out? I do. I wrote an article about it, and I stand by being appalled at the fact that the Grammys commemorated the three-year anniversary of him beating his girlfriend by giving him an award. However, our outrage shouldn't stop there. Where were the people voicing their concern for Madonna during her recent reunion with Sean Penn, or calling out Sean Penn for not apologising to Madonna in either of his Oscar speeches? Crickets.

When Chris Brown spoke out about this double standard literally a year ago, a lot of people shrugged him off, because who wants to hear what he has to say? His immaturity invalidated his credibility. However, that doesn't mean he was wrong. When Charlie Sheen (who has been arrested numerous times for assault) locked a sex worker in a closet, did we voice concern for the woman or for Charlie's ex-wives, who have experienced similar abuse at his hands? No. *The View* openly mocked that woman, we had a Comedy Central roast to celebrate it, and people even paid to see Sheen 'live in concert.' Sheen built a third career out of the press, being cast as an anti-hero out of the Paddy Chayevsky mould and a surrealist media darling. At no point were we told it wasn't okay to laugh, or that we should be outraged at Sheen's history of abuse becoming a public spectacle.

If you remember, Sheen wasn't even let go from *Two and a Half Men* over being an abuser; he was fired for insulting his boss. Unlike Brown (who gets routinely boycotted), Sheen's antics helped land him a new gig on FX, as the star of *Anger Management*, a show that pulled in record numbers during its premiere. Sheen was then rewarded with a 90-episode order from the network, good for nine more seasons. The only people who seemed that upset about it were critics – because (like *Two and a Half Men* before it) *Anger Management* is an awful, awful show – and we allow him to make light of his abuse week after week without much backlash.

I've said it before and I'll say it again: I can't stand Chris Brown. Not only is he an abuser, but he's also proven himself to be not winning as a human being – from his consistently homophobic tweets to his disregard for the wellbeing of both other humans and windows. I think the criticism of him is justified, but it concerns me that we constantly make an example out of Chris Brown and associate him with his history of abuse in a way we don't with other celebrities. Part of this is because Chris Brown has been woefully unrepentant, but neither Sheen nor Penn showed a great deal of remorse either. But as Brown was the only celebrity I listed above who is not white, the other part is due to our society's demonisation of black males and the constant media blaming of rap culture. Almost any study on media bias ever conducted tells you that our society discursively frames black people (especially men) in a very particular context, and a 2011 report from Meyer Communications showed that the 'largest block of news stories involving black men and youth were about crime – 86 per cent of the news broadcasts and 37 per cent of the newspaper stories'. When you took out stories about crime, a similar Pew report showed 'there were few other stories about black males'. Thus, Chris Brown simply fits into the media's narrative of racialised violence in a way that Charlie Sheen and Ben Roethlisberger did not.

On one hand, I'm glad to see the media leading a discussion of violence against women, as the media functions as an agenda-setting tool for society. However, rather than using the Rihanna scandal as a tool to spread awareness about abuse, we continue to demonise Brown at the expense of a larger dialogue. This is a conversation we desperately need to have, especially with this being Domestic Violence Awareness Month. According to statistics from the Kansas Coalition Against Sexual and Domestic Violence, 'one in three women has been beaten, coerced into sex or otherwise abused during her lifetime', 'more than three women are murdered by their husbands or boyfriends in [the US] every day' and 'domestic violence is the leading cause of injury to women between the ages of 15 and 44 in the United States'. These are grim statistics that aren't done justice by tabloid navel-gazing. If we are going to do justice to the women (and men) who experience partner violence every day, this discussion needs to be larger than singling out one person and making Chris Brown the poster boy for abuse. When we make the entire discussion about domestic violence in the media about only Chris Brown, we don't open up a discursive space to talk about the daily violence that people face: we make it more difficult by continuing to narrow that focus. We make the conversation worse. Instead, we need to have a conversation that raises the issue responsibly and compassionately. We need to learn to see the ways that these conversations avoid an actual discussion of abuse, which mirrors the larger silencing of victimisation in society. We need to recognise our role in fostering a culture where partner and intimate violence can be discussed and learn how to be allies to those who need our support. And if we ever hope to make a difference in their lives, we need to be outraged when every person is abused, not just when it's one of the biggest pop stars in the world.

1 Explain what types of crimes are discussed in this article.
2 In this case, do you think the crime committed deserved the punishment given?
3 Discuss the punishment given and state whether you would change it.

Watch the following documentary on children behind bars.

While watching the documentary take notes and report back on your thoughts to the class.

www.documentarystorm.com/kids-behind-bars/

'Children should receive the same punishment as adults for their crimes.'

Punishment

Punishment can be defined as the infliction of a penalty for retribution for an offence. The strongest arguments in favour of punishment are those that try to prove that punishment is good for the offender. The major reasons for punishment are reform, deterrence, compensation and retribution.

Reform aims to assist the offender to rehabilitate, and to help them to learn from their mistakes and understand the need to follow the law.

Deterrence works on the principle that potential offenders may think twice about committing a crime once they are aware of the possible punishments.

Compensation may be sought by the offended party as a means of a just punishment for the crime or crimes that have been committed.

Retribution is the belief that the offender deserves to suffer for the crime they have committed.

1 Discuss the four reasons for punishment.

2 In your opinion, which is the strongest argument for punishment? Why?

Capital Punishment Is Dead Wrong

Olivia H.

Murder is wrong. Since childhood we have been taught this indisputable truth. Ask yourself, then, what is capital punishment? In its simplest form, capital punishment is defined as one person taking the life of another. Coincidentally, that is the definition of murder. There are 36 US states with the death penalty, and they must change. These states need to abolish it on the grounds that it carries a dangerous risk of punishing the innocent, is unethical and barbaric, and is an ineffective deterrent of crime versus the alternative of life in prison without parole.

Capital punishment is the most irreparable crime governments perpetrate without consequence, and it must be abolished. 'We're only human, we all make mistakes' is a commonly used phrase, but it is tried and true. Humans, as a species, are famous for their mistakes. However, in the case of the death penalty, error becomes too dangerous a risk. The innocent lives that have been taken with the approval of our own government should be enough to abolish capital punishment.

According to Amnesty International, 'The death penalty legitimises an irreversible act of violence by the state and will inevitably claim innocent victims.' If there is any chance that error is possible (which there always is), the drastic measure of capital punishment should not be taken. Also, it is too final, meaning it does not allow opportunity for the accused to be proven innocent, a violation of the Fifth Amendment which guarantees due process of law.

District Judge Jed S. Rakoff of the United States Second Circuit Court of Appeals in Manhattan argued against the death penalty: 'In brief, the Court found that the best available evidence indicates that, on the one hand, innocent people are sentenced to death with materially greater frequency than was previously supposed and that, on the other hand, convincing proof of their innocence often does not emerge until long after their convictions. It is therefore fully foreseeable that in enforcing the death penalty a meaningful number of innocent people will be executed who otherwise would eventually be able to prove their innocence.'

As humans, we are an inevitable force of error. However, when a life is at stake, error is not an option. The death penalty is murder by the government. As a nation, we have prided ourselves in our government, its justice and truth. However, can we continue to call our government fair if we do not hold it to the same rules we do its people? Murder by a citizen will have consequences, yet a government-approved murder is not only acceptable, but enforceable. What message do we send the American people, and other countries, for that matter, if we continue to be a nation that kills its citizens, a nation that enforces the most barbaric form of punishment?

The Illinois Coalition to Abolish the Death Penalty states, 'We don't cut off the hands of thieves to protect property; we do not stone adulterers to stop adultery. We consider that barbaric. Yet we continue to take life as a means of protecting life.' No person, government-affiliated or not, has the right to decide if another human is worthy or unworthy of life. Our natural rights as humans, which cannot be taken away by the government, include the right to life. Humans are not cold metal coins that lose value; no act, no matter how heinous, can make a person less of a human being. However, for most it is easy to forget that each of the 1,099 executed since 1977 are fellow humans, not just numbers.

According to Amnesty International, 'The death penalty violates the right to life.' Capital punishment contradicts our moral beliefs and claims of a fair and just government. The US must join its political allies – including Europe, Scandinavia, Russia, South Africa and most of Latin America – that have abolished the death penalty.

The death penalty is favoured by some as an effective deterrent of crime; however, it is proven that states with the death penalty actually have higher murder rates than those without. It is proven that our nation does not need this extreme threat of punishment to prevent crime. In 2006, the FBI Uniform Crime Report revealed that the area of the US that was responsible for the most executions (the South, with 80 per cent) also had the highest murder rate, whereas the Northern areas that had the fewest executions (less than 1 per cent), had the lowest murder rates.

It can be said that the death penalty is the most overlooked form of government hypocrisy; we murder people who murder people to show that murder is wrong. It is this contradiction in policy that confuses criminals and undermines any crime deterrence capital punishment was intended to have.

Many people favour the death penalty as reparation for the wrong done to a victim's family; however, in most cases, closure is not the result. Losing a loved one, no matter how that person is lost, is unbearable, irrevocable, and shattering. Pain like this is shocking and the victim's family holds onto the hope that the execution of the murderer will bring relief and closure. Nevertheless, when execution day arrives, the pain is not eased. No relief can be gained, for their pain is an unavoidable, natural process of life. Victims' families have founded such groups as the Murder Victims Families for Reconciliation and The Journey of Hope, which oppose the death penalty. They believe that they are different from those who have taken their loved ones and they demonstrate their difference by refusing to sink to a murderer's level.

Capital punishment is immoral and a violation of natural rights. It is wrong for everyone involved: the prosecuted innocent, criminals, victims' families, and our nation. We need to replace the death penalty and capital punishment with life without parole, a safer and more inexpensive option. The death penalty does not guarantee safety for innocent victims, it does not follow the goals and promises of our nation, it does not effectively deter crime, and it does not give closure to victims' families. Nothing good comes of hate, and nothing good can ever come from capital punishment. It cannot continue to be accepted by a nation that claims to have liberty and justice for all. The death penalty is murder on the sly and it's dead wrong.

1. Look at the first two paragraphs in the article about the death penalty (p. 149). Outline the reasons why the author is against capital punishment
2. Do you agree that 'we're only human, we all make mistakes'?
3. Comment on what Amnesty International says about the death penalty (paragraph 3).
4. What argument is put forward in paragraph 4?
5. Comment on what the author says about the government in paragraph 5.
6. Do you agree with the Illinois Coalition that the death penalty is barbaric?
7. Why, do you think the death penalty does not act as a deterrent?
8. Do you agree with the author when she says that the death penalty does not ease the pain of the victim's family?
9. Do you think the author makes a strong argument against capital punishment? Give reasons for your answer.

Capital Punishment

Capital punishment can be defined as the legally authorised killing of a person as punishment for a capital crime. Capital punishments throughout history have included stoning, hanging, firing squad, electrocution, gas chamber and lethal injection.

Stoning

For execution by this method, female offenders are buried up to their shoulders and male offenders are buried up to their waist. Stones are then thrown at the offenders by volunteers. Stones are selected on the basis of size. The stones must be large enough to cause physical harm but not to kill instantly. The average execution can last up to 20 minutes.

Hanging

For execution by this method, the inmate may be weighed the day before the execution and a rehearsal is done using a sandbag of the same weight as the prisoner. This is to determine the length of 'drop' necessary to ensure a quick death. Immediately before the execution, the prisoner's hands and legs are secured, he or she is blindfolded, and the noose is placed around the neck. The execution takes place when a trap door is opened and the prisoner falls through. The prisoner's weight should cause a rapid fracture/dislocation of the neck.

Firing Squad

For execution by this method, the inmate is typically bound to a chair with leather straps across his or her waist and head, in front of an oval-shaped canvas wall. The chair is surrounded by sandbags to absorb the inmate's blood. A black hood is pulled over the inmate's head. A doctor locates the inmate's heart with a stethoscope and pins a circular white cloth target over it.

Standing in an enclosure 20 feet away, five shooters are armed with .30 calibre rifles loaded with single rounds. One of the shooters is given blank rounds. Each of the shooters aims his rifle through a slot in the canvas and fires at the inmate. The prisoner dies as a result of blood loss caused by rupture of the heart of a large blood vessel, or tearing of the lungs.

Electrocution

In a typical execution using the electric chair, a prisoner is strapped to a specially built chair, their head and body shaved to provide better contact with the moistened copper electrodes that the executioner attaches. Usually three or more executioners push buttons, but only one is connected to the actual electrical source as the real executioner is not known. The jolt varies in power from state to state and is also determined by the convict's body weight. The first jolt is followed by several more in a lower voltage.

Gas Chamber

For this method, the condemned person is strapped to a chair in an airtight chamber. Below the chair rests a pail of sulphuric acid. A long stethoscope is typically affixed to the inmate so that a doctor outside the chamber can pronounce death. Once everyone has left the chamber the room is sealed. The warden then gives the signal to the executioner who flicks a lever that releases crystals of sodium cyanide into the pail. This causes a chemical reaction that releases hydrogen cyanide gas. The prisoner is instructed to breathe deeply to speed up the process.

Lethal Injection

This involves the continuous intravenous injection of a lethal quantity of three different drugs. The prisoner is secured on a gurney with lined ankle and wrist restraints. A cardiac monitor and a stethoscope are attached, and two saline intravenous lines are started, one in each arm. The inmate is then covered with a sheet. The saline intravenous lines are turned off, and sodium thiopental is injected, causing the inmate to fall into a deep sleep. The second chemical agent, pancuronium bromide, a muscle relaxer, follows. This causes the inmate to stop breathing due to paralyses of the diaphragm and lungs. Finally, potassium chloride is injected, stopping the heart.

1. Comment on the methods used for capital punishment.
2. Why, do you think, has there been a development in the methods used (from stoning to lethal injection)?
3. Write a summary of each method used in the death penalty.

Journal your response to the methods used in capital punishment.

Various methods used in capital punishment

Rank	Country	Number executed in 2011
1	People's Republic of China	Officially not released. In the thousands, may be up to 4,000.
2	Iran	360+
3	Saudi Arabia	82+
4	Iraq	68+
5	United States	43
6	Yemen	41+
7	North Korea	30+
8	Somalia	10
9	Sudan	7+
10	Bangladesh	5+

1. Examine the table showing the countries that use the death penalty. What do you notice about the countries listed?
2. Look at the top five countries in the list. What conclusions could you come to about them?
3. In your opinion, what are the main differences between the western and eastern countries in the list?
4. Statistically, US states that have the death penalty also have higher murder rates than US states without the death penalty. Why, do you think, this might be?
5. Statistically, people from lower socio-economic backgrounds are more likely to commit murder. Why do you think this is?

Moral Debate on the Death Penalty

Many people believe that the death penalty is morally acceptable in certain circumstances. Some of the following arguments have been made.

- ★ Retribution is important in terms of compensating the victim of an offence.
- ★ The death penalty is intended to discourage would-be offenders (deterrence).
- ★ There are financial benefits to imposing the death penalty as punishment for crimes.
- ★ The death penalty is important for the safety of common good.

Many people believe that the death penalty is never morally acceptable. Some of the following arguments have been made.

- ★ Mistakes cannot be undone.
- ★ Statistics show that the death penalty does not act as a deterrent.
- ★ There are financial drawbacks to imposing the death penalty: it costs more money for death row and appeal services.
- ★ Most capital crimes are not pre-meditated.
- ★ Capital punishment will not deter people who are under the influence of alcohol or drugs, or who may have a mental health issue.

1. Consider the opinion you held on the death penalty *before* you read this section. Has it changed? Explain why/why not.
2. In your opinion, which of the arguments is strongest?
3. Do you believe that the death penalty is a human rights issue? Explain.
4. What do you think of the death penalty as an effective method of punishment?
5. How would you feel if one of your family members was placed on death row?
6. Can you suggest any alternatives to the death penalty as a means of punishment?

Podcast

Below is a website which contains many podcasts on different topics related to death row.

www.deathpenaltyinfo.org/podcasts

The following is a fictional case study.

The Crime

One summer morning in the US in the late 1980s Anthony Farrell, who was manager of an international bank, received a phone call from his wife Christina. She explained that there was someone who wanted to speak with him. An unknown voice came on the phone and explained that Anthony was to gather $50 and $100 bills and put them in a briefcase. He was instructed to go to the local shopping centre with the briefcase in exactly 45 minutes. He was then told that if he did not follow these instructions it would 'all be over'.

Mr Farrell called his assistant and instructed him to gather the money. Meanwhile, Mr Farrell called the FBI. Ten minutes later, police arrived at the Farrell family home to find Christina Farrell dead. She had been shot in the head.

Plain-clothes police officers accompanied Mr Farrell to the agreed meeting point at the local shopping centre. Mr Farrell brought the briefcase, as instructed. Nobody turned up at the meeting point.

The Farrell home was cordoned off, since it was now an official crime scene. The house was searched and forensics found unknown fingerprints and one hair. Some casings from bullets were also retrieved. A door-to-door investigation took place later that day but no information was received.

The Suspect

A substantial reward of $100,000 was offered to anyone who had information that would lead to an arrest. Two days after the reward notice was issued, a man in his early twenties was brought to the local police station by his uncle, who said that the young man had information.

When the young man was interviewed he told police that on the same day that Christina Farrell was killed his roommate, a man named John Roberts, had asked him to hide a briefcase that contained a gun. John Roberts informed his roommate that he and a mutual friend, George Nixon, had had a plan to get 'easy money' but that it had gone wrong and that George had had to kill a woman.

On this information, Roberts and Nixon were arrested.

The Trial

George Nixon's trial took place in the spring of the following year. The state's evidence was largely circumstantial. The fingerprints did not match Nixon's.

Witnesses testified that Nixon had told them that he owned a .22 pistol – this was the gun used in the murder.

John Roberts testified similar information. He also testified that it was Nixon who had entered the Farrell home that day and shot Christina Farrell. He explained that it was all part of a plan to get their hands on money quickly.

The defence presented no witnesses. The jury returned a verdict of guilty against George Nixon.

The jury found that Nixon acted deliberately and that he represented a future danger to society. The court sentenced him to die.

The Defendant

George Nixon was in his late twenties when the crime took place. He had a string of previous offences. He was involved in the making of gun silencers. He also had charges of robberies on pharmacies. It was thought that he was looking to raise money to flee the country to avoid incarceration.

However, the defence failed to bring some facts to the court. Nixon had previous injuries from childhood, which meant that he was legally blind in one eye and had also lost the use of the four fingers on his left hand and the use of his thumb on his right hand. These injuries would make it very difficult for Nixon to carry out the crime.

Details from Nixon's medical records were not presented to the jury, either. Nixon was a physically and emotionally abused child who attempted to succeed but who failed many times. However, he had been attending counselling to deal with his issues and he spoke openly with his counsellor about wanting to be a better person.

The Family

Christina Farrell's family were happy with the jury's decision that Nixon would face the death penalty. They stressed that this was not out of revenge, but about justice. Christina's daughter said: 'This man took a life. He took a lot of things. My mom was a lot of things to a lot of people. He took her away from a lot of people and left a big hole in a lot of people's lives, as well as depriving Mom of the pleasure of living.'

1 What do you think about the crime committed?
2 Do you think Nixon committed the crime or was he framed?
3 Do you think a person should face more lenient charges because of their physical or emotional state?
4 Do you think John Roberts should have also faced the death penalty?

The following is a fictional case study.

The Crime

One winter's morning in the early 1990s in the southern states of the US, 18-year-old Alison Douglas opened the laundrette shop where she worked. On this morning she was working on her own. She served customers for over an hour. After 11am customers who entered the shop reported that she was not behind the counter. When a search took place, Alison was discovered in the yard behind the shop. She had been sexually assaulted and killed. Money had been taken from the cash register in the shop.

The police carried out an investigation of the crime scene. However, the local police were not properly trained to do this and so they ruined a lot of evidence that could have been recovered.

When forensics finally arrived on the scene, they realised quickly that the local police had ruined the crime scene with their inexperience. They had also taken Alison's body to the funeral home, making impossible any accurate fingerprinting or examination of other elements at the scene, including fibres, hairs, exact location of the body, facial expression and similar evidence.

In the coroner's report it was discovered that Alison had been shot three times. It was clear that she had been sexually assaulted but the coroner was unable to gather forensic evidence in relation to this for the trial.

The Suspect

Many suspects were interviewed but the crime remained unsolved for seven months. At this time, a local man named Christopher Skeen was interviewed about the crime. Skeen was himself serving a sentence for a similar crime in the county. He stated that a black man from the area, Raymond Foster, had committed the crime. Two other police informants were said to agree with this statement. Raymond Foster was said to be a marijuana dealer and was dating a white woman from the area. He had a minor criminal record. He was arrested in relation to this case.

The Trial

Because of widespread publicity, the trial was moved out of the county in which it took place. The county in which the trial took place had a very small population of black residents.

At the trial, Skeen said that he and Foster drove to the local village the day of the crime and parked near the laundrette where Alison was working. Skeen said that he was accompanying Foster into the village, since Foster wanted to run some errands. Skeen said he heard popping sounds while he waited in the car for Foster. He went to investigate and found Foster in the laundrette standing over the body of Alison with money in his hands.

A local man testified to seeing Foster and Skeen drive away from the laundrette on the day of the crime. Another witness testified to recognising Foster and his truck in the village on the morning of the crime.

In Foster's defence, six witnesses came forward to testify that he was at home on the morning of the crime and that he was taking part in a church barbecue.

Foster did not testify. However, he told his attorney that he did not know Skeen at all and had never met him. He was found guilty of first-degree murder during a robbery. He was sentenced to the death penalty.

The Defendant

Raymond Foster was a middle-aged man who worked as a farm hand. He did not earn much money and he sold marijuana on the side. He was having an affair with a white woman. Foster's wife found out about this affair during the course of the trial but she stood by him and struggled to raise the money for his attorney. She still protests Foster's innocence, saying that she was with him on the morning of the crime.

The Family

The family of Alison Douglas had one comment to make: 'This man took our daughter's life and should pay with his own.'

1 In your opinion, what happened to Alison Douglas?
2 Do you think Christopher Skeen was telling the truth?
3 Do you think Raymond Foster committed the crime?
4 What do you think about the evidence for and against Raymond Foster?
5 Do you think justice was done in this case? Explain.

Roman Catholic Teaching on the Death Penalty

The Roman Catholic Church teaches that the death penalty is no longer necessary if it can be replaced with imprisonment. This is made clear in the Catechism of the Catholic Church.

> *'If bloodless means are sufficient to defend human lives against an aggressor and to protect public order and the safety of persons, public authority must limit itself to such means, because they correspond to the concrete conditions of the common good and are more in conformity to the dignity of the human person.'*
>
> *CCC 2267*

Death Penalty and World Religions

Christianity teaches that the death penalty is not morally acceptable. In 1988 the Anglican Bishops of England condemned the death penalty. The Methodist churches also condemn capital punishment, saying that it cannot accept retribution or social vengeance as a reason for taking human life.

Judaism teaches that the death penalty is acceptable in principle but the proof needed for the death sentence is so strict that it is practically impossible to impose.

Islam holds that the death penalty is allowed but that the family of the victim has the right to pardon the accused. Under Shari'a Law, execution is allowed for some specified crimes.

Hinduism and **Buddhism** teach that misdeeds in this life will have repercussions in the next, rendering punishment in this life unnecessary.

End of Section Summary

- Justice involves people being treated fairly and treating others fairly.
- There are secular and religious points of view on justice.
- All world faiths have teachings on justice.
- Peace can come about as a result of people acting in a just way.
- The Just War theory originated with the Greeks and the early philosophers. It was later developed by Christian theologians such as St Thomas Aquinas to outline what was deemed acceptable in the case of war.
- All human beings have rights; however, with these rights come responsibilities.
- The UN put together a Declaration on Human Rights in 1948.
- The UDHR outlines thirty rights for every human being.
- A further charter was put forward by the UN to protect the rights of the child (UNCRC).
- Human rights abuses include third world debt, child soldiers and homelessness.
- Consideration of crime and punishment is integral in looking at issues of justice.
- One form of punishment is the death penalty; this is punishment for a capital crime.
- In countries that allow the death penalty, the following may be used: stoning, hanging, firing squad, electrocution, gas chamber and lethal injection.

End of Section Activities

1. Write a critique of the Just War theory.
2. Do you think punishment works in preventing crime?
3. How do you think children should be punished for crimes they commit?
4. Do you agree with the death penalty as a form of punishment for capital crimes? Explain your reasons.
5. Can you think of alternative forms of punishment that could work within a functioning society.

'We get what we deserve in life.'
'Detention centres are effective forms of punishments for children.'
'Child offenders who are almost 18 years old should be subjected to the same punishments as adult offenders.'
'Africa is to blame for its own debt.'

1 Research the book of Job in the Old Testament and write an account of what it teaches about justice.

2 In the Gospel of Mark, find examples of Jesus taking a stand for justice. Compare these stories to a modern-day issue of justice in the world.

3 Choose one country that exercises the death penalty and research the history of the death penalty in that country.

4 Compare and contrast the use of the death penalty in the US today with its use twenty years ago.

5 Explain how racism, sexism and other forms of discrimination are contrary to religious living.

6 Explain how care for the earth is linked to religious faith.

★ Imagine that you are a child soldier. Write a diary entry of one day in your life.
★ Imagine you are a governor of a state in America and you wish to abolish the death penalty in your state. Journal your ideas on how you might achieve this.

Compile a list of questions for an interview that you could have with someone who is on death row.

Films

★ *Hotel Rwanda*
★ *Blood Diamond*
★ *Remember the Titans*
★ *Erin Brockovich*
★ *Philadelphia*
★ *Schindler's List*
★ *Rabbit-Proof Fence*
★ *Gandhi*
★ *The Shawshank Redemption*
★ *The Long Walk Home*
★ *The Green Mile*
★ *The Life of David Gale*
★ *Dead Man Walking*
★ *The Thin Blue Line*
★ *True Crime*

Weblinks

★ www.humanrights.com
★ www.focusireland.ie
★ www.simoncommunity.ie
★ www.homeless.org.au
★ www.warchild.org.uk
★ www.unicef.org
★ www.un.org
★ www.amnesty.ie
★ www.amnesty.org
★ www.hrw.org

Celebrating Faith

Section 5

Context

In this section, we have the opportunity to explore the idea of ritual in our lives. We will consider secular and religious rituals. Contemporary examples of ritual from several different faiths will be examined. We will also be introduced to the different types of prayer.

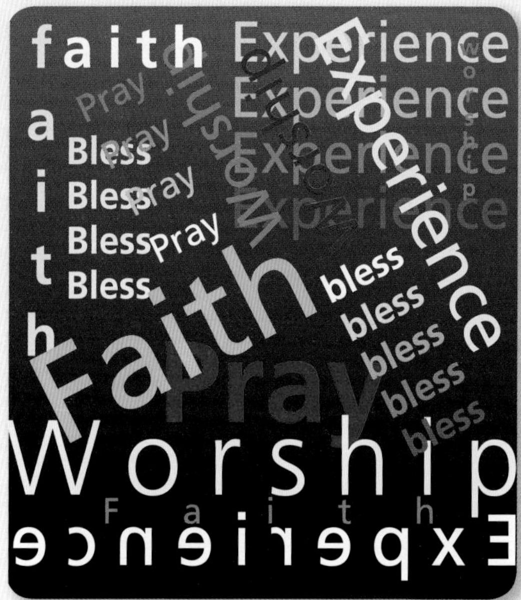

The Ritual Maker Within: An Adolescent Initiation

Edith Sullwold

It was autumn in Los Angeles, and out in the courtyard of a children's clinic few leaves were swirling in the brisk wind. Something in the air called for a bonfire in the imagination of the 9-year-old boy with whom I was spending an hour. The boy, whom I will call Peter, had been suffering from explosive flare-ups of temper at home and at school that seemed to erupt suddenly and without any apparent external cause. On this day Peter led me outside to see what we could construct on the only available inner city space, a large concrete area. A few sticks and some brown leaves served and soon a small fire was crackling.

As I watched, I saw that Peter's interest was not so much in the fire itself, but in his ability to control it – ignite it, fan and feed it, check its boundaries, and eventually put it out. It was as though Peter was acknowledging the fire as a force in itself with its own life, his work being to relate to this dynamic force with careful attention and skill. This process of building the fire, controlling, and extinguishing it was repeated many times.

My concentration on his work was so intense that I didn't notice two other boys joining Peter. They had been in rooms also opening on the courtyard and were fascinated by this fire-making process. Quietly, and without discussion, they entered the scene. At one point when it seemed a satisfactory blaze, one of the new attendants at this fire-becoming-ritual went inside and brought out an empty coffee can. He turned it upside down and began hitting it in a steady, rhythmic beat. Again without a word, the other new boy went to one side of the courtyard and made a stunning leap over the fire. Invited, Peter also went to the beginning place, hesitated a moment, and leaped over. For almost an hour, the three took turns beating the drum, tending the fire and jumping over it. Then seeming satisfied, they together put out the fire with sand, swept the courtyard and returned to their rooms.

The event was followed by two other appearances of fire as a symbol in a ritual action for young boys or adolescents. A week later another boy, aged 12, shared a dream in which he found himself with friends at a beach at night. In an area of big sand dunes his friends dug a deep pit in which they carefully built a fire, asking him to leap over it. He did this with both fear and the excitement of victory. A few days later another adolescent boy entering a private school described an actual event in which the new students were accepted by the older classmates only after having successfully leaped over a big bonfire which he had helped them build.

These events point to the reality of the spontaneous emergence of ritual action in puberty and adolescence. Ritual action acknowledges a major event in the life of the individual or the group for us today as well as in traditional cultures. Like habit, it is action that may be repetitive, but unlike habit is beyond ordinary, everyday behaviour. Most often the event which the ritual celebrates is transitional, marking a stage in an individual life such as birth, puberty, marriage or death, or a change affecting a group, such as the seasonal cycles or a new leadership. The action is initiatory in intent, helping to bring the individual or the group into a new state of being. The ritual actions are symbolic of such transitions and are intended to effect a real transformation in the participants.

The experience which I observed raises the possibility that the need for such ritual actions is so profound that it is in the very nature of the human being to create forms for them. In the traditional societies, societies which are cohesive in social structure, the honouring of such transitions generally took the form of elaborate rituals with strict procedures in which the individual and often the whole society took part. In a society such as ours, which is not cohesive, the external individual and collective rituals are becoming more and more neglected. However, the emergence of the fire-building ritual indicates that even without previous instruction or experience these ritual forms and symbols can be created from within the psychic structure of the individual.

It was of course important that I, as a witness to this event, carried a sense of its significance for the boys – a sense of its meaning – and a sense of awe surrounding its intensity. This support provided an atmosphere of safety and understanding that honoured their creative and dynamic process of ritual making.

1 Why, do you think, was Peter so intrigued by the fire?
2 In your opinion, how did Peter's controlling of the fire help him with his anger issues?
3 What kinds of rituals did Peter and his friends engage in?
4 What does the author say about ritual?
5 Why, do you think, does the author feel that these events are significant for the boys?

What is a Ritual?

A ritual can involve words spoken, actions performed or clothes that are worn that help people to express something that is deeply important to them.

1 Identify as many different rituals as you can.
2 List these rituals in two columns: religious and secular.
3 Have you any experience of these religious and/or secular rituals?

As humans, we have always been ritual makers. Before any formal religion was formed, people within their own cultures created rituals. Some of the earliest of these would include sacrifice of an animal or worship of the sun or moon. The performing of rituals was important for lots of reasons. It gave people the opportunity to mark important moments or events in their lives. As time went on, world religions began to be formed and with them came new sets of rituals.

People with religious beliefs wanted to express and celebrate their faith through rituals. Rituals are performed in a prescribed order according to the traditions of each faith. This allows for all members to engage in meaningful worship.

Religious Rituals

Religious rituals are a key part of all religious faiths. Within every world religion important moments such as birth, marriage and death are marked by some kind of religious ceremony. Normally during these rites of passage special clothes are worn, important words are spoken and symbolic gestures are performed. People with religious beliefs express and celebrate their faith through these rituals.

Exploring Religious Rituals from Around the World

Judaism: Coming of Age

The following is an interview with a Jewish boy, Noah, who has recently experienced his Bar Mitzvah.

Did anything important happen recently?
I had my Bar Mitzvah. This means I now have the same rights as a grown Jewish man. I am now responsible for all my actions. That's the scary part!

What does becoming a Bar Mitzvah mean?
It means I have become 'Son of the Commandments'. This means that I must now uphold all the commandments. It will be difficult but I have watched my older sister uphold the commandments for the last two years since her Bat Mitzvah when she was 12, so I know I can do it.

Does every Jewish boy celebrate this ritual?
Every Jewish boy automatically becomes a Bar Mitzvah at the age of 13. However, most Jewish boys celebrate this occasion with a religious ceremony in the synagogue and a party afterwards.

Did you have to prepare for your Bar Mitzvah?
From a very early age I have been taught the importance of the Torah and following the commandments. Yet I started more detailed preparation for my Bar Mitzvah months ago with my Rabbi in the synagogue. A lot of this time involved learning and reading passages from the Torah. As the weeks went by I had to lead certain prayers during religious services. I also had to raise money for a charity of my choice. I chose to raise money for my local homeless shelter.

What happens on the day of your Bar Mitzvah?
That morning I had to wear special clothes. I wore a suit with a white shirt and tie. Once in the synagogue, I had to put on a skullcap (*kipah*) and a prayer shawl (*tallit*). On the day, the most important thing to happen is the *aliyah*. This involved me reciting blessings from the Torah. This is a big deal and I was very nervous in case I messed up. My family were all there with me and they were honoured with more blessings. The highlight of the day for me was when my father passed his Torah down to me which was given to him by his father.

What happened next?
All of my family and friends came together to share a meal and help me celebrate the day. There was music and dance after the meal.

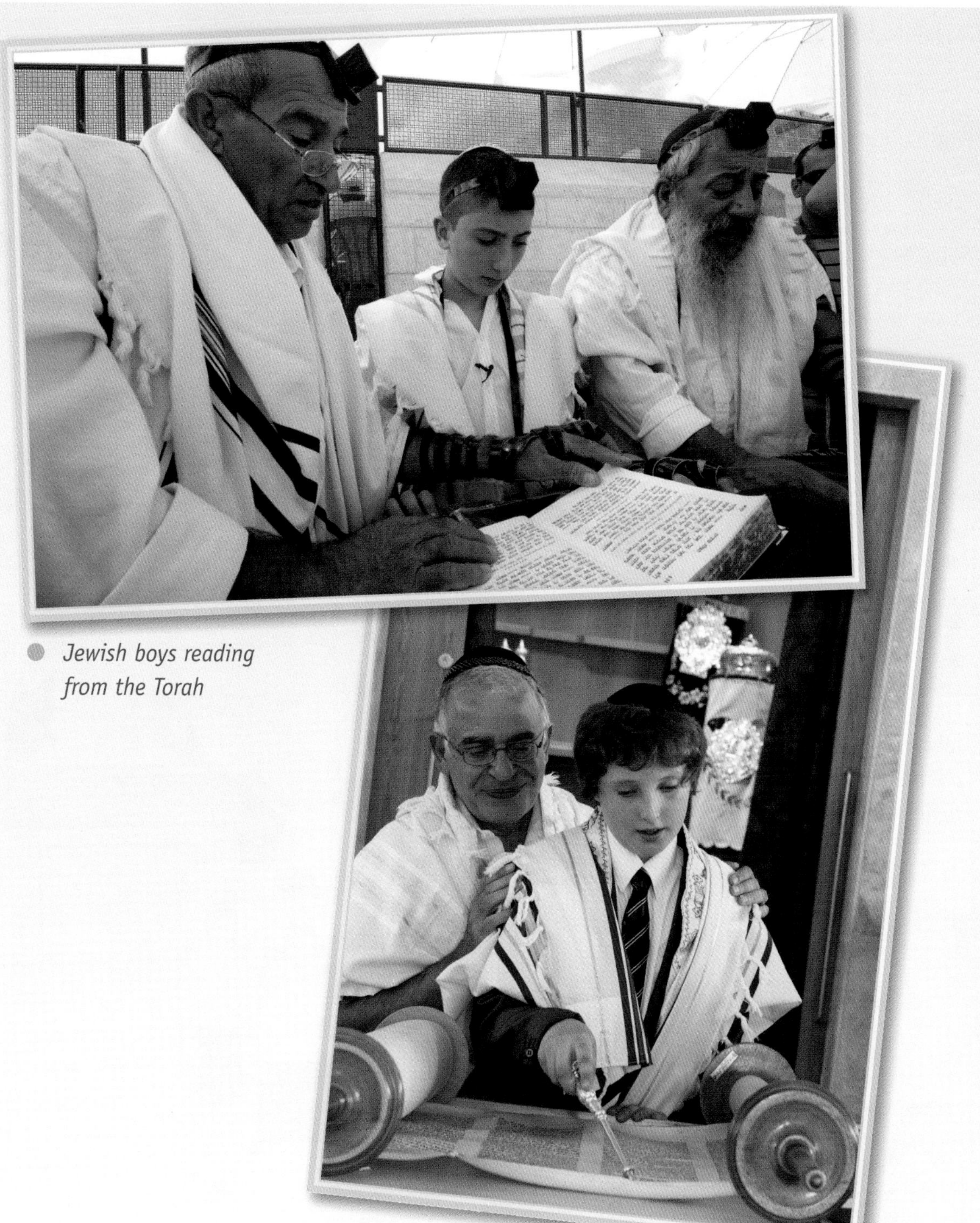

Jewish boys reading from the Torah

Go to *chabad.org* and search for the video on 'The Bar Mitzvah'.

Christianity: Death

- *Family and friends gather to receive the coffin into the church.*

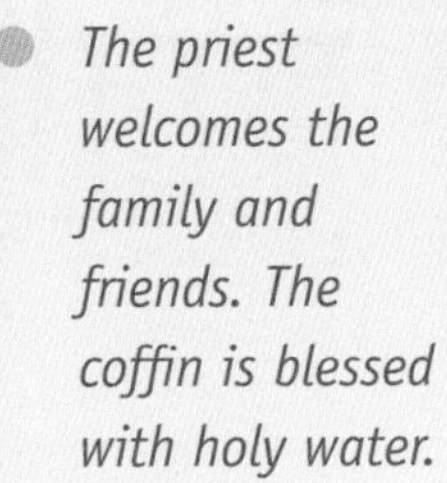

- *The priest welcomes the family and friends. The coffin is blessed with holy water.*

- *Liturgy of the Word – readings from the bible are usually read by family and friends.*

- *Homily – The priest says a few words about the life of the person and the meaning of life.*

- *The coffin is blessed again before it leaves the church for the final journey with family and friends.*

- *Burial – The Rite of Committal – final prayers are said before the coffin is lowered into the ground.*

Islam: Birth

There are certain rites that all Muslims follow when welcoming a new child into the world. It normally involves the following.

1. The first words the baby must hear are the *adhan*: 'God is great; there is no God but Allah. Muhammad is the messenger of Allah.' These words are whispered into the baby's right ear by the father.
2. The next step should involve the baby tasting something sweet. The parents may rub some honey or juice from a date along the baby's gums. This process is thought to help with the child's digestion.
3. After seven days, in order to show that the baby is a servant of Allah, the baby's hair is shaved. The hair is then weighed and measured in silver, and this amount of silver is then given to charity.
4. On the seventh day it is tradition to choose a name for the baby.
5. Also on the seventh day, a ceremony called the *aqeeqah* is carried out. This involves the sacrifice of a sheep. The meat is then divided up among family, friends and the poor.
6. At some point after the seventh day and before puberty, Muslim boys must be circumcised. This is stated in the *Sunnah* and one of the main purposes is cleanliness.

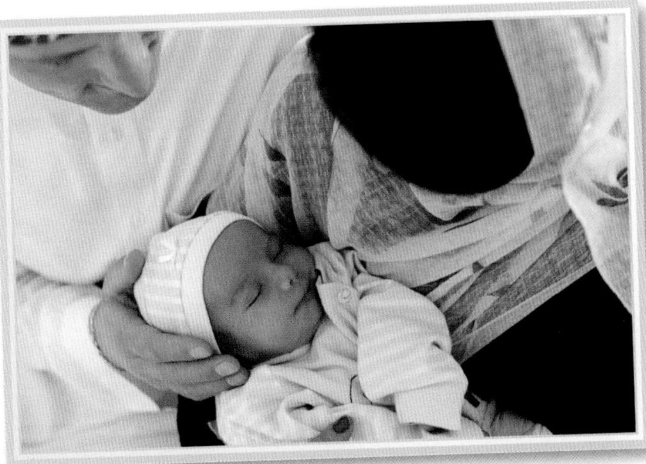

Hinduism: Birth

Hindu rituals are an important part of welcoming a child into the world; however, the ritual of welcoming begins even before the baby is born. The following steps normally occur.

1 Shortly after a couple are married a prayer called *Garbhadhana* is said in the hope that the couple will conceive.

2 Three months into the pregnancy, a ceremony called *Pumsavana* is held. This is done in the hope that the foetus will grow healthy.

3 During the seventh month a ceremony called the *Simantonnayana* is performed. This is like a baby shower. Prayers are said for the wellbeing of the unborn baby's mental health.

4 When the child is born, honey is placed in the baby's mouth and God's name is whispered into the baby's ear. This is called *Jatakarma*.

The following rituals are also very important for each baby:

★ Naming ceremony (Namkaran)
★ First trip out (Nishkramana)
★ First taste of solid food (Annaprasana)
★ Ear-piercing ceremony (Karnavedha)
★ First haircut (Mundan).

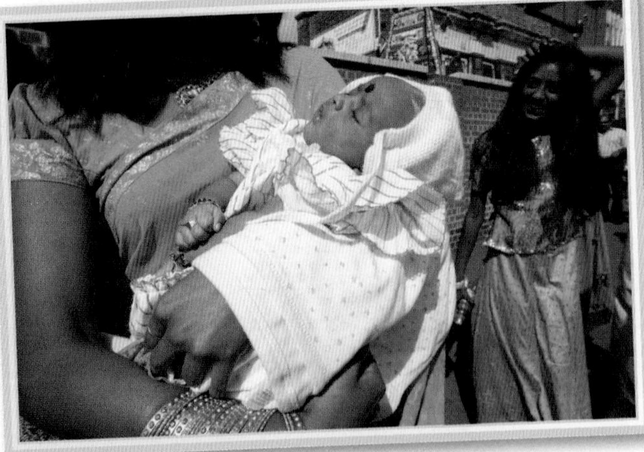

Research the birth rituals in other world faiths.

Buddhism: Marriage

'If a man can find a suitable and understanding wife, and a woman can find a suitable and understanding husband, both are fortunate indeed.'

Buddha

Within the Buddhist faith, marriage is not a religious duty: it is up to each person to choose whether they want to get married and have children or not. The Buddha gave advice on how to be happily married. His guidance focused on the importance of being faithful, loyal, generous and content. He also spoke about the importance of honouring one's parents and the teachings of dharma.

Buddhist monks are not permitted to marry, nor are they allowed to attend or perform wedding services. However, they can offer blessings on a couple getting married.

Search for the video 'Karma brought us together', a highlight video of a Buddhist Japanese wedding.

Research wedding rituals from several different world faiths. Compare and contrast two of these rituals.

Journal your views on the importance of ritual in world faiths.

Secular Rituals

Rituals are not confined to the religious world only. People perform rituals everyday but sometimes they may not be aware of this. Many rituals become so routine and such a part of everyday life that we do not even notice them any more.

The following rituals are familiar in our society:

- ★ Graduation ceremony
- ★ Minute's silence
- ★ Singing the national anthem
- ★ Breaking a bottle off the side of a new ship
- ★ Cutting a cake
- ★ Singing 'Happy Birthday'
- ★ Cutting the 'grand opening' ribbon at a new building.

1 In your opinion, why are rituals important?

2 Do rituals play a role in your everyday life?

Prayer

One important example of ritual for most faiths is the ritual of prayer. Prayer is communication with God. If we want a deep relationship with our God, communication is essential. When people pray they are acknowledging the existence and the greatness of their God. Prayer shows true admiration for a God that is good. You can pray to God silently or vocally. Silent prayer includes meditation and reflection. Vocal prayer is the way most people learn to pray initially. This is prayer using words – either saying these words aloud or in one's head.

Communication is a two-way process, we must listen to God's answers when we pray and not just turn to God when we want help. This would lead to a very unbalanced relationship. When we pray we must have a firm belief that our God cares enough for us to want to communicate with us. For people of religious faith, prayer can be a source of comfort, support, guidance and help in everyday life.

Prayer can be experienced individually or communally. People can pray formally (using set prayers) or informally (talk to God like they would a friend). For a person to engage in prayer with God, they can either chose to go to a sacred place or somewhere they feel comfortable, i.e. their own home.

There are many different kinds of prayer.

★ Petition is when a person asks God for help in their life.
★ Intercession is when a person asks God's help for others, e.g. a sick relative.
★ Thanksgiving is when a person gives thanks to God for all the good in their life.
★ Penitence is when a person asks God for forgiveness for their sins.
★ Praise is when one praises their God for the good that he or she does.

Prayer Questionnaire

By completing this questionnaire you should have a good understanding of your own attitude to prayer.

1 What were the first prayers you learned when you were very young?

2 Who taught them to you?

3 When did you use them?

4 Do you remember the way in which prayers were said in your primary school?

5 At what times of the day? Which prayers? Did you understand the words?

6 As you celebrated First Confession, First Holy Communion and Confirmation, did you learn anything new about prayer?

7 Did your prayer pattern change?

8 Did you still continue to pray at home? Why?

9 Were your prayers mostly prayers of asking, or of thanks, or what?

10 As you started post-primary school, what form did prayer take in your school day?

11 Did you learn any new prayers?

12 Had you forgotten any of the prayers that you had already learned in primary school?

13 If so, how do you think this happened?

14 Do you still pray at home?

15 Which prayers do you say most often?

16 What, do you think, helps you to pray? What is unhelpful?

17 Are your prayers mostly prayers of thanks, of asking, of sorrow?

18 Why do you pray/not pray?

19 Do you think God hears your prayers? Explain your answer.

20 What would you say to someone who said: 'I believe in prayer.'?

1 Compose your own prayer (for private use).

2 Journal the contents of an email that you might send to God about your thoughts on prayer.

Two Traditions of Prayer: Judaism and Islam

Why They Pray

- ★ Jewish people pray to build a relationship with God, to express their faith, to be part of a worshipping community and to obey God's commandments.
- ★ Muslim people pray for similar reasons, and because they were told by their God, Allah, that prayer was very important.

How They Pray

- ★ Jewish people pray with total concentration and from the heart.
- ★ Muslim people must perform *wudu* before they begin *Salat* (second pillar of faith). They must pray on a prayer mat if they are not in a mosque and they also pray in the direction of Mecca. Muslims pray as if they are in the presence of Allah. When they pray there are movements to go with the words of their prayers. Muslim prayer involves body, mind and soul.

What They Pray

- ★ Jewish people pray to give thanks, request something and to praise their God.
- ★ Muslim people pray set prayers taken from the *Qur'an*, their sacred text.

When They Pray

- ★ Jewish people are expected to pray three times a day: morning, afternoon and evening. These prayers are contained within the Jewish prayer book, the *Siddur*.
- ★ Muslim people pray five times a day: dawn, midday, late afternoon, just after sunset and between sunset and midnight.

Where They Pray

- ★ Jewish people usually recite prayers publicly in the synagogue.
- ★ Muslim people usually recite prayers in the Mosque and in their homes.

Reflection

'Whatever is true, whatever is honourable, whatever is right, whatever is pure, whatever is lovely, whatever is of good repute, if there is any excellence and if anything is worthy of praise, dwell on these things.'

Philippians 4:8

'The real man smiles in trouble, gathers strength from distress, and grows brave by reflection.'

Thomas Paine

'The unexamined life is not worth living.'

Socrates

1 What are the speakers attempting to communicate in these quotes?
2 What do you think reflection is?
3 Do you reflect on past experiences?
4 Why do you think it might be important to do this?

Reflection is when one looks back on their experiences in a meaningful way. Due to the stresses and strains of everyday life, reflection is becoming increasingly important. It is vital to take time out and think of the following:

Who are you as a person?

Do you like who you are becoming?

Where do you see yourself going in life?

These are important questions that one should give time to on a regular basis. It is essential for young people to reflect, since the choices you make at this stage of your life can determine the person you may become and the path that you choose to follow.

Life Reflection

Take some time to think about your own life and reflect on it before answering the following questions.

1. Think of a person who makes or made a positive difference in your life. What qualities does that person have that you would like to develop?
2. Imagine twenty years from now – the most important people surround you in your life. Who are they and what are you doing?
3. If a steel beam (6 inches wide) were placed across two skyscrapers, for what would you be willing to cross? A thousand Euro? A million? Your pet? Your brother? Fame?
4. If you could spend one day in a great library studying anything you wanted, what would it be?
5. List ten things you love to do. It could be singing, reading, drawing, dancing, playing football, daydreaming ... anything you absolutely love to do!
6. Describe a time when you were deeply inspired.
7. Five years from now, your local paper does a story about you and they want to interview three people... a parent, a brother or sister, and a friend. What would you want them to say about you?
8. Think of something that represents you...a song, an animal, a flower. Why does it represent you?
9. If you could spend an hour with any person who ever lived, who would that be? Why that person? What would you ask them?
10. Everyone has one or more talents. Which of the following are you good at? (You may write some that are not listed.)
    - Good with numbers
    - Creative thinking
    - Making things happen
    - Mechanical
    - Working well with people
    - Decision making
    - Accepting others
    - Speaking
    - Dancing
    - Singing
    - Sharing
    - Trivia
    - Good with words
    - Athletics
    - Sensing needs
    - Artistic
    - Memorising things
    - Building things
    - Predictions
    - Writing
    - Listening
    - Humorous
    - Music

Meditation

Meditation is one way in which you can reflect.

Watch the video 'An Introduction to Easy Meditation' at theguardian.com

1 What do you know about meditation?
2 Have you ever meditated? Why/Why not?

Meditation is a type of silent prayer. It is known to be a prayer of the mind. Through meditation we try to centre our hearts and thoughts on the mystery of God. This allows God to reveal to us the mysteries of life.

Initially, meditation was associated with the Buddhist faith. It has been associated with the Christian tradition since the twelfth century. However, meditation can be practised by any person, whether or not they choose to be part of religious faith. In today's society, meditation is becoming increasingly popular because of its ability to reduce feelings of anxiety and phobias and to help people become more self-aware.

Buddhism and Christianity approach meditation quite differently. In Christianity, the main purpose of meditation is to be at one with God and encounter him or her in a real way. In Buddhism, the main purpose is to examine one's own thinking and to become peaceful in oneself.

The two traditions give thanks for different things. For Christians, meditation allows them to give thanks to God for what they have been given. In Buddhism, meditation centres on being thankful for life, birth and existence.

1 Match each of the following statements on meditation with one of the speakers below.

1. 'Things can go bad once you stop meditating.'
2. 'Meditation can help you find your soul-mate.'
3. 'Meditation may help you quit smoking.'
4. 'Meditation can help you deal with everyday stress.'
5. 'Meditation can help you prepare for a starring film role — or just prepare, in general.'
6. 'Meditation can help you deal with anxiety.'
7. 'I find meditation in sitting on the floor with the kids colouring for an hour, or going on the trampoline.'
8. 'It has given me energy, strength, health, wisdom, and access to my own inner stillness, inner silence, inner bliss. It is my connection to myself; it is my connection to the universe.'

Angelina Jolie	**Adrian Brody**	**Howard Stern**	**Tiger Woods**
Russell Simmons	**Eva Mendes**	**Hugh Jackman**	**Russell Brand**

Solutions: 1 = Tiger Woods, 2 = Russell Brand, 3 = Howard Stern, 4 = Eva Mendes, 5 = Adrian Brody, 6 = Hugh Jackman, 7 = Angelina Jolie, 8 = Russell Simmons.

Meditation in the Christian Tradition

Christians meditate in order to get a deep connection with their God. They want to be at one with God and open themselves up to him or her through their minds. Christian meditation is reflecting and thinking God's thoughts. Christians believe that God is good and so, in their meditation, giving thanks to God is a key component. This form of silent prayer takes a lot of discipline. It is not something that can be achieved easily; it takes time and effort to get the practice right.

In the Christian tradition there are different ways to meditate, but before any one person can meditate the following steps need to be taken.

★ Find a suitable space.
★ Sit comfortably or lie down.
★ Gently close your eyes.
★ Relax the body, using relaxation techniques.
★ Cultivate an awareness and openness to God.

Christian meditation can involve the use of scripture or guided meditation.

★ Using scripture: For this type of meditation, a quote, verse or word from the Bible can be used. This is then said over and over again (a mantra).
★ Guided meditation: This is when a person (or a person on a CD or other recording) leads the meditation. An imaginary situation or a story from the Bible is read out.

It Was Meditation Integrated With the Scriptures That Healed My Life

Rhonda Jones

Life is not just about surviving, but thriving. However, many years ago surviving was how I lived each day for a period of four years in which I suffered from a deep depression. I was a Christian at the time and did everything humanly possible to get relief. I prayed that God would take this heaviness away. I would play praise music and dance around the room. I went and saw both secular and Christian counsellors. I even took anti-depressants, but nothing worked for any lasting time.

Then one day I was sitting in my dark green mini-van in the parking lot of my kid's school. I was so wretched with emotional pain that you could cut it with a knife. For some reason, I just started doing these deep breathing exercises and with each exhalation I would repeat silently to myself, 'I release pain.' I said this over and over and in about a 10-minute timeframe, all the pain was gone.

There was a peace and stillness I had not experienced in a very long time. In that peace, God spoke to my heart and told me that the reason I was so depressed was because of my chronically negative thoughts. As I listened to my thoughts, which were unconscious to me before this incident, I noticed that I was continually putting myself down. I was saying things like 'I hate myself' over and over and over, all day long.

This was when my healing began. Within the next few months, using relaxation techniques and integrating them with scriptures I learned how to quiet my mind, eliminate my negative thinking and restore my peace of mind. Also, in the process of spending extended time in silence and solitude with God, my intimacy with Him increased as well.

1. What do you think of meditation?
2. What do you think of Rhonda's experience?
3. How do you think meditation helped her?

Class Activity: Guided Meditation

Make sure you are sitting comfortably...two feet on the ground, back straight and your hands on your lap or by your side...Close your eyes and allow your body to relax...Take a deep breath in and breath out all the tension or worry that you are carrying at the moment...Try to leave these worries aside for now and focus on your body...breathing in slowly through your nose...holding it...and slowing breathing out through your mouth.

Imagine doing a scan of your body and notice where you feel tense...is it your shoulders... your stomach...your legs...imagine breathing peace and relaxation into these areas and feel your body completely relax...

Again take a deep breath in through your nose...imagining you are breathing in peace and relaxation...and gently exhale through your mouth...breathing out any stress or tension that you are feeling...

Now...using your imagination...imagine you are out on a country road...
It is around three o'clock in the afternoon...

★ What type of weather is it?
★ What can you see, smell and hear?
★ Is there anything special about this day?

You are by yourself so you have a chance to think about your life and where you are going...

★ Is there something on your mind at the moment?
★ What brings you happiness?
★ What makes you unhappy?
★ What are your hopes?

You have walked quite a distance... You see somebody far away... As you get closer, you see their face and you think: 'It's nice to meet someone on this journey.'

★ What are you thinking?
★ How do you feel?

This person smiles and says hello. You notice something different about this person. They sound very warm-hearted and they politely ask if they can join you for part of the way. You say yes.

★ What do the two of you talk about for the first 10 minutes?

You feel this person is very genuine and caring. They show this by the way they talk and listen to you. You feel you can trust them. You mention to them what you were thinking about earlier.

★ What do you mention?
★ How does the person react?

★ What do they say?
★ How do you feel now?
★ Is there anything else you would like to say to this person?

The two of you continue talking for some time and by now you have travelled some distance. It is time for you to return home.

The person lives in a nearby cottage. They assure you that if you ever want to talk to someone at any time, they will be there for you.
★ What do you say?
★ What are you feeling?

The person goes off towards their cottage and you start back on your way home.

Think back over your journey for a minute or so. Now come to where you are at this time, here in this place. Slowly open your eyes.

Allow 1 minute of silence. Meditate silently on your own intentions.

Meditation in the Buddhist Tradition

In order for a Buddhist to practise their faith, meditation plays an important role in reaching enlightenment. The Buddha taught his followers that the eight-fold path was the way to reach enlightenment. Within the eight-fold path (the moral code of Buddhism) the last part, right concentration, relates to meditation. For Buddhists, the main objective of meditation is to examine their own thinking. This enables them to concentrate fully on their meditation and to reach awareness.

Within Buddhism there are many types of meditation. Two of the most common are mindfulness of breathing (*anapanasati*) and loving kindness (*metta bhavana*) meditation.

★ Mindfulness of breathing: For this type of meditation, Buddhists need to follow the four Ps: place, posture, practice and problems. This means finding a suitable place, getting the correct posture, focusing on your breathing and, if you find yourself distracted, returning to your breath. If you continue to practise this form of meditation it will eventually become easier and the distractions will become less.
★ Loving kindness meditation: You cannot start this type of meditation until you have completed the first part (above). For this type of meditation you must pay attention to yourself and your wellbeing. A series of questions must be asked of yourself. Then when this is done, you must also think of others: people you like, people you are indifferent towards, people you don't know and people you don't like. You must wish all of these other people

well. It is hoped that through this type of meditation a person will become happier within themselves and have respect for others and the wellbeing of others. This in turn will hopefully make them a better person.

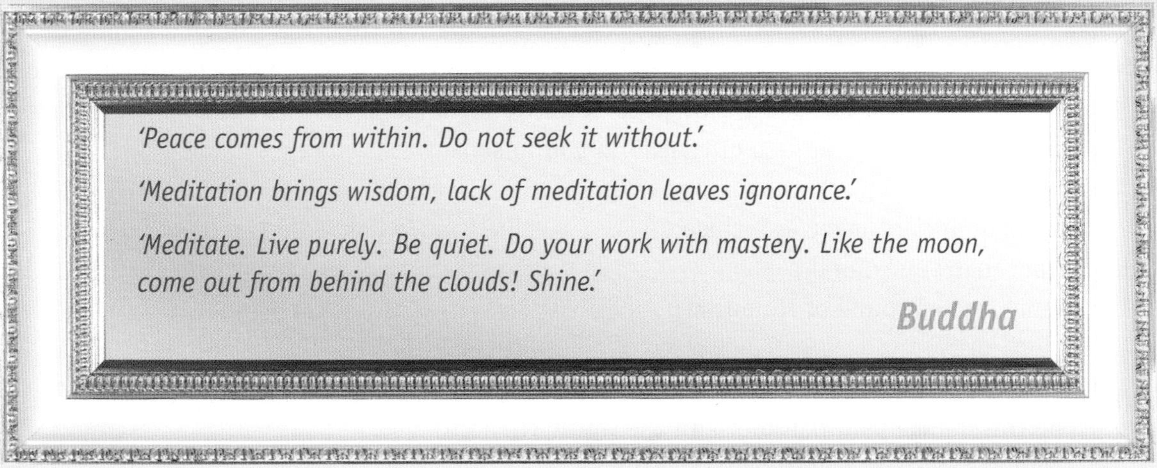

'Peace comes from within. Do not seek it without.'

'Meditation brings wisdom, lack of meditation leaves ignorance.'

'Meditate. Live purely. Be quiet. Do your work with mastery. Like the moon, come out from behind the clouds! Shine.'

Buddha

1 What do you think the Buddha was trying to say about meditation?

2 What do you think are the main differences between Christian and Buddhist meditation?

A community of Buddhist monks meditating

Go to www.vipassanadhura.com and read up on 'How to Meditate'.

Mantra

It is an ancient tradition to repeat words, verses, phrases or quotes while meditating. This is called *mantra*. These words however, must be of a sacred nature and really mean something to you. They can be from a sacred text, they can be a quotation from a person you admire or they can simply be your own thoughts and feelings that might help you overcome a situation you find yourself in. They must be short enough to be easily repeated again and again. The ultimate desire is that these mantras will help or transform you in some way.

Examples of ancient mantras include:

★ 'I am that I am' (Torah)
★ 'Aum' (sacred sound of Hinduism).

Examples of modern mantras include:

★ 'Be the change you wish to see in the world' (Gandhi)
★ 'Forgive me' (your own thoughts/feelings).

1 List five of your own modern mantras.
2 Explain why the five mantras mean something to you.

Contemplative Tradition

The contemplative tradition is closely connected with contemplative prayer. Contemplative prayer is one of the most difficult types of prayer; it is sometimes described as prayer of the heart. It has been described as the feeling of having God's overwhelming love within. St Gregory the Great at the end of the sixth century described contemplation as 'resting in God'. One witness of the Christian contemplative tradition is St Teresa of Avila.

St Teresa of Avila

Go to learnoutloud.com and listen to 'The Life of St Teresa'.

Teresa was born in Avila in Spain in 1515. From a young age Teresa was a very religious person. Her parents taught her to pray and she would often go somewhere quiet to say her prayers. Teresa had a very strong bond with her mother. Teresa was devastated when her mother passed away, especially since Teresa's father was quite strict.

Teresa felt a huge void in her life and began to devote herself to the Virgin Mary.

> *'I threw myself down in despair before an image of the Mother of God. With many tears, I implored the Holy Virgin to become my mother now. Uttered with the simplicity of a child, this prayer was heard. From that hour on, I never prayed to the Virgin in vain.'*

At the age of 16, Teresa was sent to a convent in order to be educated. This allowed her interest in religion to flourish further. Spiritual life now held great interest for Teresa and she became determined to become a nun. Teresa joined the Carmelite order in 1535. It was here that Teresa started to teach others about the benefits of contemplative prayer.

Soon after joining the Carmelites, Teresa got malaria and was left in great pain and her legs were paralysed for three years. During this time of suffering, Teresa began to experience visions and an inner sense of peace. These visions seemed to overcome the physical pain.

> *'I bore these sufferings with great composure, in fact with joy, except at first when the pain was too severe. What followed seemed to hurt less. I was completely surrendered to the will of God even if he intended to burden me like this forever…The other sisters wondered at my God-given patience. Without him I truly could not have borne so much with so much joy.'*

As Teresa got better, she told people about these visions. Some clergy were disparaging and for a time she lost her confidence in prayer and spiritual life. It was not until she was 41 that she met a priest who told her to persevere with prayer and make that connection with God again. While it took some time to engage in a meaningful way, Teresa eventually got her ability back to engage in contemplative prayer. She felt the love of God overpower her at times.

Two years later Teresa set up her own convent and dedicated the rest of her life setting up convents in Spain. She passed away when she was 67. A fellow nun commented as follows on Teresa's death.

> *'She remained in this position in prayer full of deep peace and great repose. Occasionally she gave some outward sign of surprise or amazement. But everything proceeded in great repose. It seemed as if she were hearing a voice which she answered. Her facial expression was so wondrously changed that it looked like a celestial body to us. Thus immersed in prayer, happy and smiling, she went out of this world into eternal life.'*

As well as establishing convents all over Spain, Teresa also wrote a body of works. Below is one of her most famous poems: it sums up the relationship that a person can have with God.

God alone is enough.

Let nothing upset you,
let nothing startle you.
All things pass;
God does not change.
Patience wins
all it seeks.
Whoever has God
lacks nothing:
God alone is enough.

1 In your own words, explain contemplative prayer.
2 Explain how St Teresa is a person of the contemplative tradition.
3 What do you think St Teresa is saying in the poem?

Student Activity on Contemplative Prayer: Prayer of the Heart/The Jesus Prayer/ The Prayer of Quiet

The Prayer of the Heart is also called The Jesus Prayer and The Prayer of Quiet. It is part of the spiritual tradition of the Orthodox Church.

St Simeon gives these directions.

- Sit down alone and in silence.
- Close your eyes.
- Breathe out gently and imagine yourself looking into your own heart.
- Carry your mind, i.e. your thoughts, from your head to your heart.
- As you breathe in say in your mind: 'Jesus Christ, Son of God.'
- As you breath out say: 'Have mercy on me, a sinner.'
- Try to put all other thoughts aside.
- Be calm and patient and repeat the prayer process very frequently.

It is said that the tradition was developed in the monasteries on Mount Sinai and later on Mount Athos. It is a powerful summary of all prayer. We call Jesus 'Lord'. We recognise him as the Christ, the Messiah. And we express the great truth about our relationship with him. We confess our sinfulness and plead for pardon and peace.

'I will remind you of only one thing: one must descend with the mind into the heart, and there stand before the face of the Lord, ever present, all-seeing within you. The prayer takes a firm and steadfast hold, when a small fire begins to burn in the heart. Try not to quench this fire, and it will become established in such a way that the prayer repeats itself and then you will have within you a small murmuring stream.'

Bishop Theophan

Journal your experience of the Prayer of the Heart.

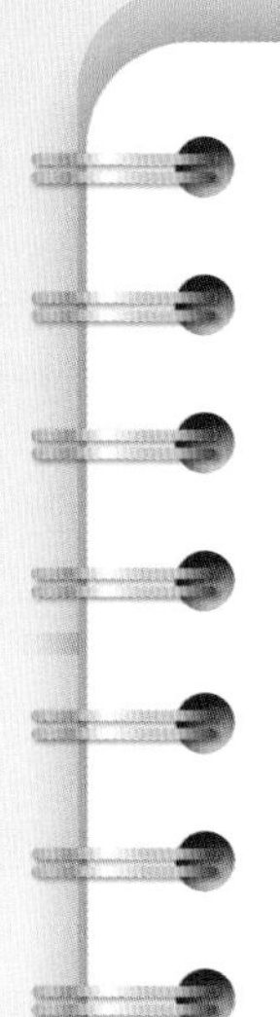

End of Section Summary

- A ritual can involve words spoken, actions performed or clothes worn to express something that is deeply important to people. Humans have always been ritual makers.
- Religious rituals are a key part of religious faith.
- Rituals are not only confined to the religious world: people perform them every day.
- One religious ritual all faiths engage in is prayer.
- Contemplation and meditation are examples of a silent prayer that involves a lot of dedication.
- Mantra is an ancient tradition of repeating words, verses, phrases or quotes while meditating.
- St Teresa of Avila is an example of a person from the contemplative tradition.

End of Section Activities

1. Explain the difference between secular and religious rituals.
2. What do you think of prayer?
3. Discuss the different types of prayer and how they could be used.
4. Describe 'reflection' in your own words.
5. Explain the difference between Christian and Buddhist meditation.

- 'Nobody listens to prayers.'
- 'Meditation is necessary for inner peace.'
- 'Contemplative prayer cannot be proven.'

1 Research the ritual of marriage in the five major world religions.
2 Research two other rituals from the Buddhist and the Hindu faiths.
3 Write a profile of St Teresa of Avila, focusing on the contemplative tradition.

Journal your memories of partaking in any religious ritual.

Compile a list of questions for an interview that you could have with a person of faith. Ask them to recount their memories from a religious ritual.

Books

★ *A Path with Heart* – Jack Kornfield
★ *Seeking the Heart of Wisdom: The Path of Insight Meditation* – Joseph Goldstein and Jack Kornfield
★ *Anam Cara: A Book of Celtic Wisdom* – John O'Donohue

Websites:

★ www.sacredspace.ie
★ www.worldprayers.org
★ www.thechristianmeditator.com
★ Go to www.catholic.org and read about Saint Marguerite d'Youville

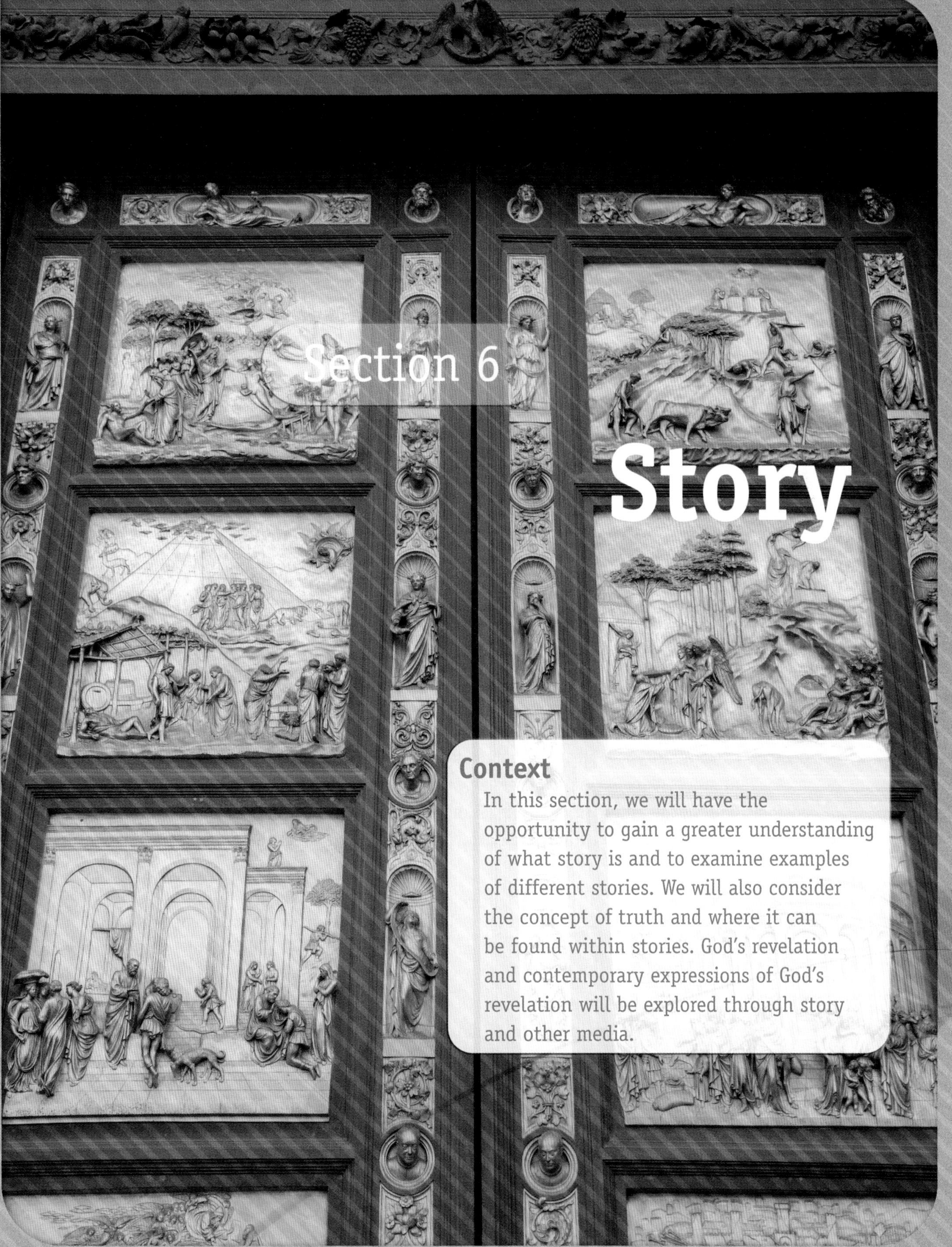

Section 6

Story

Context

In this section, we will have the opportunity to gain a greater understanding of what story is and to examine examples of different stories. We will also consider the concept of truth and where it can be found within stories. God's revelation and contemporary expressions of God's revelation will be explored through story and other media.

Story

Consider the following questions.

- ★ Imagine a world with no music, TV, books or films. What would you do with your free time?
- ★ Where would your entertainment come from?
- ★ Could you imagine yourself sitting down to listen to someone telling a story?
- ★ In your life today, what is your experience of story?

Stories have been around since the beginning of time and have always played an important role in people's lives. A story is a means of communication. Each story tells us something.

Ancient storytellers enthralled listeners with their tales. They passed on their traditions, customs, knowledge and wisdom. Storytelling was hugely important to people in the past. Stories travelled to others through word of mouth. This would have been the only method of sharing stories.

Today, story has evolved from its origins of one person telling stories to others. Story can now be experienced in many different media, including films, books, advertisements, music and art. These media allow stories to be communicated instantaneously to millions of people worldwide.

There are many different types of stories:

- ★ Fairy tale: a story involving fantasy (mostly aimed at children)
- ★ Folk tale: a story passed on orally from older generations
- ★ Fable: a short story that teaches a lesson (usually involving animal characters)
- ★ Saga: a long narrative that tells a story about some historical figures
- ★ Legend: an unproven story handed down from earlier times

★ Myth: a traditional story, especially one concerning the early history of a people or explaining some natural or social phenomenon, and typically involving supernatural beings or events
★ Parable: a story that contains a deeper or hidden meaning.

1 Can you remember the first story you were told?
2 In your opinion, why was storytelling important in the past?
3 How do you think storytelling has changed over time?
4 Do you think the seven types of stories are still relevant today? Why/why not?
5 What do you think of modern methods of storytelling?

'It is an ancient need to be told stories.'

Alan Rickman

'It's all about letting the story take over.'

Robert Stone

'After nourishment, shelter and companionship, stories are the thing we need most in the world.'

Philip Pullman

'The purpose of a storyteller is not to tell you how to think, but to give you questions to think upon.'

Brandon Sanderson

1. What do you think Alan Rickman is trying to communicate in his quote?
2. How can a story 'take over'?
3. Do you agree with the quote by Philip Pullman?
4. Have you ever heard or read a story that made you stop and think?

Go Ask Alice

Anonymous

An unnamed 15-year-old diarist, whom the novel's title refers to as Alice, starts a diary. With a sensitive, observant style, she records her adolescent woes: she worries about what her crush Roger thinks of her; she loathes her weight gain; she fears her budding sexuality; she is uncomfortable at school; she has difficulty relating to her parents. Alice's father, a college professor, accepts a teaching position at a different college and the family will move at the start of the New Year, which cheers Alice up.

The move is difficult. While the rest of her family adjusts to the new town, Alice feels like an outcast at school. Soon she meets Beth, a Jewish neighbour, and the two become fast friends. Beth leaves for summer camp and Alice goes to live with her grandparents. She is bored, but reunites with an old friend, Jill, who invites Alice to a party. At the party, Alice unwittingly drops LSD and experiences a fantastic drug trip. Though curious, she vows not to do drugs again.

Alice happily experiments with more drugs and loses her virginity while on acid. Roger and his parents show up unexpectedly to visit her grandfather, who has had a small heart attack. Alice is enthralled with Roger but feels guilty about her drug use and loss of virginity. She doesn't know to whom she can talk about drugs. She is worried that she may be pregnant. Alice goes home and her family accepts her warmly. Unable to sleep, she receives powerful tranquilisers from her doctor. Beth returns from camp, but Alice finds that Beth has changed. In a boutique, Alice meets Chris, a hip girl. Alice's parents worry about Alice's ' hippie' appearance.

Alice and Chris are both dissatisfied with the establishment and their own families. Alice gets a job working with Chris, and the two become best friends. At school, they use drugs and are popular. Chris's friend Richie, a college boy, turns Alice on to marijuana. To make more money for drugs, she and Chris sell drugs and do whatever they can to help Richie and Ted (Chris's boyfriend and Richie's roommate). Alice and Chris discover Richie and Ted having sex with each other and flee to San Francisco. Alice turns Richie in to the police and vows to stay clean with Chris. They move into a cramped apartment. Chris secures a job in a boutique with a glamorous older woman, Sheila, and Alice gets one with a custom jeweller. Sheila invites the girls to a party at her house.

At Sheila's swanky party, the girls use drugs again. They continue to party with Sheila until one night, when trying heroin, Alice realises that Sheila and her boyfriend have been raping and brutalising them. The girls kick their drug lifestyle. They find a new apartment in Berkeley and open a jewellery shop there, which turns into a hangout for the neighbourhood kids. Alice misses her family. She returns home for Christmas, and the holiday spirit and family camaraderie revive her. She begins school and resists drug advances from old friends, though some are aggressive. Chris smokes marijuana with her, and Alice goes back on drugs. The police raid Chris's house while she and Alice use drugs. The girls are put on probation, and Alice will be sent to a psychiatrist.

Alice continues to do drugs without her family's knowledge. She hitchhikes to Denver (recording her diary entries on scraps of paper without dates). She travels to Oregon with other drug users but soon loses them. A janitor directs her to a mission similar to the Salvation Army. Alice is cleaned up and meets a young sufferer of lifelong sexual abuse, Doris, who lets her stay at her apartment. They get sick from malnourishment and hitchhike to Southern California, where Alice takes more drugs, even prostituting herself for them. Alice talks with a priest about teen runaways, and he calls her parents. They want her to come home. In the city, Alice meets several other runaways and talks to them about why they left home. She imagines she may go into child guidance or psychology some day to help out others, and she vows to quit drugs.

Alice comes home and is excited to renew her life with her family. Alice loses consciousness and drifts off into a reverie that she thinks is either a flashback (caused by LSD residue in the spinal cavity) or a schizophrenic episode. Otherwise, Alice is happy with her family and with herself, except for her social isolation: she can't hang out with drug users, and 'straight' kids don't want her around. Alice's grandfather dies in a coma from a stroke. She agonises over the thought of worms and maggots eating his dead body underground. Her relationship with her father matures. Someone plants a joint in Alice's purse, and she leaves school to go to his office. He consoles her, and gets her permission to study at the university library.

Alice meets a freshman at the university library, Joel; his father is dead, his mother is a factory worker, and he works as a janitor to pay for school. He and Alice get to know each other better, as does her family. She fantasises about marrying him. Pressure to use drugs at school intensifies, as the kids harass Alice and her family. Alice's grandmother dies. After the funeral, Joel has a long talk with her about death that makes her feel better, and they kiss. She opens up to Joel about some of her past, and he is kind and supportive.

Alice writes in her undated diary from a hospital. She is unsure how she has ended up here and can only think of the worms she thinks are eating her alive. She has chewed her fingers to the bone, and clawed up her face and body. Her father says that someone dosed with LSD the chocolate-covered peanuts Alice was eating while she was baby-sitting. Alice finds out she is being sent to an insane asylum. Her father tells her that her case was brought before a juvenile court and that Jan and another girl testified that Alice had still been on drugs and was selling them. Alice registers at the State Mental Hospital. She is frightened by the ugly building and by the inmates. She meets a little 13-year-old girl, Babbie, a former prostitute and drug user with a history of sexual abuse.

Life in the asylum drains Alice. A visit from her parents brings a warm letter from Joel. Her father reports that Jan has retracted her statement, and they're trying to get the other girl to do the same to free Alice. Alice returns home and is happy to be with her family. The family takes a vacation together, and when they return, Alice is invited swimming by Fawn, a 'straight' kid. She has a fun time with Fawn's friends and hopes that they haven't heard stories about her. Joel makes a surprise visit and gives her a friendship ring, which she vows to wear her whole life. She is worried about starting school again but feels stronger with the support of her new friends and Joel. She comments that she no longer needs a diary, for she now has people in her life with whom she can communicate.

In the epilogue, we are told that Alice died three weeks later of an overdose—whether it was premeditated or accidental remains unclear—and that she was one of thousands of drug deaths that year.

1. What do you think of Alice's story?
2. Do you think it's a story that should be told?
3. Alice's story is in the form of a diary. Do you think she would have wanted her story to be told?
4. Do you think young people could identify with Alice's story and her insecurities?
5. Although this is just a summary of Alice's story, does it make you stop and think about life?

The Man, the Boy and the Donkey

Aesop's fable

A man and his son were once going with their donkey to market. As they were walking along by its side a countryman passed them and said: 'You fools: what is a donkey for, but to ride upon?'

So the man put the boy on the donkey and they went on their way. But soon they passed a group of men, one of whom said: 'See that lazy youngster: he lets his father walk while he rides.'

So the man ordered his boy to get off, and got on himself. But they hadn't gone far when they passed two women, one of whom said: 'Shame on that lazy lout to let his poor little son trudge along.'

Well, the man didn't know what to do, but at last he took his boy up before him on the donkey. By this time they had come to the town, and the passers-by began to jeer and point at them. The man stopped and asked what they were scoffing at. The men said: 'Aren't you ashamed of yourself for overloading that poor donkey of yours and your hulking son?'

The man and boy got off and tried to think what to do. They thought and they thought, till at last they cut down a pole, tied the donkey's feet to it, and raised the pole and the donkey to their shoulders. They went along amid the laughter of all who met them till they came to Market Bridge, when the donkey, getting one of his feet loose, kicked out and caused the boy to drop his end of the pole. In the struggle, the donkey fell over the bridge, and his fore-feet being tied together, he was drowned.

'That will teach you,' said an old man who had followed them.

The moral of this Aesop's fable: *Please all, and you will please none*.

1. A fable teaches a lesson. In your own words, describe the lesson of this fable.
2. Can you think of a time you listened to others instead of doing what you thought was right?
3. Do you think a fable is an effective way to teach a lesson?

The Story of Cain and Abel

Old Testament (Genesis 4:1–16)

After Adam and Eve had sinned in the Garden of Eden, they were sorry and they asked God how they could make it up to him. Even though they sinned, God still loved them. After some time, Eve gave birth to two sons. Cain was born first and then Abel. Cain was a farmer and Abel was a shepherd.

God asked Adam and Eve to sacrifice something that was important to them to show God that they were sorry for their sins. Adam and Eve told Cain and Abel about this message from God. Both Cain and Abel were to sacrifice something to God also. Abel chose his best lamb to be sacrificed. He wanted to make sure that God knew how much he appreciated all he had done for him. Cain decided to offer up some of his excess wheat from that year's crop. Cain thought that Abel was mad to sacrifice his best lamb.

The day of offering the sacrifice arrived. Abel's lamb burnt completely on the altar while Cain's wheat never really caught fire. God welcomed Abel's sacrifice but rejected Cain's. Cain had made no real effort and had been selfish, while Abel gave willingly to show his love for God. God would have welcomed Cain's offering no matter what it was, if it had been offered up with the best intentions.

Cain became very jealous, even though he only had himself to blame. He felt that God preferred Abel. Cain's jealousy turned to anger and then to rage. One day while he was walking with his brother, Cain struck Abel and killed him. Cain was relieved when he looked around and realised that no one had seen him.

And then the Lord spoke, 'Cain, where is your brother?'

Cain shrugged, 'I dunno! Am I my brother's keeper?'

God replied, 'Cain, how could you be so cruel to your only brother? He has done nothing, but try his best for Me, for his parents... and for you.'

Cain fell to the ground sobbing. Finally, he felt the horror of what he'd done. And he had to live with that feeling and the knowledge that he'd murdered his little brother for the rest of his life.

1. What is this story trying to tell us?
2. Can you relate to the actions of Cain?
3. This story was written over 4,000 years ago. Do you think it is still valuable today in teaching us important life lessons?

Truth

When a person reads a story, they are looking for meaning and engagement. People look for the truth within these stories. Truth can be defined in many ways but perhaps one of the best ways of defining it comes from the Greek word '*aletheia*', which means 'unhide' or ' hiding nothing'. This shows that the truth does exist in the world but it is up to each human to uncover it for themselves. Truth can be found in a number of different ways. For some people truth can be found in religion and for others it can be found in science.

1 What do you think is meant by religious truth?

2 Explain what you understand scientific truth to be.

Religious Truth

Religion is about having a belief in the existence of something greater than humans. This belief can be expressed by a person having faith in the existence of God/Gods. A person of religious faith must follow the standards that have been set out by its original creator. People of faith accept that the God/Gods they believe in cannot be proved through science. People who have this faith believe that it is helping them to uncover the truth about life. In a religion, revelation is essential in understanding God and spirituality. Sacred scriptures can inform people of religious truths, including why the world was created and how God wants people to live their lives.

Scientific Truth

Everything to do with science can be measured, observed and proved. Scientific experimentation is the key to scientific truth. Anything that can be proved through an experiment a number of times is considered to be scientific truth. Science can provide answers as to how the world was created and how humans evolved. Some theories have been put forward to explain the above, including the Big Bang theory and Charles Darwin's theory of evolution.

Religious truth and scientific truth are examples of different kinds of truth. Both are considered to be correct, depending on your personal beliefs.

1 Explain the difference between religious and scientific truth.

Research what Charles Darwin *and* Galileo Galilee said about the creation story.

Go to www.pbs.org to watch some videos on evolution or use the link below.
www.pbs.org/wgbh/evolution/educators/teachstuds/svideos.html

God's Story: Revelation

'Blessed are you, Simon son of Jonah, for this was not revealed to you by man, but by my Father in heaven'

Matthew 16:17

1 Explain what you understand from this quote from Matthew 16:17.

2 What do you think God's story is about?

In the context of the Christian faith, God's revelation is how God revealed himself to mankind. God's revelation is the essence of Christian religious truth. This is how God revealed his existence to mankind. The knowledge that one knows about God is given from God as he is the one who has shown himself to be true. God's revelation can be seen in his creations.

'What can be known about God is plain to them, for God Himself made it plain. Ever since God created the world, his invisible qualities both his eternal power and his divine nature, have been clearly seen; they are perceived in the things that God has made. So those people have no excuse at all.'

Romans 1:20

Christians believe that we, as humans, are made in the image and likeness of God.

'So God created mankind in his own image, in the image of God he created them; male and female he created them'.

Genesis 1:27

Christians believe that it is through God that humans have the ability to have faith and to be spiritual.

'For God does not show favouritism. All who sin apart from the law will also perish apart from the law, and all who sin under the law will be judged by the law. For it is not those who hear the law who are righteous in God's sight, but it is those who obey the law who will be declared righteous. (Indeed, when Gentiles, who do not have the law, do by nature things required by the law, they are a law for themselves, even though they do not have the law. They show that the requirements of the law are written on their hearts, their consciences also bearing witness, and their thoughts sometimes accusing them and at other times even defending them.) This will take place on the day when God judges people's secrets through Jesus Christ, as my gospel declares'.

Romans 2:11–6

It is believed that God's final revelation was through Jesus Christ. It is human nature to question that which cannot be proved. However, through the Bible, Christians can have their beliefs in God affirmed as the Bible tells the complete story of God's revelations. 'God's final revelation is shown to us through his son Jesus.' This final revelation was the most profound, since it allowed humans to experience God's revelation in a real way.

Jesus came on earth to be a living testament to the existence of God in the world. Jesus is the living embodiment of God's revelation. Jesus spent his earthly life teaching us how to live in the image and likeness of God.

God's revelation is clearly explained in the Gospels. The following Bible references are examples of this.

> *'I myself did not know him, but the reason I came baptising with water was that he might be revealed to Israel.'*
>
> **John 1:13**

> *'For this people's heart has become calloused; they hardly hear with their ears, and they have closed their eyes. Otherwise they might see with their eyes, hear with their ears, understand with their hearts and turn, and I would heal them.*
>
> **Matthew 13:15**

From God's revelation, humans made a decision to believe and accept or not. The following are examples of man's response and acceptance to God's revelations.

> *'So I say to you: ask and it will be given to you; seek and you will find; knock and the door will be open to you.'*
>
> **Luke 11:9**

> *'Others, like seeds sown on good soil, hear the word, accept it, and produce a crop 30, 60 or even 100 times what was sown.'*
>
> **Mark 4:20**

Journal your response to this section on God's revelation.

God's revelation can also be seen in the stories in the Gospels. Through the parables, Jesus attempted to show people God's presence in the world. The parable of the Prodigal Son is an example of God's presence working through people.

Go to godtube.com and watch the animated clip on the prodigal son parable.

The Parable of the Prodigal Son

There was a man who had two sons. The younger one said to his father, 'Father, give me my share of the estate.' So he divided his property between them. Not long after that, the younger son got together all he had, set off for a distant country and there squandered his wealth in wild living.

After he had spent everything, there was a severe famine in that whole country, and he began to be in need. So he went and hired himself out to a citizen of that country, who sent him to his fields to feed pigs. He longed to fill his stomach with the pods that the pigs were eating, but no one gave him anything. When he came to his senses, he said, 'How many of my father's hired servants have food to spare, and here I am starving to death! I will set out and go back to my father and say to him: "Father, I have sinned against heaven and against you. I am no longer worthy to be called your son; make me like one of your hired servants."'

So he got up and went to his father. But while he was still a long way off, his father saw him and was filled with compassion for him; he ran to his son, threw his arms around him and kissed him. The son said to him, 'Father, I have sinned against heaven and against you. I am no longer worthy to be called your son.'

But the father said to his servants, 'Quick! Bring the best robe and put it on him. Put a ring on his finger and sandals on his feet. Bring the fattened calf and kill it. Let's have a feast and celebrate. For this son of mine was dead and is alive again; he was lost and is found.' So they began to celebrate.

Meanwhile, the older son was in the field. When he came near the house, he heard music and dancing. So he called one of the servants and asked him what was going on. 'Your brother has come,' he replied, 'and your father has killed the fattened calf because he has him back safe and sound.'

The older brother became angry and refused to go in. So his father went out and pleaded with him. But he answered his father, 'Look! All these years I've been slaving for you and never disobeyed your orders. Yet you never gave me even a young goat so I could celebrate with my friends. But when this son of yours who has squandered your property with prostitutes comes home, you kill the fattened calf for him!'

'My son,' the father said, 'you are always with me, and everything I have is yours. But we had to celebrate and be glad, because this brother of yours was dead and is alive again; he was lost and is found.'

1 Where can you see God's presence at work in this parable?
2 From what you have studied about God's revelation, explain how parables can make this topic easier to understand.

Expressions of God's Revelation

Today there are many expressions of God's revelation. These expressions make it easier to understand God's story and his message. God's message can be found in many areas, such as art, poetry, music and film. However, it is important to note that within each of these methods, individuals can freely take their own understanding and meaning from them. Part of God's revelation is the recognition that each person is unique. Due to this uniqueness, not everyone will experience God's revelation in the same way.

Art

Art can be a valuable method for people to express their deepest thoughts, through painting, sculpture, sketching and pottery. There is great freedom within the medium of art, which allows a piece of work to evoke feelings and emotions in others. Three artists who deal with God's revelation in different ways are Elizabeth Wang, Jane Macneill and Giotto.

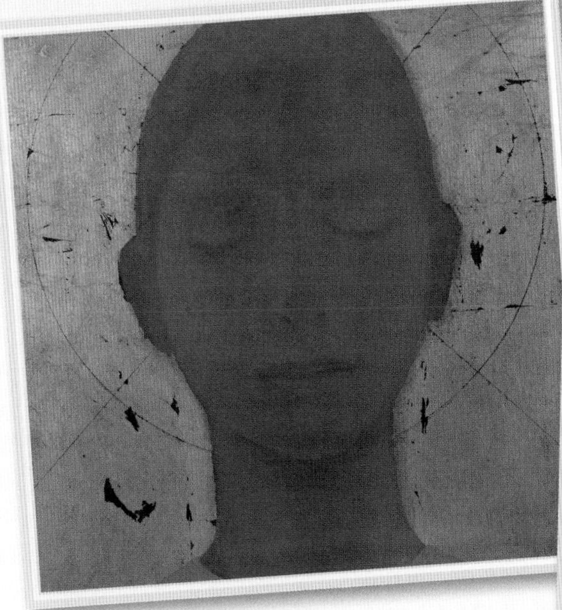

Moment I, Jane MacNeill

God the Father loves us as his children with a tender and unfailing love, Elizabeth Wang

1. Explain how God's revelation can be seen in the paintings by Elizabeth Wang and Jane MacNeill.
2. What do you think Giotto's painting is about?
3. What feelings are evoked in you on looking at these paintings?
4. Which image is closest to your understanding of God's revelation?

St. Jerome checking the Stigmata on the Body of St Francis, Giotto

Poetry

Poetry is one way to engage meaningfully with God's revelation. Two poets who deal with this theme in their work are John Donne and Gerard Manley Hopkins. In the following sonnet, John Donne asks God to 'batter' his heart. He says that God only knocks gently and seeks to mend. However, Donne feels that he needs God to use more force to make him like 'new'. At the end of the poem, Donne wants God to take him prisoner ('Take me to you, imprison me'), since he feels he will not be free or chaste until God 'ravishes' him.

Batter My Heart

John Donne

Batter my heart, three-personed God; for, you
As yet but knock; breathe, shine, and seek to mend;
That I may rise, and stand, o'erthrow me, and bend
Your force, to break, blow, burn, and make me new.
I, like an usurp'd town, to another due,
Labour to admit you, but oh, to no end.
Reason, your viceroy in me, me should defend,
But is captived, and proves weak or untrue.
Yet dearly I love you, and would be loved fain,
But am betroth'd unto your enemy,
Divorce me, untie or break that knot again,
Take me to you, imprison me, for I,
Except you enthrall me, never shall be free,
Nor ever chaste, except you ravish me.

1. Write down what you think the poet is saying about his relationship with God.
2. Why does the poet want God to 'batter' his heart?
3. The poet wants to be punished by God for the wrongs that he has done. Do you think God would want this?
4. What do you think the poet means by 'imprison me'?

Story

In the following poem, Hopkins describes God's revelation through nature. As each creature speaks of itself, it is speaking of its origins in God. Hopkins also explores God's revelation in humans. He explains that God's grace is at work in the 'just man'. This is also a sign that Christ is working through that person.

As Kingfishers Catch Fire

Gerard Manley Hopkins

As kingfishers catch fire, dragonflies draw flame;
  As tumbled over rim in roundy wells
  Stones ring; like each tucked string tells, each hung bell's
Bow swung finds tongue to fling out broad its name;
Each mortal thing does one thing and the same:
  Deals out that being indoors each one dwells;
  Selves – goes itself; myself *it speak and spells,*
Crying What I do is me: for that I came.

I say more: the just man justices;
  Keeps grace: that keeps all his goings graces;
Acts in God's eye what in God's eye he is –
  Christ – for Christ play in ten thousand places,
Lovely in limbs, and lovely in eyes not his
  To the Father through the features of men's faces.

1. What is the poet saying in lines 1–8?
2. Who does the poet credit with the creation of life?
3. Explain what the poet is saying about humans in the final six lines.
4. Give your definition of a 'just man'.

Music

The Fray

Music is another way for people to express their beliefs and thoughts on God and his revelation.

Listen to the following songs on youtube or grooveshark.com

You Found Me

The Fray

I found God on the corner of 1st and Amistad
Where the West was all but won
All alone, smoking his last cigarette
I said, 'Where you been?' He said, 'Ask anything'

Where were you when everything was falling apart?
All my days were spent by the telephone that never rang
And all I needed was a call that never came
To the corner of 1st and Amistad

Lost and insecure, you found me, you found me
Lying on the floor surrounded, surrounded
Why'd you have to wait? Where were you? Where were you?
Just a little late, you found me, you found me

But in the end everyone ends up alone
Losing her, the only one who's ever known
Who I am, who I'm not and who I wanna be
No way to know how long she will be next to me

Lost and insecure, you found me, you found me
Lying on the floor surrounded, surrounded
Why'd you have to wait? Where were you? Where were you?
Just a little late, you found me, you found me

The early morning, the city breaks
And I've been calling for years and years and years and years
And you never left me no messages
You never sent me no letters
You got some kind of Man taking all I want

Lost and insecure, you found me, you found me
Lying on the floor, where were you? Where were you?

Lost and insecure, you found me, you found me
Lying on the floor surrounded, surrounded
Why'd you have to wait? Where were you? Where were you?
Just a little late, you found me, you found me

Why'd you have to wait to find me, to find me?

1 Explain what you think this song is about.
2 Highlight the lyrics that show God's revelation.

Joan Osborne

If God Was One of Us

Joan Osborne

If God had a name, what would it be
And would you call it to His face
If you were faced with Him in all His glory
What would you ask if you had just one question

And yeah, yeah, God is great
yeah, yeah, God is good
yeah, yeah, yeah, yeah, yeah

What if God was one of us
Just a slob like one of us
Just a stranger on the bus
Trying to make His way home

If God had a face what would it look like
And would you want to see
If seeing meant that you would have to believe
In things like heaven and in Jesus and the Saints
And all the Prophets

And yeah, yeah, God is great
yeah, yeah, God is good
yeah, yeah, yeah, yeah, yeah

What if God was one of us
Just a slob like one of us
Just a stranger on the bus

Trying to make His way home
He's trying to make His way home
Back up to heaven all alone
Nobody calling on the phone
Except for the Pope maybe in Rome

And yeah, yeah, God is great
yeah, yeah, God is good
yeah, yeah, yeah, yeah, yeah

What if God was one of us
Just a slob like one of us
Just a stranger on the bus
Trying to make His way home
Just trying to make His way home
Like a holy rolling stone
Back up to heaven all alone
Just trying to make His way home
Nobody calling on the phone
Except for the Pope maybe in Rome

1 Explain what you think this song is about.
2 Highlight the lyrics that show God's revelation.

Film

For people today, film is a popular form of entertainment. However, many important social issues can be dealt with through film. God's revelation is seen by many people through the medium of film. For example, in *Bruce Almighty* the main character rages against God and God responds. The film *Patch Adams* looks at the work of an individual who has unique ideas on how to help others despite opposition.

People can experience God's revelation in their own lives at various times. God can be revealed through personal experiences. Ringo Starr and Elton John are two people who have experienced God's revelation in their own lives.

Ringo Starr admits: 'I have found God'

Ringo Starr, the Beatles' drummer, has admitted he has 'found God' after taking what he described as a winding life of enlightenment. The reformed rock legend, who turns 70 in July, admitted he had lost his way when he was younger, first as a Beatle then later after the group broke up.

He experimented with LSD and marijuana when he was a Beatle in the 1960s, then later in the 1970s suffered alcohol and cocaine problems. In an interview with the *Los Angeles Times*, Starr, who is now a teetotal and has quit his sixty-a-day cigarette habit, said that religion was one of the most important aspects in his life.

'I feel the older I get, the more I'm learning to handle life. Being on this quest for a long time, it's all about finding yourself,' Starr told the paper at a Grammy Museum event in Los Angeles. 'For me, God is in my life. I don't hide from that ... I think the search has been on since the sixties. I stepped off the path there for many years and found my way [back] onto it, thank God.'

1. What do you think Ringo means when he says 'I have found God'?
2. Why, do you think, did it take Ringo so long to find God?

Love is the Cure

The first story I'd like to tell you is an amazing one. To understand the AIDS epidemic, to understand my passion for ending it, you need to know about Ryan White. It all goes back to my friend Ryan.

Ryan came into this world with a rare and terrible genetic disease, haemophilia, which prevents the blood from clotting and leads to uncontrollable bleeding. Haemophilia is a manageable condition today, but in the early 1970s, when Ryan was born, it was a dangerous and often fatal disease. As an infant, and then as a child, Ryan was in the hospital again and again.

Then, as if the hand he'd been dealt wasn't difficult enough, the poor boy contracted HIV, the virus that causes AIDS, through a treatment for his haemophilia. At age thirteen, the doctors gave Ryan a grim prognosis: less than six months to live. He held on for more than five years. And in that short span, Ryan accomplished what most could not hope to achieve in a thousand lifetimes. He inspired a nation, changed the course of a deadly epidemic, and helped save millions of lives. Imagine, a child doing all of that, a sick boy from a small town in Middle America. It sounds like a movie script, like a bedtime story, like a miracle. And it was a miracle. Ryan's life was an absolute miracle.

It must have been 1985 when I first learned about Ryan. I was at a doctor's appointment in New York. I forget why I was there. I picked up a magazine from a stack in the waiting room. I was mindlessly flipping through the pages when I came across an article that would change my life. I couldn't believe what I was reading, that a boy was being kept out of school, and his family was being shunned and tormented, because he had AIDS.

Ryan lived with his mother, Jeanne, and his younger sister, Andrea, in the small town of Kokomo, Indiana. Jeanne worked at the local General Motors car factory for twenty-three years. The Whites were a blue-collar family through and through, much like my own family growing up, which is perhaps why I instantly connected with them when we finally got to know one another.

In 1984, around Christmastime, Ryan was in particularly bad shape with a rare form of pneumonia. But tests at the hospital revealed a far worse diagnosis: he had full-blown AIDS. The pneumonia was an opportunistic infection attacking his badly weakened immune system.

As it turned out, Ryan had contracted HIV from a treatment for his haemophilia called factor VIII, a clotting agent derived from donated blood. A single dose of factor VIII could include plasma pooled from thousands of people, and some of them had HIV. Because the HIV virus itself wasn't identified until the mid-1980s, there was no way to screen for the disease. That's how HIV-contaminated factor VIII was administered to patients in the United States and throughout the world in the early '80s, including Ryan. Thousands of haemophiliacs became HIV-positive in this way before pharmaceutical companies and the government put measures in place to test and purify factor VIII.

Jeanne waited until after Christmas to tell Ryan that he had AIDS. When he found out, Ryan knew exactly what it meant: he was going to die.

Everyone was aware of AIDS by 1984, especially haemophiliacs. While it was still a very new and frightening disease, the medical community had already figured out the basics. They had identified the HIV virus itself that year, and they knew that it was spread only by sex or by direct blood exposure. More to the point, they knew it couldn't be transmitted through casual contact, such as sharing water fountains or toilet seats, drinking from the same glass, eating with the same utensils, or even kissing. There was simply no risk of infection from being around someone with AIDS.

But there was fear. There was so much fear. It was everywhere, a ghost that shadowed Ryan's every move and haunted him throughout his life.

When Ryan was told about his condition, that he might not have very long to live, he made an extraordinary decision: to live out the rest of his days, however many there might be, as ordinarily as he could. He wanted to go to school, to play with his friends, and to spend time with his mom, Andrea, and his grandparents. He just wanted to be like any other child, even if his disease meant that he wasn't. When he first learned of his prognosis, Ryan asked Jeanne to pretend that he didn't have AIDS. He didn't want special treatment; all he wanted was a sense, however brief, of normality.

But that would not be his fate. Ryan was never allowed to live a normal life, let alone die a normal death. Shortly after he was diagnosed, a local paper discovered that Ryan had AIDS. They ran a story about it, and suddenly the whole town – and then the whole nation – knew about his condition. After that, everything changed for Ryan and his family. As a child with haemophilia, Ryan had been treated with compassion. As a child with AIDS, many treated him with contempt.

Ryan missed the majority of seventh grade, thanks to his bout with pneumonia. He was too weak to return to school that year, in the spring of 1985. By the summer, however, he was much better. He even had a paper round. He was eager to be back in school, to play with his friends, to have a semblance of a normal life. But in late July, a month before the beginning of the new school year, the superintendent of Ryan's school district announced that Ryan would not be allowed to attend classes in person, due to the widespread fear that he posed a health risk to his schoolmates – that by being near them, he might somehow infect them. It was decided that Ryan would attend school by phone instead.

The fear, I suppose, was understandable. AIDS was a fatal illness at the time, without exception. But it was well known that Ryan couldn't transmit the virus to others just by being around them. After all, Jeanne and Andrea lived with Ryan. They drank out of the same glasses, ate off the same dishes, hugged him, kissed him. They were with him constantly, especially when he was most sick. Yet even their intimate proximity to Ryan hadn't resulted in their contracting HIV. Besides, the U.S. Centers for Disease Control and Prevention (CDC) and the Indiana State Board of Health had assured the school district that Ryan posed no threat to teachers, students, or staff, and they offered guidelines for him to safely return.

Logic and science couldn't contain the fear, however. Ryan was effectively quarantined. But he wasn't a quitter; he never, ever gave up. Not being allowed to attend school was unacceptable to him. He decided to fight to return.

Ryan and Jeanne sued the school. They had the national medical community and the State Board of Health on their side. But the judge dismissed Ryan's lawsuit. He said that the boy's lawyers had to appeal the school superintendent's decision to the Indiana Department of Education first. Ryan's days were numbered as it was, and here was a technical decision that would further delay his going back to school. In the meantime, a special phone link was set up, and Ryan dialled into school every day.

The appeals process that ensued was long, nasty, and public, with Ryan, now fourteen years old, at the centre of it all. The local school board and many parents of Ryan's schoolmates were vehemently opposed to him attending school. More than a hundred parents threatened to file a lawsuit if Ryan was allowed to return. In late November, the Indiana Department of Education ruled in Ryan's favour and ordered the school to open its doors to him, except when he was very sick. The local school board appealed, prolonging Ryan's absence from the classroom. Months later, a state board again ruled that Ryan should be allowed to attend school with the approval of a county health official.

With more than half the school year gone, Ryan was officially cleared to return to classes on 21 February, 1986. The thrill of victory, though, was short-lived. On his first day back, he was pulled from the classroom and brought to court. A group of parents had filed an injunction to block his return, and the judge issued a restraining order against him. When the judge handed down his verdict, the room packed with parents began to cheer, while Ryan and Jeanne looked on, shocked and scared. It seemed like a modern-day witch hunt, and Ryan was to be burned at the stake.

Ryan's lawyers fought the restraining order, and he again won the right to go back to school. This time the decision was final. On 10 April, 1986, with hordes of press on his heels and some students picketing nearby, Ryan returned to classes. He was not allowed to participate in gym class, and he was made to use a separate bathroom and water fountain, and disposable utensils in the cafeteria. These were needless precautions, but Ryan agreed to them in order to assuage the fears about his misunderstood disease. Still, twenty-seven children were withdrawn from school that day. Two weeks later, parents opened an alternative school, and twenty-one of Ryan's schoolmates were enrolled so as not to be in the same building as Ryan daily.

Back at school, and nearly everywhere he went in his hometown, Ryan was teased and tormented. He was called a 'fag' and other homophobic obscenities in public. His school locker and possessions were vandalised, and terrible rumours were spread about him. One anonymous teenager wrote a letter to the local paper accusing Ryan of threatening to bite and scratch other children, spitting on food at a grocery store, even urinating on bathroom walls. These were lies, of course, but it didn't matter. Having AIDS made Ryan a freak, and regardless of what he did or didn't do, he was considered as such.

If you can believe it, adults treated him even worse than children did. People on Ryan's paper round cancelled their subscriptions. When he and his family went out to eat, local restaurants would throw away the dishes they used. The parents of Ryan's girlfriend forbade her from seeing him. At one point during the Whites' legal battle with the school district, a group of school parents demanded that the county declare Jeanne an unfit guardian in order to have Ryan taken away from her, and thus taken out of school.

It wasn't just Ryan who was subjected to ill treatment and ostracism – his entire family suffered. The tyres were slashed on Jeanne's car. A bullet was shot through a window of the White family's home. Ryan's extended family was harassed, too, and even non-relatives who defended Ryan were subjected to abuse. When the local paper supported Ryan's right to attend school, the publisher's house was egged. A reporter at the paper even received death threats.

Somehow, Ryan's disease brought out the very worst in people, and there was little refuge for him and his family. Not even at church. The Whites were people of deep faith and Christian convicition. Each night, Ryan and Jeanne prayed together before bed. But after Ryan's illness became public, the community at their Methodist church began to shun them. The parishioners were so afraid of catching AIDS from Ryan that he and his family were asked to sit in either the first pew or the last. People wouldn't use the church bathroom after Ryan. Parents told their children to avoid him.

In his autobiography, Ryan tells the story of his family going to church on Easter Sunday in 1985, shortly after his diagnosis. At the end of the service, people turned to those sitting around them to shake hands and say, 'Peace be with you,' an Easter tradition at Ryan's church. No one would shake his hand this time. Not a single person would offer this sick child a blessing of peace on Easter. As they left the church that morning, Jeanne's car broke down. She tried to stop members of the congregation leaving the church car park, but no one would help her.

Despite the ostracism he suffered from his church and his community, and despite the terrible pain and physical distress he experienced his entire life, Ryan was full of faith and Christian love until the end. Only a year before he died, Ryan told the Saturday Evening Post that he wasn't afraid of dying because of his faith in God. Even after he had endured so much abuse from fraudulent zealots, and as he was growing sicker, Ryan's faith was stronger than ever. 'There's always hope with the Lord,' Ryan told the Post. 'I have a lot of trust in God.'

As a boy, I loved Sunday school. I loved hearing stories from the Bible, stories full of hope. To this day, while I do not practise any religion, I do take the compassionate teachings of Jesus to heart, and I have great respect for all people of faith. I am inspired by Jesus the man because he loved unconditionally, because he forgave unconditionally, and because he died for the sake of others. The same can be said of Ryan White. He was a true Christian, a modern-day Jesus Christ. That's a bold statement, I know; some might even take offence to it. But to know Ryan's story, and to have witnessed his extraordinary qualities as I did, is to come to no other conclusion.

The White family put their Christian faith to practice. They were upset at being treated so terribly by their community, of course, but they understood the fear. They knew it was caused by ignorance and misunderstanding. And so they responded with the compassion that they themselves never received. They worked hard to educate their community, to teach others about AIDS. In the end, Ryan wound up reaching far more than those in Kokomo, Indiana. He reached the entire nation.

The story of an ill young man who was kept out of school and shunned by his community wouldn't stay hidden in a small Midwestern town for long. Ryan's plight quickly became national news, and soon he was a household name. Ryan was on national talk shows and nightly news broadcasts. He was on the cover of People magazine. He was actually quite a shy boy, and Jeanne, a wonderfully unpretentious woman, certainly wanted no attention for herself. But the Whites felt it was their duty to speak out, to tell the world what they were experiencing. They wanted to make life better for thousands of others who were suffering in the same way – and not just other haemophiliacs who had contracted HIV but everyone living with the disease.

While bigots such as the famous preacher Jerry Falwell and the American politician Jesse Helms were spreading the hateful message that AIDS was a curse from God against gays, here was a dying teenager and his mother, thrust into the spotlight, standing shoulder-to-shoulder with all people living with HIV/AIDS. It was the height of bravery, the height of compassion. I love them for it to this day. By speaking out, Ryan and Jeanne helped to normalise the epidemic and relieve some of the terrible stigma and fear surrounding it. In doing so, they also hastened the government response and increased the urgency of medical research. What's more, they demonstrated what we now know to be the truth – that we must love all those living with HIV/AIDS if we are ever going to eradicate the disease itself.

Like millions of people, when I read about Ryan in that magazine, sitting in the doctor's waiting room, I was incensed. More than that, I was overcome with the desire to do something for him and his family. 'This situation is outrageous,' I thought. 'I've got to help these people.'

As angry and motivated as I was, I hadn't a clue what I could do for them. I suppose I was thinking that I would help raise awareness about what the White family was going through, or perhaps raise money to fight AIDS. But how could I help others when I couldn't help myself?

The truth is, I was a huge cocaine addict at the time. My life was up and down like a yo-yo. My sense of values was buried under my self-destruction. I was still a good person, a kind person, underneath – otherwise I would have never reached out to the Whites in the first place. All I hoped was that somehow I could bring this boy and his family some comfort and support.

It turned out, in the end, the Whites would do far more for me than I ever did for them.

In the spring of 1986, after Ryan won his right to return to school, he and Jeanne came to New York to attend a fund-raiser for AIDS research and to appear on Good Morning America. I saw their interview, and I called Jeanne the next morning. I wanted to meet Ryan. I wanted to help. I invited Ryan and his family to one of my concerts.

Ryan was too sick to attend the first concert I planned to bring him to, but eventually I was able to fly the Whites to Los Angeles. They came to two of my shows, and then I took the family to Disneyland, where I had arranged a private tour and a party for Ryan. I wanted to give him an adventure – limos, planes, fancy hotels – a carefree time to take his mind off his pain and his difficult circumstances. But what I remember most about that visit is that I had at least as much fun as Ryan, if not more.

I felt instantly comfortable with the Whites, instantly connected to Ryan. While we came from different countries, we really were cut from the same cloth. The Whites were commonsense, straight-shooting people. They were caring and humble and always grateful. What I did for them on that trip, and subsequently, was out of the pure love I had for this family. And that's really what it was: love. I fell in love with the Whites right away.

Getting to know the family put into stark relief what a terrible mess I was. You can't imagine how selfish I was at the time, what an asshole I had become. It was partly the drugs, partly the lifestyle I had created, partly the people around me, who indulged my worst instincts. I had everything in the world – wealth, fame, everything – but I'd throw a fit if I didn't like the curtains in my hotel room. That's how upside down I was. That's how pathetic I had become.

Ryan, on the other hand, was dying. His family had been tormented. And yet, during his trip to L.A. and every time I was with him from then on, he was relentlessly upbeat. At Disneyland, Ryan was so weak that I had to push him around in a wheelchair for part of the time. For a child, being wheelchair-bound at Disneyland must be incredibly frustrating, not to be able to run around and play at one of the world's largest playgrounds. But Ryan loved every minute of it. He loved life. Ryan wasn't thinking about dying; he was thinking about living, and he was getting on with it. His time was too precious to feel sorry for himself. I was with Ryan quite a lot over the years, and I can't remember a single time when he complained about anything. I know he wasn't a perfect child; there's no such thing. But Ryan was special.

So are his mum and sister. Jeanne was going through the most torturous episode any parent could imagine: watching her child die a slow and painful death, and not being able to do anything about it. But she never asked, 'Why me?' She embodied forgiveness and acceptance and perseverance at every turn, even though she must have suffered greatly in her most private moments.

Andrea was just like Jeanne; you couldn't get her down, and you never heard her complain. The youngest in the family often gets all the attention, especially someone like Andrea, a beautiful teenage girl, an athlete, a wonderful student. But Andrea's life took a backseat to Ryan's illness. She had to give up competitive roller-skating, her passion, for financial reasons. Like Ryan, she lost friends and was teased. She had it very rough. I was amazed by how she dealt with the reality of her family's situation with maturity and wisdom well beyond her years.

This family inspired me in a way that I cannot fully explain. Being around the Whites touched me at my very core. I guess you could put it this way: I wanted to be like them. I wanted to be part of their family. They made me want to change, to be a better person, to be the person I knew I was on the inside. But this wasn't an easy thing to do, because of my addictions, because of my lifestyle. I was beginning to open my eyes to reality, but it took Ryan's death to open them completely. When his eyes closed, mine opened. They've been open ever since.

After the Whites came to L.A., from then on, I did whatever I could for them. Little things, mostly. Ryan came to more concerts. I sent gifts and flowers and cards. I called to check in. In 1987 Jeanne decided to move the family to Cicero, Indiana, a small town outside Indianapolis. She knew it was the right thing to do after Ryan confided in her that he didn't want to be buried in Kokomo. They needed to escape the place that had caused them such grief – that much was clear. One day, Jeanne called. With a great deal of hesitation in her voice, she asked if I might loan her part of the down payment she needed for her new home in Cicero.

To that point, Jeanne had never asked for a single thing. That she was now coming to me for help meant she badly needed it. I knew how desperate she was to give Ryan and Andrea a better life, so I told her to forget about a loan, I would simply send her the money. But Jeanne absolutely insisted on a loan. In fact, she made both of us sign a home-made contract stating that she would pay me back! Sure enough, years later, I received a cheque from Jeanne. I put the money straight into a college savings account for Andrea. Jeanne resisted, of course, but I told her that I wanted to help, that it meant something to me to support her family in this way. Looking back on it, I think she was being more charitable in continuing to accept my assistance than I was being supportive in giving it.

The Whites had a completely different life in their new home in Cicero. They were welcomed with open arms. Ryan did have a few friends in Kokomo, but in Cicero he became something of a local hero. The Whites were not only accepted but embraced, and Ryan thrived in his new school, making the honour roll as well as making many good friends.

It's not the case that the residents of Cicero were better or kinder human beings than the residents of Kokomo. My own opinion is that people are more or less the same all around the world; and besides, these two towns are only thirty miles apart. In fact, people in Cicero had many of the same questions, and shared many of the same fears, as people in Kokomo. Was it safe for the other children to be around Ryan? Did he pose a health risk to the community ? The difference was that Cicero knew more about HIV/AIDS by the time Ryan arrived.

For one thing, Ryan had done much to educate the entire nation. Everyone knew his story, and in learning about Ryan's plight, America learned about AIDS as well. In addition, Ryan's new school held extensive AIDS education classes for the entire student body as well as the staff. The school board even sponsored conferences for parents and other members of the community to learn about AIDS, all before Ryan ever set foot in the classroom. He also had a champion and a wonderful friend in Jill Stewart, the president of the school student body, who happened to live down the street from the Whites.

Thanks to Jill's efforts, and the community's, Ryan's classmates were compassionate toward him, not fearful. Parents understood that their children weren't at risk, and they were able to ease any concerns among Ryan's classmates. Some children even taught their nervous parents about the disease. In the end, people weren't afraid; they were supportive. Cicero was able to see beyond Ryan's illness and focus on the amazing person he was.

Ryan found a bit of peace in Cicero, though not from his disease. He never wanted to give up – that goes without saying – but his fragile body had endured too much. In the spring of 1990, toward the end of his junior year of high school, Ryan was hospitalized with a severe respiratory infection. Jeanne called to tell me that Ryan was on life support. I immediately flew to Indiana. NFL star Howie Long and actresses Judith Light and Jessica Hahn were on the same US Airways flight. They had befriended Ryan and taken up his cause as well.

I spent the last week of Ryan's life by his hospital bedside, supporting Jeanne and Andrea in any way I could. Mostly that meant playing the family receptionist, and I was honoured to do it. Many people were trying to reach Ryan by phone and by mail – friends, celebrities, politicians, everyone wanted to express their support. Ryan was in and out of consciousness, but he was awake when Michael Jackson called. Michael was the biggest star in the world at the time, perhaps the most famous man on the planet. Years earlier, he had befriended Ryan as well, and one of Ryan's prized possessions was a red Ford Mustang that was a generous gift from him. As Ryan lay dying, he was so weak that he couldn't speak to Michael. I held the phone to his ear as Michael offered him kind words of comfort and love.

I grew very close to Jeanne during the final week of Ryan's life. She described me then as her guardian angel, since I was able to help the family during this terrible moment by handling logistical details, and by simply being there for them. But it was the other way around. Jeanne and her family were guardian angels to me. And the message they were sent to deliver was very clear: it might be my deathbed next.

I had all the money in the world, but it didn't matter, because I didn't have my health. I wasn't well. But unlike Ryan, a cure existed for my substance abuse, for my self-destructiveness. As I stood next to Ryan's hospital bed, holding Jeanne's hand, seeing his bloated and disfigured body, the message was received. I didn't want to die.

As it happened, on the evening of 7 April, I was scheduled to play a massive concert in Indianapolis, not far from Riley Hospital for Children, where Ryan was being treated. The show was called Farm Aid IV, the fourth in a series of concerts meant to raise awareness and donations for family farmers in America. Months earlier, I had happily agreed to join Garth Brooks, Guns N' Roses, Neil Young, Jackson Browne, Willie Nelson, John Mellencamp, and many other amazing performers to put on this show. But at that moment, with Ryan near death, I didn't want to leave his side.

I rushed to the Hoosier Dome and hurried onstage. Other performers were in their usual stage dress, but I was wearing a baseball cap and a Windbreaker. I was so upset that I didn't care what I looked like, and it showed. Even 60,000 screaming fans couldn't chase away the grief I felt then. Since there were many musicians, each of us performed only a few songs. I started with 'Daniel' and then played 'I'm Still Standing.' Before my third song, I told the crowd, 'This one's for Ryan.' They burst into applause. The news of Ryan's hospitalization was a national story, and everyone knew he didn't have long to live. I played 'Candle in the Wind,' and the response was overwhelming. I looked out into the crowd, and people were holding up their lighters, thousands of little vigils flickering in the darkness for my dying friend.

When I finished the song, I ran offstage and rushed back to the hospital, back to Ryan's bedside. That's where I was, hours later, when Ryan died on the morning of 8 April 1990.

I'll never forget the funeral. I'll never forget the numbness of tragedy. I'll never forget what he looked like in the open casket, or the drive from the service to the cemetery. It was raining. We drove very slowly, in both grief and caution. I'll never forget Jeanne thanking me, in the middle of the greatest loss of her life, taking the time to acknowledge my being there with her. How surreal it all felt, like an awful dream.

It was the end of a very long week. It was the end of a very long fight.

Jeanne had asked me to be a pallbearer and to sing a song at Ryan's funeral. I wasn't sure that I would be able to keep my composure, but I agreed to do the song. I couldn't say no to her, but I didn't know what to sing. I didn't know what would be appropriate for such a tragic and painful occasion.

I ended up going back to my very first album, Empty Sky, and to the song 'Skyline Pigeon,' which Bernie Taupin and I wrote together. It's always been one of my favorites, and I thought it was the best track on that first album, maybe even the best track we had written to that point. It's a song about freedom and release, and it seemed fitting for Ryan's funeral. Now that he had passed away, I figured that Ryan was free to go wherever he wanted, his soul was free to travel, his spirit was free to inspire people around the world.

1. What did you think of this story?
2. Do you think that God was at work throughout this story? How?
3. How did Ryan White change Elton John's life?
4. Why, do you think, had Ryan such a strong faith?
5. Can you think of a time when you saw God reveal himself through the actions of other people?

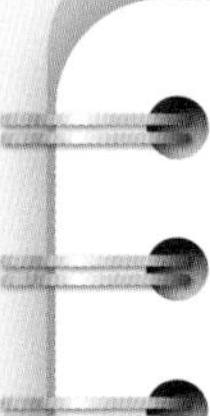

End of Section Summary

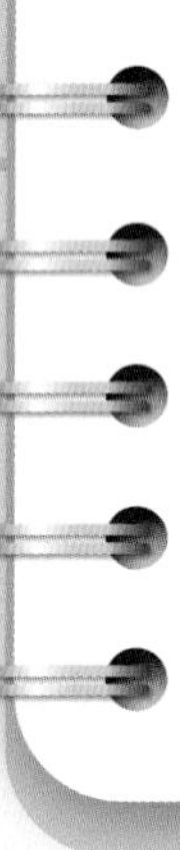

- Stories are means of communication.
- Types of stories include fairy tale, folk tale, fable, saga, legend, myth and parable.
- Truth can be defined in many ways, but one of the best ways comes from the Greek work 'aletheia' which means 'unhide' or 'hide nothing'.
- Science and religion can both provide answers that give the truth about the creation of the world.
- God's revelation is how God revealed himself to humankind.
- God's revelation can be seen in his creations.
- God's final revelation was through Jesus Christ.
- God's revelation is accounted for in the Bible.
- God's revelation can be seen in the contemporary world today through story, poetry, music, art and film.
- People can experience God's revelation in their own lives at various times. God can be revealed through personal experiences.

End of Section Activities

1. Read the summary of *Go Ask Alice* (p. 194). In your own words, explain Alice's downfall.
2. Rewrite the story of Cain and Abel in a modern-day setting.
3. Write a detailed account of God's revelation including all three components.
4. Read the article by Elton John. Write a letter to the editor of the newspaper, outlining your response to the article.

★ 'There is no need for religious truth now that we have scientific truth.'

★ 'God's story is a work of fiction.'

1. Find another Aesop fable and rewrite it in your own words.
2. Use the internet to find examples of modern-day stories where people have experienced God's revelation.
3. Look up references from the Bible that refer to God's revelation and write an essay on your research.
4. Choose one contemporary expression of God's revelation. Research this topic and present your findings to the class.

Keep a journal for at least a week. Each night, write down the influence of story on your day.

- ★ Compile a list of questions for an interview that you could have with a young person. Ask them what they know about story and what meaning they think it brings to their life.
- ★ Compile a list of questions for an interview that you could have with an older person. Ask them to recall stories from their own life. Analyse these stories and present your findings to the class.

Books

- ★ Fairy tale: 'The Emperor's New Clothes'
- ★ Folk tale: 'Jack and the Beanstalk'
- ★ Fable: 'The Boy Who Cried Wolf'
- ★ Saga: The *Twilight* saga/*Harry Potter* series
- ★ Legend: *Bigfoot*
- ★ Myth: 'The Trojan Horse'
- ★ Parable: 'The Parable of the Fig Tree'

Films

- ★ *Toy Story*
- ★ *Shrek*
- ★ *Out of Africa*
- ★ *My Left Foot*
- ★ *Not Without My Daughter*
- ★ *Alive*
- ★ *Fly Away Home*

Glossary

A

abortion	The deliberate termination of human pregnancy

C

cloning	Making an identical copy of
conscience	An inner feeling or voice viewed as acting as a guide to the rightness or wrongness of one's behaviour

D

disciple	A follower of a teacher
drug	A chemical substance that affects the processes of the mind or body

E

euthanasia	The painless killing of a patient suffering from an incurable and painful disease, or in an irreversible coma

I

in-vitro fertilisation	A procedure during which eggs from a woman's ovary are removed. They are fertilised with sperm in a laboratory and then the fertilised egg is implanted in the woman's uterus

J

justice	Just behaviour or treatment

K

kingdom of God	The spiritual domain over which God is sovereign

M

mantra	A word or sound repeated to aid concentration in meditation
meditation	A form of silent prayer that involves focusing the mind upon a sound, object, visualisation or the breath
Messiah	The anointed one (*Christos* in Greek)
miracle	A highly improbable or extraordinary event that is considered to be divine intervention in human affairs
morality	Principles concerning the distinction between right or wrong, or good and bad behaviour

P

pacifism	The refusal to participate in war or military service on a point of principle
parable	A story told by Jesus that contained a deeper meaning
peace	Freedom from disturbance
persecution	The act or practice of persecuting, harassing or punishing in a manner designed to injure
prayer	Communication with God
prophet	A spokesperson for God/A person regarded as an inspired teacher of the will of God

R

resurrection	Rising from the dead
revelation	The revealing of some form of truth or knowledge through communication with a deity or other supernatural entity
rituals	A series of actions performed according to a prescribed order during religious ceremonies

S

Sanhedrin	The highest court of justice and the supreme council in ancient Jerusalem
spirituality	The quality or condition of being spiritual; attachment to or regard for things of the spirit as opposed to material or worldly interests
symbol	A thing that represents or stands for something else, especially a material object representing something abstract

Acknowledgements

'A Level Playing Field with Israel?' by Jan Benvie, written while working as a human rights monitor in Al Khalil/Hebron in Palestine.

'Capital Punishment is Dead Wrong', Olivia H, reprinted with permission by Teen Ink magazine and TeenInk.com.

'Designer Babies: Ethical? Inevitable?', Robert Roy Britt, reproduced by permission of Live Science.

'Exploring Surrogacy: The Legal Situation in Ireland', reproduced by permission of *Independent Newspapers*.

Go Ask Alice Sparknotes, copyright Sterling Publishing.

'Homeless People: Rebecca's Story', reproduced by permission of Rebeccas Community.

'If cocaine was legal, Katy French might still be alive', Louis Jacob, reproduced by permission of *Independent Newspapers*.

'I'm trying to fight a winning battle but I'm nearly certain I'm not winning', Vincent Hogan, reproduced by permission of *Independent Newspapers*.

Information on drugs in Section 3 was reproduced with permission of www.drugs.ie.

'Judge jails C case rapist for "dreadful evil act"', Tomás Mac Ruairí, reproduced by permission of *Independent Newspapers*.

'Juliet's Journey: From Child Soldier to Global Campaigner', reproduced by permission of War Child.

'Life is sweet for Brian Keenan', Joanna Moorhead, copyright Guardian News & Media Ltd 2009.

Love is the Cure, Elton John, reproduced by permission of Hodder.

'Marie Fleming partner says he would be willing to help her die', Ruadhan Mac Cormaic, reproduced by permission of *The Irish Times*.

My Olympic Dream, Katie Taylor, reproduced by permission of *Simon & Schuster*.

'One of Us', words and music by Eric Bazilian, © 1996 Human Boy Music (ASCAP), all rights administered by WB Music Corp.

'Potential dangers of human cloning', Gary Wickham, reproduced by permission of Health Guidance.

'Raising Domestic Violence Awareness: Why Talking About Chris Brown Isn't Enough' by Nico Lang, courtesy of *The Huffington Post*.

'Redemption Stories: The Girl with the Arms', John Spain, reproduced by permission of *Independent Newspapers*.

'Ringo Starr admits: "I have found God"', Andrew Hough, reproduced by permission of *Independent Newspapers*.

The child-friendly (unofficial) text of the United Nations Convention on the Rights of the Child was developed by and provided with the permission of the Canadian UNICEF Committee.

'The Everyday Lives of the Early Christians: An Interview with Carl J. Sommer', Carl Olson, reproduced by permission of Carl J. Sommer, Adjunct Professor of Church History at Kenrick Glennon Seminary and author of *We Look for a Kingdom: The Everyday Lives of the Early Christians.*

'The impact of Meditation on Rhonda Jones' Life: It Was Meditation Integrated With the Scriptures That Healed My Life' by Rhonda Jones courtesy of www.thechristianmeditator.com.

'The long road home for surrogate babies', Carl O'Brien, reproduced by permission of *The Irish Times*.

'The Ritual Maker Within at Adolescent Initiation', Edith Sullwold PhD, reprinted by permission of Open Court Publishing Company, a division of Carus Publishing Company, dba ePals Media, Chicago, IL, from *Betwixt & Between: Patterns of Masculine and Feminine Initiation*, edited by Louise C. Mahdi, Steven Foster, and Meredith Little, copyright ©1987 by Open Court Publishing Company.

'The Search for Meaning' by Dr Linda Sapadin, first published at www.PsychWisdom.com, reprinted with the kind permission of the author.

'The X Case and the letter of the law', Linda Kelly, reproduced by permission of the author.

'What does it mean to be a spiritual person?', Dr. Margaret Paul, reproduced by permission of the author. Margaret Paul, Ph.D. is a best-selling author of 8 books, relationship expert, and co-creator of the powerful Inner Bonding® process – featured on Oprah. Are you are ready to heal your pain and discover your joy? Click here for a FREE Inner Bonding course: http://www.innerbonding.com/welcome and visit our website at http://www.innerbonding.com for more articles and help. Phone Sessions Available. Join the thousands we have already helped and visit us now!

The Twelve Steps are reprinted with permission of Alcoholics Anonymous World Services, Inc. Permission to reprint the Twelve Steps does not mean that AAWS has reviewed or approved the contents of this publication, or that AAWS necessarily agrees with the views expressed herein. A.A. is a program of recovery from alcoholism only – use of the Twelve Steps in connection with programs and activities which are patterned after A.A., but which address other problems, or in any other non-A.A. context, does not imply otherwise.

Universal Declaration of Human Rights, Plain Language Version: 'The United Nations is the author of the original material'.

'You Found Me', The Fray, reproduced by permission of Hal Leonard Corporation.